LEARN
Adobe Animate CC
for Multiplatform Animations

SECOND EDITION

Adobe Certified Associate Exam Preparation

Joseph Labrecque
Rob Schwartz

Adobe

LEARN ADOBE ANIMATE CC FOR MULTIPLATFORM ANIMATIONS SECOND EDITION
ADOBE CERTIFIED ASSOCIATE EXAM PREPARATION
Joseph Labrecque
with **Rob Schwartz**

Adobe Press is an imprint of Pearson Education, Inc. For the latest on Adobe Press books, go to www.adobepress.com. To report errors, please send a note to errata@peachpit.com. For information regarding permissions, request forms and the appropriate contacts within the Pearson Education Global Rights & Permissions department, please visit www.pearsoned.com/permissions/.

Adobe Press Editor: Laura Norman	**Compositor:** Kim Scott, Bumpy Design
Development Editor: Victor Gavenda	**Proofreader:** Becky Winter
Senior Production Editor: Tracey Croom	**Indexer:** Valerie Haynes-Perry
Technical Editor: Russell Chun	**Cover & Interior Design:** Mimi Heft
Copyeditor: Liz Welch	**Cover Illustration:** Markovka/Shutterstock

ISBN 13: 978-0-13-489266-5
ISBN 10:   0-13-489266-6

1 18

The battle itself is worth it—regardless of outcome.
The fact that we fight at all speaks more
than the result of any particular conflict.

Acknowledgments

Adobe Animate CC is an application that has personally (and professionally!) always been a joy to use. It is such a uniquely rich, creative powerhouse, enabling designers across the world to produce rich assets, expressive animations, and even interactive projects—all within this single creative environment.

Like many others, I began my journey with all things "Flash-y" under Macromedia and have continued with it during the transition to Adobe and up to the present day. Animate CC, as Flash Professional, reached superstar status at one point, and now stands poised to reclaim its crown as the premier multiplatform animation and interactive powerhouse. It is a new era for Animate CC...and you, as the reader of this book, get to be at the forefront.

No work of this scale can be attributed to a single individual. Thanks go to Rob, who has contributed his writing to this book in order to make present a great amount of design and theory knowledge. Thanks go as well to my editor, Victor, and my reviewer, Russell. It would be impossible to do this correctly without you both. I'd also like to express my thanks to the wider Peachpit, Adobe Press, and BrainBuffet/ACATestPrep teams...and special thanks to everyone on the Adobe Animate team and the greater creative community for the work you all do in both building and using Animate CC!

In closing, I need to acknowledge the patience and support of my wife Leslie and of our daughters Paige and Lily. It's a hard thing to manage a business and a family while working full time, teaching, recording, and writing...but they make it all much, much easier.

I hope you all enjoy this book.

About the Authors

Joseph Labrecque is a creative developer, interactive designer, and educator with over 15 years of experience building expressive web, desktop, and mobile solutions. He regularly teaches classes on Animate CC, web animation, graphics production, and mobile application design for the University of Denver, where he is also employed as a senior interactive software engineer.

Joseph is also the principal of Fractured Vision Media, LLC, a digital media production company, technical consultancy, and distribution vehicle for a variety of creative works. He is founder and sole member of the studio recording project: *An Early Morning Letter, Displaced.*

Over the past decade, Joseph has authored a number of books, articles, and courses on design and development technologies, tools, and concepts through publishers such as Adobe Press, Peachpit Press, Lynda.com, LinkedIn Learning, Pluralsight, and more. He is an Adobe Education Leader (AEL) and Adobe Community Professional. He received the Adobe Education Impact Award in 2010 and serves on the AEL Advisory Board.

Joseph regularly speaks about Animate CC and related topics at conferences such as Adobe MAX and is eager to share his expertise in venues both large and small.

Rob Schwartz (author of Chapters 10 and 11) is an award-winning teacher with 20 years of experience in technical education. In addition to holding several Adobe Certified Associate certifications, Rob is an Adobe Certified Instructor. As an Adobe Education Leader, Rob won the prestigious Impact Award from Adobe, and in 2010 he ran the Top Certifying Academic Center for the Adobe certification exams and was named #1 Instructor Worldwide in the Adobe Certified Associate World Championship. Rob gives presentations worldwide about Adobe certifications. Find out more about Rob at his online curriculum website: brainbuffet.com.

Contents

Getting Started

We design and develop a number of exciting projects that consist of vector shapes, bitmap images, text, and code to help you learn the basics of interactive media creation with Adobe Animate CC—along with other design and project management skills that you will need for a creative career in interactive media. Adobe Animate CC (formerly known as Adobe Flash Professional CC) is a powerful program for building a wide assortment of animated and interactive project types with sophisticated transitions, effects, and interactive elements. You can use Animate CC to export projects to an ever-growing array of platforms and targets, including web browsers, desktop computers, and mobile devices, through a variety of native application and web technologies.

About this book and video

Learn Adobe Animate CC for Multiplatform Animations was created by a team of expert instructors, writers, and editors with years of experience in helping beginning learners get their start with the cool creative tools from Adobe Systems. Our aim is not only to teach you the basics of the art of interactive media with Animate CC but to give you an introduction to the associated skills (like design principles and project management) that you'll need for your first job.

We've built the training around the objectives for the Adobe Certified Associate (ACA) exam in Multiplatform Animations Using Adobe Animate CC, and if you master the topics covered in this book and video series you'll be in good shape to take the exam. But even if certification isn't your goal, you'll still find this training will give you an excellent foundation for your future work in video. To that end, we've structured the material in the order that makes most sense for beginning learners (as determined by experienced classroom teachers), rather than following the more arbitrary grouping of topics in the ACA Objectives.

To aid you in your quest, we've created a unique learning system that uses video and text in partnership. You'll experience this partnership in action in the Web Edition, which lives on your Account page at peachpit.com. The Web Edition contains 10 hours of video—the heart of the training—embedded in an online eBook that supports the video training and provides background material. The eBook material is also available separately for offline reading as a printed book or an eBook in a variety of formats. The Web Edition also includes about a hundred interactive review questions you can use to evaluate your progress. Purchase of the book in *any* format entitles you to free access to the Web Edition (instructions for accessing it follow later in this section).

Most chapters provide step-by-step instructions for creating a specific project or learning a specific technique. Other chapters acquaint you with other skills and concepts that you'll come to depend on as you use the software in your everyday work. Many chapters include several optional tasks that let you further explore the features you've already learned.

Each chapter opens with two lists of objectives. One list lays out the learning objectives—the specific tasks you'll learn in the chapter. The second list shows the ACA exam objectives that are covered in the chapter. A table at the end of the book guides you to coverage of all of the exam objectives in the book or video.

Conventions used in this book

This book uses several elements styled in ways to help you as you work through the projects.

Text that you should enter appears in bold, such as:

> In the Link field in the Property inspector, type **http://www.adobe.com/ animate.**

Terms that are defined in the Glossary appear in bold and in color, such as:

> The **web font** that's used in the header of the page is just what the client is looking for. That's a great thing.

▶ Video 5.1 *Project Overview*

Links to videos that cover the topics in depth appear in the margins.

The ACA objectives covered in the chapters are called out in the margins beside the sections that address them.

★ *ACA Objective 2.1*

Notes give additional information about a topic. The information they contain is not essential to accomplishing a task but provides a more in-depth understanding of the topic.

> **NOTE**
>
> *Notice the effect of the vanishing point, which is used to provide perspective to the artwork as it's moved through the simulated 3D environment.*

OPERATING SYSTEM DIFFERENCES

In most cases, Animate CC works the same in both Windows and macOS. Minor differences exist between the two versions, mostly due to platform-specific issues. Most of these are simply differences in keyboard shortcuts, how dialog boxes are displayed, and how buttons are named. In most cases, screenshots were made in the macOS version of Animate CC and may appear somewhat differently from your own screen.

Where specific commands differ, they are noted within the text. Windows commands are listed first, followed by the macOS equivalent, such as Ctrl+C/Cmd+C. In general, the Windows Ctrl key is equivalent to the Command (or Cmd) key in macOS and the Windows Alt key is equivalent to the Option (or Opt) key in macOS.

As lessons proceed, instructions may be truncated or shortened to save space, with the assumption that you picked up the essential concepts earlier in the lesson. For example, at the beginning of a lesson you may be instructed to "press Ctrl+C/Cmd+C." Later, you may be told to "copy" text or a code element. These should be considered identical instructions.

If you find you have difficulties in any particular task, review earlier steps or exercises in that lesson. In some cases if an exercise is based on concepts covered earlier, you will be referred back to the specific lesson.

Installing the software

Before you begin using *Learn Adobe Animate CC for Multiplatform Animations*, make sure that your system is set up correctly and that you've installed the proper software and hardware. This material is based on the original 2018 release of Adobe Animate CC and is designed to cover the objectives of the Adobe Certified Associate Exam for that version of the software.

The Adobe Animate CC software is not included with this book; it is available only with an Adobe Creative Cloud membership, which you must purchase, or it must be supplied by your school or other organization. In addition to Adobe Animate CC, some lessons in this book have steps that can be performed with Adobe Media Encoder and other Adobe applications. You must install these applications from Adobe Creative Cloud onto your computer. Follow the instructions provided at helpx.adobe.com/creative-cloud/help/download-install-app.html.

ADOBE CREATIVE CLOUD DESKTOP APP

In addition to Adobe Animate CC, this training requires the Adobe Creative Cloud desktop application, which provides a central location for managing the dozens of apps and services that are included in a Creative Cloud membership. You can use the Creative Cloud desktop application to sync and share files, manage fonts, access libraries of stock photography and design assets, and showcase and discover creative work in the design community.

The Creative Cloud desktop application is installed automatically when you download your first Creative Cloud product. If you have Adobe Application Manager installed, it auto-updates to the Creative Cloud desktop application.

If the Creative Cloud desktop application is not installed on your computer, you can download it from the Download Creative Cloud page on the Adobe website (creative.adobe.com/products/creative-cloud) or the Adobe Creative Cloud desktop apps page (adobe.com/creativecloud/catalog/desktop.html). If you are using software on classroom machines, be sure to check with your instructor before making any changes to the installed software or system configuration.

CHECKING FOR UPDATES

Adobe periodically provides updates to software. You can easily obtain these updates through the Creative Cloud. If these updates include new features that affect the content of this training or the objectives of the ACA exam in any way, we will post updated material to peachpit.com.

Accessing the free Web Edition and lesson files

Your purchase of this book in any format includes access to the corresponding Web Edition hosted on peachpit.com. The Web Edition contains the complete text of the book augmented with hours of video and interactive quizzes.

If you purchased an eBook from peachpit.com or adobepress.com, the Web Edition will automatically appear the Digital Purchases tab on your Account page. Click the Launch link to access the product.

If you purchased an eBook from a different vendor or you bought a print book, you must register your purchase on peachpit.com:

1   Go to www.peachpit.com/register.

2   Sign in or create a new account.

TIP

For a video walk-through of the registration process, see www.peachpit.com/ LearnACAanimate.

3 Enter the ISBN: **9780134892665**.

4 Answer the questions as proof of purchase.

5 The Web Edition will appear under the Digital Purchases tab on your Account page. Click the Launch link to access the product.

To work through the projects in this product, you will first need to download the lesson files from peachpit.com. You can download the files for individual lessons or download them all in a single file.

The Lesson Files can be accessed through the Registered Products tab on your Account page. Click the Access Bonus Content link below the title of your product to proceed to the download page. Click the lesson file links to download them to your computer.

Project fonts

All fonts used in these projects are either part of standard system installs; can be found on the web for free or downloaded from Typekit, an Adobe service that is included with your Creative Cloud membership; or can be accessed through Google Web Fonts as a service tied to Animate CC.

Additional resources

Learn Adobe Animate CC for Multiplatform Animations is not meant to replace documentation that comes with the program or to be a comprehensive reference for every feature. For comprehensive information about program features and tutorials, refer to these resources:

Adobe Animate CC Learn & Support: helpx.adobe.com/animate.html is where you can find and browse Help and Support content on Adobe.com. Adobe Animate Help and Adobe Animate Support Center are accessible from the Help menu in Animate CC. Help is also available as a printable PDF document. Download the document at helpx.adobe.com/pdf/animate_reference.pdf.

Adobe Forums: forums.adobe.com/community/animate lets you tap into peer-to-peer discussions, questions, and answers on Adobe products.

Adobe Animate CC product home page: adobe.com/products/animate.html provides information about new features and intuitive ways to create professional layouts for print, tablets, and eBooks.

Adobe Exchange: adobeexchange.com is a central resource for finding tools, services, extensions, code samples, and more to supplement and extend your Adobe products.

Resources for educators: adobe.com/education and edex.adobe.com offer a treasure trove of information for instructors who teach classes on Adobe software at all levels.

Adobe certification

The Adobe training and certification programs are designed to help designers and other creative professionals improve and promote their product-proficiency skills. The Adobe Certified Associate (ACA) is an industry-recognized credential that demonstrates proficiency in Adobe digital skills. Whether you're just starting out in your career, looking to switch jobs, or interested in preparing for success in the job market, the Adobe Certified Associate program is for you! For more information visit edex.adobe.com/aca.

Resetting the preferences to their default settings

Animate CC lets you determine how the program looks and behaves (like tool settings and the default unit of measurement) using the extensive options in Edit > Preferences (Windows) or Animate CC > Preferences (macOS). To ensure that the preferences and default settings of your Adobe Animate CC program match those used in this book, you can reset your preference settings to their defaults (the Animate CC Help file calls this procedure "re-creating your preferences"). If you are using software installed on computers in a classroom, don't make any changes to the system configuration without first checking with your instructor.

To reset your preferences to their default settings, follow these steps:

1   Quit Adobe Animate CC.

2   Hold down the Ctrl+Alt+Shift keys (Windows) or Cmd+Option+Shift keys (macOS).

3   Continue to hold the keys and start Adobe Animate CC.

4   When the Delete Adobe Animate Preferences dialog box appears, release the keys and click OK.

   The file containing your preferences will be deleted.

CHAPTER OBJECTIVES

Chapter Learning Objectives

- Meet the Animate CC workspace.
- Understand the Stage and pasteboard.
- Discover the Properties and Tools panels.
- Explore other commonly accessed tools.
- Become familiar with the Timeline and its key components.

Chapter ACA Objectives

For full descriptions of the objectives, see the table on pages 286–291.

DOMAIN 1.0
WORKING IN THE ANIMATION INDUSTRY
1.4

DOMAIN 2.0
PROJECT SETUP AND INTERFACE
2.2

DOMAIN 4.0
CREATE AND MODIFY VISUAL ELEMENTS
4.1

CHAPTER 1

Welcome!

Adobe Animate CC (**Figure 1.1**) truly is a creative powerhouse. You're probably most familiar with content produced with this application served via the Adobe Flash Player web browser plug-in… but do you know that Animate CC can also be used to produce rich, creative content that targets HTML5 Canvas, WebGL, HD Video, SVG, iOS, Android, and more? Animate CC is a platform-agnostic application that allows you to design assets, animation, and interactive content of all kinds for a multitude of platforms—and all with the same tools and workflows!

Figure 1.1 Adobe Animate CC

In this book, you'll tackle some awesome projects that will introduce you to the application, learn some good practices for working on projects for others, and find tips and resources you can use to learn more on your own.

About the Adobe Certified Associate Series

Let's take just a second to explain what I'm trying to accomplish so I can be sure we're on the same page (pun intended!). Here's what I (and the other authors) hope to accomplish in these books and videos.

Have fun

This is seriously a goal for me, as I hope it is for you! When you're having fun, you learn more, and you're more likely to remember what you're learning. Having fun also makes it easier to focus and stick with the task at hand.

Even if the projects you create as you complete the exercises in this book aren't the kinds of things you'd create on your own, I'll make them as entertaining and fun as possible. Just roll with it, and it will make the time you spend with this book more enjoyable. Have fun, make jokes, and enjoy your new superpowers.

Learn Adobe Animate CC

This goes along with the previous item, but when you're working on the projects in this book, you have the freedom to explore and make these projects your own. Of course, you're welcome to follow along with my examples, but please feel free to change text or styles to fit your own interests. When you're sure you grasp the concepts I'm talking about, I encourage you to apply them in your own way. In some projects, you may want to even take things beyond the scope of what appears in the book. Please do so.

Animate CC: Common Terminology

★ *ACA Objective 1.4*

You'll need to become familiar with some technical terms that will come up often as you work through this book and the video course it accompanies.

- **Animation:** A change in the properties of an object over time. In Adobe Animate CC, animation can include not only visual changes in assets across time (scale, position, special effects), but also sounds and more.

- **Timeline:** In a general sense, a timeline is a sort of chart that plots events through time. Animate CC has a Timeline panel that represents such changes visually.

- **Frames:** The Animate CC timeline is based on frames. A frame is the smallest segment of the timeline and defines units of time for the project. For example, in a project that is set to 24 FPS (frames per second), each second is divided into 24 frames.

- **Authortime:** This is the work done in Animate CC itself apart from any resulting project assets or publishing formats, meaning that working on the Stage, using Animate CC tools, and manipulating the project timeline are all things that you do during authortime and are not known to the viewer.

- **Runtime:** This term can refer to either of two things. When a user views a published project outside of Animate CC, the project is now running independently of Animate itself (the authoring tool); this is *runtime*.

  Runtime is also a technical term describing a software mechanism for executing (or "playing") a project outside of Animate. Examples of this include the Flash Player and AIR (Adobe Integrated Runtime) runtimes—or even a web browser acting as a runtime for HTML5 Canvas documents.

- **Publish:** To export a finished project from Animate CC so it can be experienced outside the authoring tool. You can publish to a great variety of formats and document types from Animate CC.

Animate CC vs. Flash Professional CC

In late 2015, Adobe announced a major rebrand of its longstanding animation software, Flash Professional CC. Adobe had long been committed to elevating Flash Professional CC as the premier animation and interaction tool—but now as a platform-agnostic creativity application not restricted to any single platform. To reinforce this renewed focus, Adobe decided to rebrand Adobe Flash Professional CC as Adobe Animate CC.

"To more accurately represent its position as the premier animation tool for the web and beyond, Flash Professional will be renamed Adobe Animate CC, starting with the next release in early 2016." —Adobe

FLASH PLAYER 2020

Adobe has announced that they plan, in cooperation with browser vendors, to end-of-life Flash Player in 2020. It is important to note a few things here... this is only in regard to Flash Player and not AIR (Adobe Integrated Runtime)! AIR is a runtime and publishing mechanism for delivering applications for desktop and mobile devices that can be developed using ActionScript and additional Flash platform technologies. The AIR team has some very cool stuff on the roadmap, and AIR will continue to evolve the platform.

NOTE

One very important thing to remember is that Flash Player did pave the way for all the goodies we have in the native browser today. We have Flash Player to thank for advances in dynamic content, animation, audio and video playback, the browser-based canvas element, native 3D with WebGL, and much more.

Adobe Flash Professional CC, as Adobe Animate CC, is now poised to regain its proper place aside such giants as Adobe Illustrator CC and Adobe Photoshop CC as a top-tier application in the Adobe Creative Cloud portfolio. A new beginning with a great legacy behind it!

Preparation for ACA exam

This book, together with the video course it accompanies, covers every objective for the Adobe Certified Associate (ACA) exam, but I won't discuss them in order or make a big point of it. The authors of the books and videos in the Adobe Press Learn ACA series are teachers and trainers, and we've been doing this for a long time. We'll cover the concepts in the order that makes the most sense for *learning* and *retaining* the information best. You'll read everything you need to pass the exam and qualify for an entry-level job—but don't focus on that now. Instead, focus on having a blast learning Adobe Animate CC!

Developing your creative, communication, and cooperative skills

Aside from the actual hands-on work of learning Animate CC, this book explores the skills you need to become a more creative and cooperative person. These skills are critical for success—every employer, no matter what the industry, values creative people who can work and communicate well. This book describes the basics of creativity, how to design for (and work with) others, and project management.

A quick note on creativity

Animate CC is, by any definition of the term, creative software. You may have heard that creativity is something you're born with—and that some people have it and some don't. Not true! Creativity may come more naturally to some than to others, but all of us can become more creative people. It simply takes practice like anything else. The only way to get better at creativity is to practice, experiment, explore, and fail!

As Edwin Land said, "An essential aspect of creativity is not being afraid to fail." Failure is a *huge* part of creativity. It's a part of the process. So celebrate and enjoy your failures. Art is a very experimental activity. Even the best artists can make junk. The difference between them and the rest of us is that they learn to become comfortable with failure and recognize that it's part of the creative process. Everyone has a thousand crummy ideas in them. A creative person is just someone who's used more of them up than the rest of us!

At the end of this book, you'll explore ways to build your creativity, the same way you build your muscles. So don't worry if you feel like you aren't a very strong designer. You just need to spend some time in the creative gym!

Getting Acquainted with Animate CC

One of the great things about Animate CC is how versatile its interface is. It's flexible enough to adapt to the workflow and content the user encounters in any given project, which adds to the variety of project types that users can create with this program.

For example, some people use Animate CC only to create assets for a project, such as **spritesheets** for a game or a packaged **SWC** library for integration with a larger application. Others take advantage of the rich animation features core to the Animate CC experience. Still others develop interactive web content or even full iOS and Android apps via Adobe AIR. The creative possibilities with this application are limitless!

The Animate CC workspace

▶ **Video 1.1** *The Animate CC Workspace*

The Animate interface (**Figure 1.2**) consists of a broad series of panels, tabbed windows, and specialized dialog boxes that provide the functionality you'll need to create interactive media applications, rich animations, and engaging mobile apps.

Viewing all of these options at once would fill the screen several times over. This is why it is important to learn how to manage the workspace to show only those panels that apply to the current task.

Figure 1.2 The Animate CC interface

The Properties panel

▶ **Video 1.2** *The Properties and Tools Panels*

Multimedia elements in Animate CC have properties that you can freely adjust and animate, depending on your needs. These properties can refer to position, color, transparency, publish settings, and more.

Use the Properties panel to modify the properties of your selected object. It's a *smart* panel, so the options presented will change to reflect the element type you have currently selected.

Figure 1.3 shows the content of the Properties panel with the document itself selected. Because the Properties panel adapts to reveal the properties of any given element, you won't always see so many options available for modification.

Figure 1.3 The Properties panel

Figure 1.4 The Tools panel

A (left to right; tools marked with an asterisk * are hidden under the preceding tool on the list) Selection, Subselection, Free Transform, Gradient Transform*, 3D Rotation, 3D Translation*, Lasso, Polygon*, and Magic Wand

B (left to right) Pen, Anchor Point tools*, Text, Line, Rectangle, Rectangle Primitive*, Oval, Oval Primitive*, Polystar, Pencil, Paint Brush, and Brush

C (left to right) Bone, Bind*, Paint Bucket, Ink Bottle, Eyedropper, Eraser, Width, Camera, Hand, Rotation*, and Zoom

D (left to right) Stroke Color, Fill Color, Black and White, and Swap Colors

The Tools panel

The Tools panel (**Figure 1.4**) provides a variety of tools for creating and manipulating graphics and images within a project.

TOOLS PANEL LAYOUT

The Tools panel will appear by default as a one-column strip along the right-hand side of the interface. In the figure presented here, we are displaying the Tools panel in a different way—for the purpose of illustration—but the tools are still the same.

The panel is divided by horizontal rules into subsections that group the tools roughly by function. Options for any selected tool will vary.

Notice the tiny triangles on the bottom-right corner of some of the icons. These triangles indicate that clicking the tool will bring up an additional tool selection. This lets you access more tools that are grouped within the visible Tools panel and switch easily between them.

For instance, all the 3D tools are grouped together, but you will only ever see either the 3D Translation or 3D Rotation tool within the panel at one time—never both, since they are grouped.

Commonly accessed tools

★ ACA Objective 4.1

I'll describe most of the tools in Animate CC as you come across them in working through the various projects this book covers. A few tools are universal in terms of when you would access them, so I'll briefly describe them now.

- **Hand tool** : Use this tool to pan around the Stage. Just select the Hand tool and then drag on the Stage to pan around.

- **Rotation tool** : Allows you to rotate the Stage if you're using a tablet or similar device, giving you a more natural angle at which to create assets. To use this tool after selecting it, click anywhere on the Stage to set a pin, and then drag to rotate to your desired viewing angle.

- **Time Scrub tool** : This is a new tool in Animate CC. It allows you to easily scrub along the timeline by dragging this tool across the Stage itself.

- **Zoom tool** : As you may surmise from its name, the Zoom tool allows you to quickly zoom in and out of the Stage. Select the tool and then click either the icon marked with a + (plus sign) to zoom in or the icon with a − (minus sign) to zoom out. With either of these selected, clicking the Stage or dragging a selection rectangle with the tool will perform the requested zoom.

- **Stroke Color and Fill Color** : When dealing with shapes and text, you can define stroke and fill colors separately. Clicking either swatch here will summon a color picker that lets you redefine the selected color or even generate a new, specific color choice.

- **Black and White** : Clicking this icon once replaces the currently defined fill and stroke colors for a white fill and black stroke.

- **Swap Colors** : Clicking this icon swaps the Fill and Stroke colors. Click again to reverse.

- **Options area:** This is the area below the color tools that changes based on the currently selected tool. Notice when the Zoom tool is selected, for instance, how the + and − options then appear. Keep a close eye on this area as you work through the projects with various tools selected.

The Timeline

The **Timeline** panel (**Figure 1.5**) provides a frame-based animation and organizational structure for the interactive media authoring environment. There are a number of concepts to take note of here: layers, frames, seconds, and keyframes.

▶ *Video 1.3* The Project Timeline

Figure 1.5
The Timeline panel

- **Layers:** Much like in other programs such as Adobe Photoshop or Adobe Illustrator, layers in Animate CC are an organizational construct that allows you to stack content vertically on the Stage. Content in the uppermost layers will obscure content it overlaps in layers below.

- **Frames:** Since animation in Animate CC is measured in frames per second (fps), you can imagine that frames themselves play a big role in working with the timeline. Frames are added to the timeline within the various layers and determine how long the animation sequence will play, based on the project FPS.

- **Seconds:** Animate CC now displays seconds markers alongside frame numbers atop the timeline. These are placed at various frames in light of the selected frames-per-second (**FPS**) setting of the document. These markers make it very easy to see exactly what time you are at when viewing specific frames.

- **Keyframes:** These are special frames that contain information about a change in the properties of the object within that layer.

- **Playhead:** This indicates the current frame. You can move the playhead across frames by dragging it around. The Time Scrub tool also moves the playhead as you scrub across the Stage.

ONE ANIMATED OBJECT PER LAYER

When animating content, pay close attention to be sure that each object to be animated is on its own unique layer.

As we will see later in this book, an **instance** is a representation of an object that already exists within the project's library. You can place assets in **keyframes** on the timeline by dragging such instances from the library or by importing them to the Stage with that particular keyframe and layer selected. These assets will become visible to the user when the playhead of the animation reaches that frame.

Keyframes that include visual content will appear on the timeline with a small, filled circle inside. Keyframes with no content, or blank keyframes, appear similarly but the small circle is unfilled.

Major Interface Features

★ ACA Objective 2.2 It's a good idea, before delving into any project, to familiarize yourself with the various panels and other interface elements within Animate CC. Although many panels will not be needed at all times, some areas of the interface are so important that no matter what sort of project you are working with, you need to have them visible.

Managing panels

▶ Video 1.4
Managing Panels All individual panels or groups of panels can be minimized or maximized to make the best use of your screen area. You do this using the small double-arrow icon located in the top-right corner of the panel or panel group (**Figure 1.6**).

When a panel is collapsed, the arrows will point left; clicking the arrows will expand the panel or panel group to show the full interface.

When a panel or panel group is open, clicking the arrows will collapse the panel or panel group to icon mode.

Collapse to
Icons button

Figure 1.6
Collapsing a panel

Using workspace presets

With the number of creative options available for any given project, it makes sense that certain workspace configurations and panel sets might be better suited to certain tasks. For instance, if you're working on an animation that is not going to include any interactivity or code whatsoever, it wouldn't make sense to clutter the workspace with panels for writing code or managing code snippets.

▶ *Video 1.5* Using Workspace Presets

Animate CC ships with a number of prebuilt workspaces optimized for certain tasks (**Figure 1.7**):

- **Animator:** This workspace positions the Timeline and Stage at dead center and includes quick access to scenes and document properties.

- **Classic:** Miss the good ol' days when Flash animation on the web was king? This workspace preset replicates the panel layout of Macromedia Flash 4...or thereabouts.

- **Debug:** This workspace is extremely important for code-heavy ActionScript projects. This preset reveals the Debug Console and Variables panel, allowing simple debugging for complex interactive content.

Figure 1.7 Workspace presets

- **Designer:** This workspace is similar to the Animator preset, but with a greater emphasis on colors and tools.

- **Developer:** Quick access to the Components panel and a de-emphasis on the Tools panel are the hallmarks of this preset. It also makes the Compiler Errors and Output panels readily accessible.

- **Essentials:** This is the default workspace preset for Animate CC and aims to be balanced and uncluttered.

- **Small Screen:** This workspace provides a good example of how the various panels and panel groups can be collapsed. It's a good choice for screens with very little space.

Creating a custom workspace

Sometimes the built-in workspace presets aren't enough. For instance, maybe you have a small-screen laptop or are working across multiple monitors, or maybe you have a specific task that you do frequently that requires only a few panels to be visible.

You can create a custom workspace by opening and arranging the panels to your liking and saving the layout as a custom workspace.

1   To begin, modify the set of panels and panel groups you'd like to include in your custom workspace.

2   Choose New Workspace from the Workspace menu (sometimes called the "Workspace chooser").

3   Enter a unique name for the new workspace and click OK (**Figure 1.8**).

Figure 1.8 Naming a custom workspace

Now you'll be able to easily recall this particular workspace setup through the Workspace menu.

When customizing your workspace or simply working with panels, you should take note of a few things. The panels in the Animate CC interface have tabs that can be used to assign the panel to a group or quickly maximize and minimize the contents of the panel without collapsing the entire group.

Here are options for organizing and accessing custom workspaces:

- Drag a tab into a group to make that panel part of the group. If you drag the panel tab next to another tab, it will create a tab group.

- Drag the panel above or below another tab or tab group to create an accordion arrangement. Double-click a tab to collapse the contents of that panel vertically. Double-click again to expand the panel.

- You can also choose to lock any panel through its options menu. This prevents the panel from being moved around by mistake.

The Stage and pasteboard

The Stage (**Figure 1.9**) is the main visual layout area for the project. Objects that appear on the Stage at any given frame will be visible when someone runs the project outside of Animate CC, whether it is an HTML5 Canvas, WebGL, Adobe AIR, or Flash Player project.

Figure 1.9 The Stage and pasteboard

Stage   Pasteboard

The Stage has a number of important aspects you should be aware of. Let's start with the Stage resolution in width and height. The default resolution is 550px wide by 400px in height. Getting the Stage size right—or at least giving it an appropriate aspect ratio—is crucial when beginning a new project. The background color determines the default Stage color when there are no other elements obscuring it. The background color of the Stage is always a solid color.

NOTE
You can always create a large, rectangular shape containing a gradient or pattern or even use an imported image if your background needs to be complex.

Video 1.6
*Common Keyboard
Shortcuts*

The **pasteboard** consists of the space surrounding the Stage. You can use the pasteboard as a scratch area or a drawing surface, or even include visual elements off the Stage that will animate into the Stage at a later time. Anything on the pasteboard will still be included in the compiled files—and will add to the overall file size—so be careful. It is a versatile feature that you should definitely make use of.

> **TIP**
>
> *Many common tools and actions have keyboard shortcuts assigned to make accessing them quicker. You can view the assigned shortcuts and even create your own by choosing Animate CC > Keyboard Shortcuts (macOS) or Edit > Keyboard Shortcuts (Windows).*

Let's Get Going!

Okay—that's everything you need to know going in. You'll complete seven separate projects in this book that cover all the basics of using Animate CC for creating content targeting Flash Player, HTML5, Adobe AIR, iOS, Android, and more. The creative possibilities are truly endless—so let's get started!

CHAPTER OBJECTIVES

Chapter Learning Objectives

- Create and prepare documents.
- Create shape assets.
- Manage the timeline.
- Animate objects with keyframes and tweening.
- Emulate natural movement through easing.
- Publish a project.

Chapter ACA Objectives

For full descriptions of the objectives, see the table on pages 286–291.

DOMAIN 1.0
WORKING IN THE ANIMATION INDUSTRY
1.4

DOMAIN 2.0
PROJECT SETUP AND INTERFACE
2.1, 2.3

DOMAIN 3.0
ORGANIZATION OF DOCUMENTS
3.1, 3.2

DOMAIN 4.0
CREATE AND MODIFY VISUAL ELEMENTS
4.1, 4.3, 4.4, 4.7

DOMAIN 5.0
PUBLISHING DIGITAL MEDIA
5.2

CHAPTER 2

Design a Vector Animation

Adobe Animate CC can be used for a wide range of project types, but at its core it remains a highly capable vector animation tool. This initial project is designed to ease you into the Animate CC user interface and its tools in order to complete a series of tasks focused on vector animation.

When you're finished with this project, you will have created a short animation of a ball bouncing on a floor. Although this may not be the most exciting of projects, it will introduce you to many of Animate CC's **vector** drawing tools along with animation techniques you can use across just about every other project in this book.

One thing that Animate CC is often used for in educational settings is to create simulations for classes or reference materials. Think of this project as the simulation of a bouncing ball (because that's basically what it is).

This project will incorporate many of the fundamental concepts you'll encounter when working with animated vector content. This includes creating and preparing documents; creating shape assets; managing the timeline; animating through frames, keyframes, and tweening; making animation more natural and pleasant; and publishing your project.

Video 2.1 *Project Overview*

Keeping this project small in scope will leave us room to go over some of the other tools you might find useful when creating and working with vector shapes in Animate CC (**Figure 2.1**). These include the Pen, Brush, Pencil, and various selection and management tools. I'll discuss these tools as they become useful in the project.

Figure 2.1 Vector animation in Animate CC

Creating the Project Document

★ *ACA Objective 1.4*

Although any Animate document will be in the form of a common FLA file, the capabilities and options available to you when working on a project will depend on the specific target platform.

Whereas Animate CC used to be used solely for the creation of content that will run inside the browser-based Flash Player runtime, Adobe has been positioning the application in recent years to allow for an infinite number of target platforms. Some of the platform targets that ship natively with Animate CC are **HTML5 Canvas**, **WebGL**, ActionScript 3.0 (targeting Flash Player or Adobe AIR runtimes), plus an array of custom platforms.

Whichever document type you choose to create, there are a number of other publish options that are platform agnostic. These can include **SVG**, **HD Video**, **bitmap images**, **spritesheets**, and more.

The Animate CC document file

Before even concerning yourself with the specific properties of a document, you need to choose your eventual target platform for the current project. You have a number of great choices with Animate CC, and they all share a common document format: the FLA file.

Animate CC creates an FLA file whenever you open a new document. It acts as a package to hold the internal assets and to keep your project organized. A simple project can consist of a single FLA file that holds all necessary artwork, sound, and code. This is one of the major strengths of Animate CC: the tight integration of design and development.

Animate CC uses a variety of file types in the process of creating and displaying interactive media applications. Some of the file types are specific to the Animate CC environment; others are more generic file types, including those used for images and audio.

NOTE

An FLA is a compressed file type, meaning that all the files and folders it contains have been written to a single file. An XFL is uncompressed and exists as a series of exposed files and directories.

The ActionScript 3.0 document

Animate CC has deep roots in **ActionScript** and the Adobe Flash runtimes: Flash Player and Adobe AIR. This should come as no surprise. For the majority of its lifetime, ActionScript was the only platform supported by Animate CC. As a result, choosing any of the AS3-based document types allows for the fullest set of creative tooling and the use of a deeply mature programming language, ActionScript 3.0.

For this project, you will create a new ActionScript 3.0 document. You'll explore other document types throughout this book, but since the idea with this project is to start off simple and explore core, traditional functionality, it makes sense to employ the document type that Animate CC is most comfortable with.

★ *ACA Objective 2.1*

NOTE

Any Animate document, no matter what the target platform, will take the form of an Animate Document file with the extension of .fla (or .xfl, if that is your preferred format).

FLASH PLAYER 2020

Even though Flash Player as a web browser plugin will be going away by the year 2020, it is important to note that ActionScript, Adobe AIR, and even the SWF file format will not be going anywhere!

Setting document type and properties

▶ **Video 2.2** *Creating a New ActionScript 3.0 Document*

The first thing to do when creating a new Animate CC project is to make some decisions about document type and properties. The main properties of an Animate document include the stage size, frame rate, background color, guides, and ruler units. These properties are usually set when the document is first created, but sometimes it's necessary to adjust them afterward.

In this exercise, you'll create your first Animate document and explore some basic properties settings.

1 Start Animate CC. If you're opening the application for the first time, you should see the **Welcome Screen** (**Figure 2.2**). You can disable this feature if you like, but it provides a useful display of all the choices you can make when starting off a new project, or even continuing a project you've already been working on.

Figure 2.2 The Welcome Screen

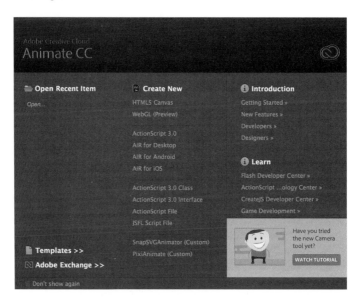

2 In the center column, under the Create New heading, click ActionScript 3.0, which is the third option from the top.

You will immediately be taken to a new Animate document that you can modify however you like (**Figure 2.3**).

Figure 2.3 A new Animate document

ALTERNATIVE DOCUMENT CREATION

Before continuing, you may want to try another way of creating a new document—directly from the Animate CC workspace when the Welcome Screen isn't open. Creating a new document this way allows you to select some basic settings, like width and height, before Animate CC opens the new document.

Choose File > New from the menu bar to open the New Document dialog box, which displays an expanded list of document types. Click Cancel to close this when finished, since you already created a new document from the Welcome Screen.

Notice that the document properties are displayed in the Properties panel for the document you've created (**Figure 2.4**). Here, you can modify some document properties and then save your document as a file.

The default width and height for a new document is 550px wide by 400px tall. This is fine for the current project, so leave these values as they are.

The default frames per second (fps) value is set at 24. This is also fine for now.

Figure 2.4 The Document Properties section of the Properties panel

3 Choose a background color for your stage. I nearly always choose black, but you can pick whatever color you like.

Now you have a new document with some basic stage properties configured.

★ ACA Objective 5.2

4 Choose File > Save to save your document. Note that you have two options here: FLA and XFL (**Figure 2.5**). An FLA file is the easiest to manage, since it's a neat little bundle and all you need to worry about is a single file. Stick with FLA, type a name for your file, and then click Save.

Figure 2.5 Choosing a file type

WHAT ARE XFL DOCUMENTS?

Recent versions of Animate CC not only allow the creation of Animate CC authoring files in FLA format but also can save projects in XFL, a format that's much easier to edit outside of Animate CC or to use with a version control system like Subversion or Git. The proper name for the file format is Flash Uncompressed Document, shortened to XFL with the X standing for XML (Extensible Markup Language) and the FL for Flash.

An alternative to the packaged FLA format, the XFL file format represents an Animate CC project as an XML document alongside a set of other folders and files. Each XFL structure has, at its heart, a file called DOMDocument.xml. If you open this file in a text editor, you'll see all of the information for your document, including timeline data, code, motion paths, and so on.

Remember that the FLA file format is simply an archived version of the XFL structures and documents. You can have a look for yourself! Just change the filename extension to .zip and open the file in a ZIP utility. The one built into Windows should handle this automatically, but macOS users may have to resort to a third-party app.

Preparing the project Stage and timeline

★ *ACA Objective 2.3*

▶ *Video 2.3*
Preparing the Project Stage and Timeline

Before moving on to creating some vector shapes and moving them around, you'll do a little project preparation to organize your document.

Almost always, I find it useful to have snapping enabled in my projects. Snapping will enable the application itself to "snap" objects to x and y coordinates based on a number of settings that you can select according to taste. It can make positioning objects in a precise way much easier. Animate CC offers a number of snapping options, and I enable them all. Whether you benefit from snapping or not will depend on how precisely you like things to be positioned on the Stage.

To enable or disable various snapping options, choose View > Snapping > Edit Snapping from the application menu (**Figure 2.6**). This will open the Edit Snapping dialog box, where you can select the snapping options for your project. Note that you can also toggle these options on and off directly from the View menu.

TIP

You can also enable both rulers and the grid from the same View menu. Experiment with all these options to see what works best for your work style.

Let's have a look at the timeline (**Figure 2.7**). You'll notice that within the timeline itself, a numbered system of frames extends horizontally along the timeline for the length of the animation, and a series of layers runs vertically down the timeline. Another series of numbers at the top of the timeline counts off elapsed

Figure 2.6 Select Snapping options here.

time in seconds calculated from the document FPS value. Note that in a new document such as you have here, you have one layer (called Layer_1) and a single frame (at the Frame 1 position). Initially, every new document includes only a single frame on the timeline.

Figure 2.7 The Animate CC timeline

1 To begin, double-click the "Layer_1" text to make its name editable, and type in **Floor**. You'll use this layer to hold the vectors drawn to represent the solid floor of the bouncing ball simulation.

2 Next, click the New Layer ( ) button at the bottom of the timeline—it looks like a sheet of paper.

This creates a new layer in the timeline, again with a default name.

3 Double-click the layer name and type **Circle** to rename it. This is the layer within which you'll draw out your bouncing ball vector shape.

Controlling layers and folders

★ *ACA Objective 3.1*

Besides the ability to create new layers, you have a number of other options at the bottom-left side of the timeline that you can use to manage layers and related items (**Figure 2.8**):

- Click the page icon ( ) to create a new layer.
- Click the folder icon ( ) to create folders for grouping layers.
- Click the trash can icon ( ) to delete unneeded layers.

Figure 2.8 Click these three icons to manage layers.

Layer management icons

Rearrange layers by dragging them above and below each other in the timeline layer stack. This will also affect the Z-order of the content on the Stage (for an explanation of Z-order—the ordering of overlapping visual objects in a project—see the sidebar "Arranging stacking order").

Setting layer properties on the timeline

Layers have several properties that can be set directly on the timeline or by right-clicking and choosing a command from the menu that appears.

★ *ACA Objective 3.2*

To set the visibility of a layer, click the bullet below the eye icon (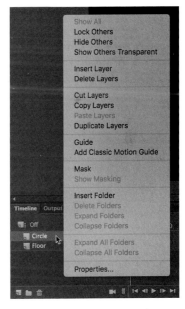). By default, Animate CC will still publish hidden layers, so this is not a way of hiding content at runtime. You might use this method when you need to focus on editing one particular set of elements by temporarily hiding the rest. If you want to toggle visibility for all layers, just click the eye icon.

Clicking the bullet below the lock icon (🔒) will lock everything within the layer. This locks only the artwork; you can still edit the keyframes within the timeline. You can also lock an element or unlock all elements from this menu by clicking the lock icon.

The bullet below the outline icon (▢) toggles the object display between normal and wireframe. Wireframe view can be useful when you're working with objects that are completely covered by other objects. It allows you to see exactly where the borders of objects lay in perspective to one another regardless of stacking order.

Right-clicking a layer opens a context menu that reveals more layer commands (**Figure 2.9**). These include commands for copying, cutting, pasting, duplicating, and working with guides. Animate CC offers a ton of options for working with layers—and a lot of them can be accessed from this menu.

Choosing the Guide property will allow the layer to display and function normally during authoring but prevent that layer from showing up in the published file. It's used only as a guide within the authoring environment itself, and it's never a part of the published project.

NOTE

An imported image reference or mockup of a project interface can be imported to a guide layer to provide a reference for placing actual interactive media elements.

Figure 2.9 The Layer commands menu

You'll see a lot of these other options as we go about creating and modifying our projects. One additional context menu item to note is the Properties command (also available by choosing Modify > Timeline > Properties). Choosing it opens the Layer Properties dialog box, where you can manage a lot of these properties through a single, unified screen (**Figure 2.10**). You can even set the outline color using the Layer Properties dialog box.

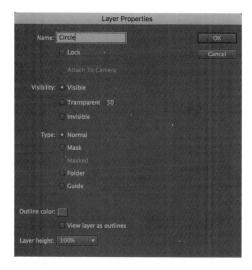

Figure 2.10 The Layer Properties dialog box

ABOUT LAYER MODES

You may notice that you are able to switch between basic and advanced layer modes by clicking a small toggle above the timeline (■: Off). For nearly all of the projects in this book, we will be using basic layers mode—but we will explore how to use advanced layers mode in Chapter 6. If you happen to switch layer modes by mistake, don't worry. You can always switch back by simply clicking the layer mode toggle once more.

Drawing Vector Assets

Okay! That should be enough background to get you going. Now that you have your Stage set up along with a number of layers in the timeline, you can begin creating your visual elements.

The drawing tools in Animate allow you to create and modify vector images. Vector images are composed of points and paths that are completely scalable without any image degradation because their appearance is calculated and rendered with every change. This differs greatly from bitmap images, which are set to a fixed resolution and can easily degrade in visual quality if enlarged or reduced in scale.

Animate CC is not restricted to vector shapes, but it works with vectors very, very well. One of the original purposes of using vectors was to keep the distributable file size as low as possible. This still holds true today.

Rectangle and Oval tools

You can create standard rectangles and ovals in Animate CC by selecting their respective tools from the Tools panel. You can set properties for these objects before you create them on the Stage or modify them later, either by selecting the objects and changing the settings within the Properties panel or by changing the properties at the bottom of the Tools panel.

Pressing and holding the Shift or Alt/Option key while drawing these objects constrains the drawing as follows:

- Pressing the Shift key forces the Rectangle tool to draw a perfect square.
- Pressing the Shift key constrains the Oval tool to perfect circles.
- Pressing the Alt/Option key causes any of these shapes to be created from the center out rather than from corner to corner. You can combine Shift keys and Alt/Option keys as necessary.

Rectangle and Oval Primitive tools

In addition to the standard Rectangle and Oval tools, Animate CC offers two tools that create primitive versions of the same shapes, with characteristics that can be modified in the Properties panel (**Figure 2.11**). When using the Rectangle tool, you have an option to create rounded corners through the Properties panel before

Figure 2.11 The Rectangle Primitive Tool Properties panel

drawing the shape or even while drawing the shape by pressing your arrow keys. Unfortunately, you cannot edit this property after you've created the shape. This is where the primitive tools come into play.

The Rectangle Primitive tool lets you create a shape object that has editable corner-rounding. This is a great feature for customizing rounded tabs; without it, you would need to keep guessing at the proper rounding value as you redrew rectangles.

The Oval Primitive tool lets you select starting angles and ending angles that create a pie chart–type graphic. You can also specify an inner radius to create a doughnut shape. This feature is often used to make elements for circular arrows that frequently show up in artwork used for preloading interactive media elements.

Merge drawing vs. object drawing

By default, the shape tools in Animate CC draw objects in standard Merge Drawing mode. The problem with drawing in this standard mode occurs when you have shapes that overlap each other. In Merge Drawing mode, you draw all shapes on the same layer, and new shapes delete anything underneath them. You can get around this by choosing Modify > Group to group shapes as you create them. Alternatively, you can draw all of them on separate layers.

TIP

You can keep track of your current location in the document hierarchy by looking at the breadcrumb trail (*) in the top-left corner of the Document window, just below the menu.*

Another solution is to draw your objects in Object Drawing mode. You can toggle this mode on and off by clicking the circular icon (Object drawing mode on) within the Properties panel or at the bottom of the Tools panel. Turning on this option forces Animate CC to draw every new shape as a separate object that is very similar to a grouped object. If you want to modify a base shape created using Object Drawing mode, first you have to double-click that object with the Selection tool to enter the object. Once inside the object, the familiar shape controls should be available.

Drawing shapes

Now let's draw some shapes.

1 To draw the Floor layer contents, do one of the following (or if you have the time, try both):

   ▪ Select the Rectangle tool and be sure that Object Drawing mode is turned on.

   ▪ Select the Rectangle Primitive tool for this project.

2 Regardless of which tool you've chosen, click the Floor layer to select it.

3 Drag across the Stage to form a rectangular floor shape (**Figure 2.12**). Don't worry about the color of your assets right now—you can change that later.

▶ **Video 2.4**
Drawing the Floor

Figure 2.12 The Floor layer.

4 Lock down this layer so you don't accidentally modify it.

5 Select one of the oval shape tools and select the Circle layer.

6 Hold down the Shift key; then drag on the Stage to create a circle. Don't make it too big—about 80–100 pixels should do fine (**Figure 2.13**).

▶ **Video 2.5** *Drawing a Ball*

Figure 2.13 The circle and floor are now present.

▶ **Video 2.6** *Using the Align Panel*

7 If the Align panel isn't visible in your current workspace configuration, choose Window > Align to access it.

8 Center the ball vertically on the Stage and then align it with the top as well. Then scoot it down about 10 pixels after aligning it to the top.

▶ **Video 2.7** *Testing the Project*

9 Now that you have drawn all of your elements, preview the content by choosing Control > Test.

ARRANGING STACKING ORDER

You can also manage the depth of interactive media elements within a single layer on the timeline. You can do so by adjusting what is often referred to as the Z-order: elements can be shifted forward or back one step at a time, or they can be forced to the front or back at once. You do this by choosing Modify > Arrange or by right-clicking an object on the Stage.

Additional vector creation tools

★ *ACA Objective 4.1*

In this project, you're using only a few of the vector creation tools available in Animate CC. Before moving on, let's have a quick look at some of the additional tools at our disposal.

LINE TOOL

The Line tool ( ) creates a shape that is entirely composed of a single stroke. There is no fill whatsoever when you're working with the Line tool. Holding down the Shift key ensures that the line you create is completely straight along the horizontal axis, along the vertical axis, or at a 45-degree angle.

PENCIL TOOL

Just as is the case with the Line tool, using the Pencil tool ( ) creates a shape consisting of one stroke only. The major difference is that the Line tool produces only straight lines and the Pencil tool is much more freeform in execution.

At the bottom of the Tools panel, you will find a Pencil Mode icon ( ), which provides options to straighten, smooth, or ink the stroke created with the Pencil tool. Selecting the Straighten option tells Animate CC to guess what type of line you were attempting to create and automatically straighten things out. The Smooth option softens the curves and smooths out your line. The Ink option creates a line exactly where you drag.

BRUSH TOOL

Similar to how the Pencil tool and Line tool will create vector shapes consisting of strokes, the Brush tool ( ) creates a shape that has no stroke and only fill. It works in a freeform way similar to the Pencil tool in that you can draw all sorts of forms with it.

At the bottom of the Tools panel you'll find options for the Brush tool that let you modify the brush size and shape (**Figure 2.14**). These options also let you selectively create the fill based on what is already on the screen. You can choose to draw additional vector content only behind the current artwork or only within a selection.

Object Drawing mode ——— ⬚ 🔒 ——— Lock Fill

Brush mode ——— ⬭ ● ——— Brush Size

Brush Shape ——— ●

Figure 2.14 Brush tool options

A final option on the Brush tool is the option to lock the fill. Choosing this causes a fill to be shared between multiple brushstrokes. How this works should be apparent when you use a bitmap fill or a gradient fill with the Brush tool.

PAINT BRUSH TOOL

This is a brand-new tool to Animate CC that expands the creative possibilities available to you. When you use the Paint Brush tool ( ), Animate CC creates a stroke and then maps vector artwork onto that stroke. The Paint Brush tool uses art brushes from the Brush Library panel (**Figure 2.15**), or you can import art brushes from the CC Libraries panel after creating them with the Adobe Capture mobile app.

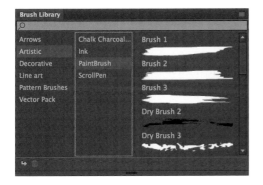

Figure 2.15 The Brush Library panel

PEN TOOL

The Pen tool ( ) is the basic tool for creating and editing Bezier curves. It works in conjunction with the Subselection tool ( ) to modify existing paths. It takes a while to master the Pen tool, but the power and control it allows make learning this tool worth the effort.

To create a curve, you can simply click your way around to create straight corner points, or you can drag a little at each anchor point to create a curved path. Clicking and holding the Pen Tool icon in the Tools panel will reveal additional editing options such as the Add Anchor Point tool and the Delete Anchor Point tool.

ADD ANCHOR POINT TOOL

The Add Anchor Point tool ( ) adds anchor points when you click the edge of a line or existing curve. This allows heavy modification of paths through increased complexity. Any vector line or curve between points is called a path. Paths can often include a stroke but do not necessarily have to in order to exist.

DELETE ANCHOR POINT TOOL

The Delete Anchor Point tool ( ) removes anchor points from a line or curve when you click them.

CONVERT ANCHOR POINT TOOL

The Convert Anchor Point tool ( ) turns a curved anchor point into a straight anchor point with a click. You can also turn a straight anchor point into a curved anchor point by clicking the anchor point and dragging out a set of handles for further manipulation.

POLYSTAR TOOL

The PolyStar tool ( ) gives you the ability to create a shape in the form of either a polygon or a star. When using this tool, you can specify many aspects of the shape, such as how many points you want the star to have or how many sides you want the polygon to have. The resulting shape consists of both stroke and fill.

Working with Vector Shapes

Animate CC has an interesting quirk that isn't seen in many other artwork programs. When a vector object is created, it can be made up of a fill and/or a stroke. Most programs treat the fill and the stroke as a single object. Animate CC lets you access the fill, the stroke, or both, depending on how you select the objects.

Similarly, various tools are available that deal specifically with either fills or strokes. Let's take a look at some of them now.

Selecting visual elements

Animate CC has a variety of tools for enabling the selection of entire elements, or even the partial selection of certain elements. For instance, you can use the Selection tool to select a stroke or fill, the Lasso tool to perform a more freeform and precise selection, or the Magic Wand to choose calculated portions of an element. You will need to select objects many times when working in Animate as this allows you to modify the properties of the selected object through the Properties panel.

★ *ACA Objective 4.3*

SELECTION TOOL

The Selection tool ( ) provides several ways to modify an existing shape. You can select the stroke, the fill, or both (by double-clicking), and drag them around the Stage. By selecting these objects, you can also access properties within the Properties panel and modifiers at the bottom of the Tools panel.

Another, less obvious use of the Selection tool involves hovering over an unselected stroke. A cursor will appear, indicating that you can bend the stroke. Pressing and dragging when you see this cursor will bend the stroke and take the fill along for the ride (**Figure 2.16**).

> **NOTE**
> *Using the Selection tool to bend strokes isn't usually the best way to approach the problem. Modifying the vectors with Bezier curves using the Subselection tool (described in the next section) provides more precise control over the resulting curve.*

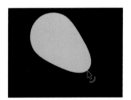

Figure 2.16 Shape-tweaking with the Selection tool

SUBSELECTION TOOL

Working with vectors can take some practice, but it is a skill that is absolutely essential for any interactive media producer. To edit a vector using the Subselection tool, you need to understand that there are two types of points that define a vector.

The first is an anchor point, represented by a square point that lies directly on the edge of an object. You can move anchor points by dragging.

The other type of point associated with vector drawings is the control point. Control points are shown as dots on the end of a line attached to the anchor point. Moving the control points around determines how the curve will pass through the anchor point.

LASSO TOOL

The Lasso tool ( ) in Animate CC lets you select content by looping the cursor around shapes or portions of shapes. The ability to do this with vector objects isn't common in creative applications, but it does show up in other Adobe products such as Illustrator.

POLYGON TOOL

The Polygon tool ( ) is similar to the Lasso tool but allows the creation of straight-edged selections. These are formed by clicking the mouse rather than dragging around the area to select. The clicks are joined by a straight-edged selection to create a polygon. You can finalize the selection by double-clicking.

MAGIC WAND

The Magic Wand ( ) lets you click an area of a shape and select all similarly colored, contiguous shapes. You can access settings to adjust the allowable color variation and overall smoothing by clicking the options setting button, directly below the Magic Wand setting.

Modifying shape color

Whether you're changing the color of a fill or a stroke, Animate CC is certainly not afraid to provide you with enough tools to get the job done. A number of tools in the Tools panel allow you to select and modify color. If that isn't enough, two panels are dedicated to this effort as well.

PAINT BUCKET TOOL

The Paint Bucket tool (![icon]) lets you fill or modify the fill of an existing shape with a different fill color as shown in the Properties panel or at the bottom of the Tools panel. Simply select a color in either of these areas, and click the area to be filled or the existing fill. Keep in mind that this will work only on a shape and only on a shape that is not currently selected.

INK BOTTLE TOOL

The Ink Bottle tool (![icon]) does exactly the same thing as the Paint Bucket tool but affects only strokes.

EYEDROPPER TOOL

The Eyedropper tool (![icon]) lets you select an existing fill or stroke and automatically sets up either the Paint Bucket tool or the Ink Bottle tool with the same settings as the shape element that you clicked.

THE SWATCHES PANEL

By default, the Swatches panel (**Figure 2.17**) is preloaded with the 216 color web-safe palette plus a few specialty fills, but it can be modified to hold only the colors or fills associated with a particular job. Pressing Ctrl/Command while clicking a color will remove a swatch, and going to a blank area of the Swatches panel with a color defined within the Color panel will let you drop that color into the Swatches panel.

Figure 2.17 The Swatches panel

NOTE

The swatch settings are stored with the FLA file itself and do not persist from document to document without additional actions.

THE COLOR PANEL

The Color panel in Animate CC (**Figure 2.18**) allows you to accurately specify colors as well as more complex fills like gradients and bitmap-based fills. Notice that the areas for defining the fill and the stroke are separate. It's a common mistake to be adjusting the stroke by accident and get frustrated when the fill color isn't changing.

Figure 2.18 The Color panel

In addition to holding simple colors, the Color panel lets you create gradients. You can add color stops within the gradient by clicking beneath the gradient window of the Color panel. Double-clicking the small square under the color stop will allow you to select the color for that area of the gradient. Dragging a color stop off the panel will delete it.

You can also use the Color panel to load bitmaps as fill areas. This lets you set an image as a fill style. Just choosing the bitmap fill from the Color Type menu (to the right of the Stroke Color box) will prompt you to select a bitmap image. If bitmaps are already loaded into your library, they'll be available as possible fill selections.

Time to Animate!

★ ACA Objective 4.7

Now you'll add some animation to your project. Since you're dealing with vector shapes, you'll be using a *shape tween* to perform the animation. When you declare a shape tween across a span of frames, you need at least two keyframes defined. This is how Animate CC knows to fill in the between frames: it calculates motion based on the change in properties between keyframes.

Frames are the basic building blocks of a timeline. They represent chunks of time defined by the frame rate of the document. If the frame rate is 24 frames per second (fps), then the playhead will move through 24 of the small squares per second. This determines the speed of the animation.

Keyframes are special frames that contain information about new content, or changes in existing content present within previous keyframes. Animate CC provides two main methods of animating content: using a frame-by-frame approach or through the Animate CC tweening system.

A keyframe with no content is called a **blank keyframe** and is represented by a frame with an unfilled circle.

NOTE

Keep in mind that only a keyframe can contain content. You cannot place content in a timeline without first inserting a keyframe. The contents of that keyframe can extend across multiple frames of the timeline.

Inserting a frame span

▶ **Video 2.8** *Frames and Keyframes*

You'll continue building this bouncing-ball project by inserting a frame span.

1   Using the mouse, select frame 30 across both the Circle and Floor layers. To do this, click the topmost frame and drag down to the bottom one.

Frame 30 of each layer should be highlighted.

2   Choose Insert > Timeline > Frame.

Animate CC not only inserts a frame at frame 30 (**Figure 2.19**) but also fills in the entire span of frames up to that point. Since we begin on frame 1 with a keyframe and there's content in that keyframe, that content is displayed across the entire span of frames from 1 to 30. You can confirm this by scrubbing the playhead through the frames in the span.

Figure 2.19 Frames inserted

Making use of keyframes

The tweening engine in Animate CC requires you to define at least two keyframes. Keyframes are special frames that hold information about shape and instance properties. In this project, you'll modify the y position of your circle shape. Animate CC will examine the number of frames between each pair of keyframes and calculate the properties for the object on each frame, based on the difference in properties between the two declared keyframes.

1   To insert a keyframe into the project, move the playhead to frame 15, making sure the Circle layer is selected.

2   Frame 15 is the midpoint of the bounce animation, so you'll move the ball shape down until it is resting on the floor. First, choose Insert > Timeline > Keyframe from the application menu.

Animate CC inserts a new keyframe, identical to the existing keyframe (**Figure 2.20**).

Figure 2.20 Keyframes created

3   Select the Selection tool. Use this tool to select the circle shape on frame 15 and drag it down to the bottom of the Stage until it rests on the floor shape.

Copying and pasting keyframes

You now have the properties set for the start and midpoint of your animation. Next, you need to take care of the end. If you want the animation to loop smoothly, then you'll need the properties of your shape on the ending keyframe to match the starting one. You could select the shape present on frame 1 and take notes regarding the positioning properties to copy bit by bit into the closing keyframe, but there's a simpler way: paste in place.

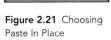

1 Move the playhead to frame 30.

2 Making sure the Circle layer is selected, choose Insert > Timeline > Blank Keyframe from the application menu to insert an empty keyframe just waiting for you to paste in some content.

3 Move the playhead back to frame 1 and use the Selection tool to select the shape there. Right-click the shape and choose Copy.

4 Move the playhead back to frame 30, right-click the Stage, and choose Paste In Place (**Figure 2.21**).

Animate CC pastes in the shape with all of its properties, filling the keyframe.

Figure 2.21 Choosing Paste In Place

Alternatively, you can copy the frame itself. To do this, right-click a keyframe and choose Copy Frames. Now you can select any frame on the timeline, right-click, and choose Paste And Overwrite Frames. It's that easy!

Navigating between keyframes

You can drag the red playhead marker across the timeline to move to any particular frame. You can also use the mouse cursor to click a specific frame within any layer and the playhead marker will jump to that position. If dealing specifically with keyframes across a certain layer, there is a better way.

If you look to the right of the layer name on whichever layer is currently selected in the timeline, you will notice the keyframe navigation control buttons (**Figure 2.22**). These allow you to jump from keyframe to keyframe easily, without having to scroll around the timeline or move the playhead all over in order to locate precise keyframes.

Figure 2.22 Keyframe navigation controls

The buttons are directional and clicking each will select the next keyframe in the desired direction relative to the current playhead position. Neat.

Creating a shape tween

Now that you've established all of your keyframes, it's time to tell Animate CC to fill in the frames between those keyframes. Remember, to make our animation more realistic we want to have the ball squash and rebound at the bottom of its bounce. To do that, we'll change its shape temporarily.

▶ **Video 2.9**
Animating with Shape Tweens

1 Click and drag across both frame spans—that is, some frames before frame 15 and some after.

2 Right-click the selected frames and choose Create Shape Tween.

> The frames in question turn a green color with a thin arrow pointing from left to right. This tells us that the shape tween has been created successfully (**Figure 2.23**).

Figure 2.23 Shape tween created

NOTE

If you try to apply a motion tween to a shape, Animate CC will prompt you to convert that shape to a symbol first. This is not a great idea, since it will create a bunch of elements in your library named symbol #. Elements without descriptive names can be hard to track as the project grows. We'll begin exploring symbols in Chapter 4.

USING SHAPE HINTS

Unfortunately, shape tweens don't always take the route from one shape to another that you might have had in mind. Sometimes it's necessary to give the shapes some guidance.

You can find shape hints in the Modify > Shape > Add Shape Hints menu. This option allows you to place alphabetical reference points on both ends of the tween to anchor areas of the shape and control the path of the shape transition. Normally, you'd need to do this only when tweening from one shape to another.

Modify Animation through Easing

If you preview the animation right now, it appears stiff and lifeless even though there's constant motion. The animation appears mechanical because it is: based on the instruction we've given it so far, Animate CC is simply calculating the motion in a strictly linear fashion to achieve the animation. You can make the animation appear much more dynamic and lifelike by taking both the easing and overall timing into consideration.

Adding some impact

★ *ACA Objective 4.4*

▶ **Video 2.10** *Squish the Ball on Impact*

Now you'll squish your circle as it impacts against the floor using the Free Transform tool. You use this tool to scale, skew, rotate, and even reposition elements on the Stage.

Figure 2.24 Circle squished using the Free Transform tool

1   Select the Free Transform tool from the Tools panel and use it to click the circle shape at frame 15. Frame 15 is a keyframe and the content is, during this frame, in visual contact with the floor.

2   Drag the small white circle at the center of the shape to the bottom of the shape. Known as the *transform point*, this allows transforms to be pinned to that specific point.

3   Next, grab the small square at the top center of the transform rectangle and pull it toward the transform point to "squish" the circle to some extent (**Figure 2.24**).

The Free Transform tool enables you to transform a shape in four essential ways:

- **Scaling** is accomplished by dragging the square dots along a shape's edges and corners. If you drag a corner point while holding down the Shift key, you preserve the aspect ratio of the original element. In other words, it will be scaled the same amount in both the horizontal and vertical directions.

- **Skewing** is achieved by dragging the edges in between the dots. The cursor changes into a skewing icon as you roll over an edge.

- **Rotation** is done by moving the cursor just off the corner points until it changes to a circular arrow and then dragging to rotate. Holding down the Shift key will constrain the rotation to 45-degree increments. Moving the round dot in the middle of the transformation selection allows you to adjust the axis of rotation. For example, you'd use this technique to rotate the hands of a clock by moving the dot to the bottom of the clock hand.

- Dragging anywhere on the graphic element other than the control edges or points allows the Free Transform tool to act just like the Selection tool.

MAKING USE OF ONION SKINNING

Animate CC has two options that let you visualize animations across frames. Onion skins and onion skin outlines, both found in the Timeline panel, serve a similar purpose by allowing you to see ghosted or outlined versions of a selected range of frames within an animation. These techniques work for all timeline animation types.

▶ *Video 2.11* Using Onion Skinning

Adding and adjusting keyframes

By default, tweens work in a linear fashion; in other words, halfway through the tween span, the properties are exactly halfway between the start and finish values. If you preview the animation, you'll notice that even though the shape does squish at frame 15, every other frame includes at least some bit of squish to it, and that's just unnatural. To remedy this:

1 Insert blank keyframes at frames 14 and 17.

2 Copy the circle shape from frame 1 and use the Paste In Place command to place the circle within both of the empty keyframes you just created (**Figure 2.25**).

Figure 2.25 Circle placed

3 In each instance, move the shape down to the top of our floor.

Now when you preview, you can see that the shape is placed in the coordinates where it would be expected to be at that frame. It can take some interpretation, so use your eye!

Applying easing for a more natural look

Applying an ease can add a nice touch to make a tween sequence look even more natural. Easing is used to determine how the properties are tweened from beginning to end. The ease will indicate whether the animated sequence will speed up, slow down, or remain steady throughout the length of the animation.

NOTE

Ease values range from –100 to 100. When you select a high positive ease value for the tween, the properties will change quickly in the beginning and then slow down at the end This is known as an "ease out." Selecting a negative value will cause the changes to accelerate through the span of the tween using an "ease in." Whenever the ease value is other than 0, a label reading "in" or "out" is displayed next to it.

1. To apply the ease to the first frame span (1–13), select any of the frames in that span, and adjust the Ease value in the Tweening Properties panel to –60.

2. For the second lengthy frame span, which covers frames 17–29, repeat step 1, applying an Ease value of 60 (**Figure 2.26**).

Figure 2.26 Adjusting the Ease value in the Tweening Properties panel

3. Preview the nearly completed animation. Everything should loop in a natural and believable way, simulating a bouncing ball on a hard surface.

Using ease presets with shape tweens

Though a linear ease can be effective in some cases, Animate CC also supports the ability to apply a robust set of ease presets to any shape tween.

1. Click anywhere between the first two keyframes on the Circle layer to select a frame within the initial shape tween.

2. In the Properties panel, look at the Tweening section. Right now, Classic Ease is selected. Click that button to view the ease type presets.

   In the dialog box that appears, you will see a list of ease types on the left. These ease types include Ease In, Ease Out, Ease In Out, and more. Selecting any of these will display individual presets such as Cubic, Quart, Sine, and Circ (**Figure 2.27**). Choosing an individual preset displays a visual graph to the right, approximating how each preset will affect your tween.

Figure 2.27 Selecting an ease preset

3. Select Ease In to reveal the individual presets within.

4. Apply the Cubic ease preset by double-clicking it.

   The ease type displayed now reads "Cubic EaseIn."

If you preview your animation, you'll notice that the Cubic EaseIn preset enables the ball to hold a bit longer at the end of the tween, making the ball appear as if it is hanging the air for a bit before falling, as a real ball would. Let's add an ease preset to the shape at the end of the animation as well to complement this.

1   Click anywhere between the last two keyframes on the Circle layer to select a frame within the final shape tween.

2   In the Properties panel, click the Ease Type button.

3   Select Ease Out to reveal the individual presets available to you.

4   Apply the Cubic ease preset by double-clicking it.

     The ease type displayed now reads "Cubic EaseOut."

Preview the animation by choosing Control > Test from the application menu. Notice how as the animation loops the ease presets chosen for our specific shape tweens add a sense of weight and realistic motion to the bouncing animation.

Adjusting the overall frame rate

The overall frame rate of an Animate CC project determines how quickly the playhead will move through the frames of the timeline and at which points the individual seconds markers appear. You set the frame rate through the Properties panel (**Figure 2.28**).

Figure 2.28 Setting frames per second (FPS) in the Properties panel

Your choice of frame rate depends largely on the capabilities of the playback device(s) you may be targeting and the nature of the interactive media content. Although higher frame rates should produce smoother animations, the use of higher frame rates can also create larger files and more work (for the animator) when using frame-by-frame animations.

Play around with the project frame rate to see how adjusting the FPS value affects the look of the animation. If you want to adjust the timing of your animation, the best way to do so is to adjust the number of frames across the timeline, effectively lengthening or shortening the animation. When you're pleased with everything, feel free to move on to publication.

Publishing the Animation for Flash Player

Once you've created your Animate document, you can preview it within the authoring environment only by using the Control > Test Movie menu command. At this point, the project is still just an authoring file and people will not be able to view your FLA project unless they have Animate CC installed on their machine as well. For most of your target audience, this will certainly *not* be the case!

So how do you get your awesome project out to the world? It's really quite easy; you need only publish the project in a widely consumable format. This could be a format that targets Flash Player, Adobe AIR, or even HTML5 Canvas or WebGL. Since this project was built with Flash Player in mind, we'll focus on that target platform.

Publishing for Flash Player

The primary output for an ActionScript document type in Animate CC is the browser-based Flash Player (**Figure 2.29**). Software that runs within Flash Player is packaged as a compiled SWF file. The acronym SWF comes from "ShockWave Flash." "Shockwave" refers to the web-distributable file type for projects created for the web with Adobe Director, an older application that had a number of similarities, initially, to Animate CC. The SWF file is typically embedded within an HTML structure and delivered via a web page.

★ ACA Objective 5.2

Figure 2.29 The Adobe Flash Player icon

Different web browser and operating systems can handle Flash Player very differently. For instance, if you're using the Microsoft Windows 10 Edge browser or Google Chrome, Flash Player is built in as a part of the native experience. If you're using the macOS Safari browser or Mozilla Firefox, you'll have to install Flash Player and manage it as a separate extension.

NOTE

As mentioned previously in this book, the days of using Flash Player in web browsers are limited. The major browser manufacturers, in cooperation with Adobe, will cease supporting the browser-based Flash Player plugin by the year 2020.

Most mobile web browsers do *not* support Flash Player in any form. If you're targeting mobile browsers via Animate CC, you should consider using HTML5 Canvas or WebGL document types. You also have the option of creating a native mobile app using Adobe AIR, but not all content is suitable as an app.

As of this writing, Flash Player is at version 29. Adobe continues to improve Flash Player features with quarterly major updates along with smaller security updates at shorter intervals to address specific problems that may arise.

ActionScript 3.0 Publish Settings

The first publishing target we'll look at in this book is for ActionScript 3.0 documents. You might be a bit confused about the naming convention here; isn't ActionScript a programming language? Yes, but it also provides the core target platform for Flash Player as well as Adobe AIR for Desktop, for Android, and for iOS.

NOTE

It is important to note that Adobe AIR, ActionScript, and the SWF file format are not affected by the announcement to end Flash Player support in web browsers by the year 2020.

Generally, if you've chosen to create an ActionScript 3.0 document in Animate CC, you're targeting the browser-based Flash Player runtime. However, you can easily switch between ActionScript-based targets by switching the Target property of the document in the Properties panel.

TIP

One of the major advantages to creating your animated content using an ActionScript 3.0 document type is that it makes testing and previewing your content easy. Choosing Control > Test will open a Flash Player–based preview window within Animate itself instead of having to open the content in a separate application, such as a web browser. This can speed up your workflow and you can always reuse the assets and animations in other documents types once you've nailed it!

The Publish Settings dialog box (**Figure 2.30**), accessed from the File menu, lets you specify how Animate CC will create the output file of an interactive media application. This dialog box lets you select the format and versioning information necessary to deliver your interactive media application to a wide variety of platforms and formats.

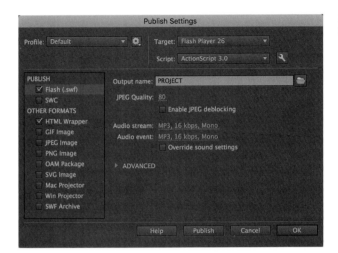

PROFILE SETTINGS

The ability to save collections of Publish Settings options as profiles is a huge time-saver for those who regularly publish to a variety of devices and platforms. Getting your settings just right can often require you to publish your document several times as you tweak the options of the Publish Settings dialog box.

By saving a profile with a descriptive name, you can quickly access those settings at a later date. For instance, you could be creating an Adobe AIR application for delivery to macOS and Windows desktop computers. Once you get the settings working properly, saving the profile as **AIR for Desktop** would allow you to quickly recall the settings that worked for you in the past.

TARGET SETTINGS

The Flash Player runtime and Adobe AIR platforms are constantly being updated to provide improved performance, capabilities, and security. Both of these playback engines attempt to update themselves continually to remain current. Adobe currently releases a major new version of the runtimes every quarter, with smaller security and stability updates in between.

Unfortunately, not all networks within companies or schools let users automatically update their software. In these cases, it may be necessary to select the lowest common denominator within an organization. Some organizations have a vetting process that a software update must go through before it is deployed to the entire network, so they might not be using the most current playback software.

SCRIPT SETTINGS

Flash Player uses a programming language called ActionScript to create interactivity within an interactive media application. This language has gone through several iterations; the latest is ActionScript 3.0.

ActionScript 3.0 can be a little more verbose than previous versions of ActionScript, but the performance and capabilities of this latest version make upgrading well worth the effort. Using ActionScript 3.0 will let you deliver to a wider variety of platforms, while also enhancing performance and security.

Animate CC no longer supports older versions of ActionScript. If you need to work with files created with an earlier version of ActionScript, you must use an older version of Animate CC.

OUTPUT NAME OPTION

The Output Name option in the Publish Settings dialog box lets you select the location and name of the output SWF file. This location defaults to the same directory as the FLA file.

JPEG QUALITY

Bitmaps within Animate CC are published using a version of JPEG. This format is a lossy compression scheme that decreases file size by sacrificing quality. When you publish a SWF file, all included images are compressed to keep everything nice and tidy. Setting the quality here will affect the quality of only the images published as part of the SWF file; lowering the image quality in the Publish Settings will have no effect on the quality of the images currently being stored as part of the FLA document itself.

An Enable JPEG Deblocking option is also available. This option helps minimize the blocky JPEG artifacts that can occur when you select lower-quality JPEG settings.

These settings affect only images that do not have a custom JPEG quality selected in the Bitmap Properties dialog box (covered in Chapter 3).

AUDIO QUALITY

You can set the quality of audio events and streams at publish time, just as you set the quality of a bitmap image. You can set compression schemes and compression values to make the files smaller.

Just as with bitmaps, you can use a custom setting for the audio or force all audio files to use the global settings established in the Publish Settings dialog box.

ADVANCED PUBLISH SETTINGS

It's good to familiarize yourself with the specifics of the advanced settings as they can help increase security, performance, and search engine visibility if used correctly.

The Advanced settings (**Figure 2.31**) include these options:

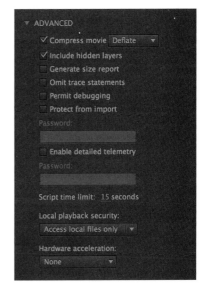

Figure 2.31 Advanced publish settings

- **Compress Movie:** This option compresses the SWF file to enable faster downloads.

- **Include Hidden Layers:** Unlike other Adobe products, Animate automatically includes hidden layers in the final output for Flash Player.

- **Generate Size Report:** This option generates a report detailing the file size and download requirements of the output.

- **Omit Trace Statements:** Trace statements are often used for debugging during Animate development targeting Flash Player. Omitting trace statements prevents the results of the trace statements from showing up in an output window. This output window is usually not available to the end user anyway, so it isn't a huge issue.

- **Permit Debugging:** This option allows the output to be viewable using the Animate debugger.

- **Protect From Import:** Password-protecting your final output prevents another user from loading and decompiling your Flash Player–based project.

- **Script Time Limit:** This setting caps the amount of time that a script can run, thus preventing an excessive or infinite loop in the code from locking up an end user's player. Good design should obviate the need to address this option.

PLAYBACK SECURITY

The Flash Player Publish Settings also include two settings that directly relate to network security and performance: Local Playback Security and Hardware Acceleration.

Local Playback Security determines whether the interactive media application can access files that are local to the published file or files that are contained served from a different domain over the web browser. You must choose one or the other, since allowing Flash Player to reach across from local to remote domains could result in serious security issues.

Hardware Acceleration determines what level of access the interactive media application has to the end user's local hardware. Your options are as follows:

- **None:** Select this option to prevent the interactive media application from accessing additional hardware that would enhance performance; this option provides the highest level of security.

- **Level 1: Direct:** This option lets the Flash Player bypass the browser and draw directly on the screen. Performance is enhanced, but the direct access could be a security issue.

- **Level 2: GPU:** This option not only allows direct access but also enables the Flash Player to use the graphics processing unit (GPU) on the end user's video card to help manage the graphics on the screen. Depending on the video card, this can be a huge improvement when working with video or other processor-intensive animations. Directly accessing the video card may present security concerns, but the added performance might be worth the risk.

PUBLISH SETTINGS: HTML

When publishing a standard Flash Player SWF file for use in a web environment, it's always a good idea to include a sample HTML file. You can customize this file to specify how the movie is displayed on the page.

> **NOTE**
>
> *This approach does not apply to publishing in an HTML5 format. It applies to SWF files embedded in HTML only.*

Setting these custom values and publishing the document will create an HTML document that you can study to determine how the SWF file was embedded and the results of the various embedding parameters.

Publishing a SWF

▶ *Video 2.14* *Publish for Flash Player*

There are numerous ways in which a SWF can be published, based on the defined Publish Settings, for any Animate CC project targeting Flash Player. In fact, if you've previewed the animation at all up to this point using Control > Test, you've already done so!

To publish a SWF in a more intentional and direct way, you can use the File > Publish command or click Publish in the Publish Settings dialog box.

Generating a projector

Animate CC lets you create self-contained applications called projectors. These projectors can be created for both macOS and Windows platforms from either macOS or Windows versions of Animate CC. To generate a projector, select Mac Projector or Win Projector under Other Formats on the left side of the Publish Settings dialog box (**Figure 2.32**).

▶ *Video 2.15*
*Generate a
Projector*

Figure 2.32 Generating a projector

Projectors don't require the use of a plugin or browser, so they're easy to use and you don't have to install additional software. This format is a popular option for delivering interactive media using USB drives, CD-ROMs, and hard drives.

> **NOTE**
> *Unlike Adobe AIR applications, projectors do not even need to be installed—they just run.*

Because it's so easy to install this format, it's a good option to consider when developing kiosks and presentations if you don't want or need the additional features or complexities of using Adobe AIR installers.

Generating a SWF archive

You can also publish all of your individual layers as separate SWF files to be imported and further manipulated in a video compositing application such as Adobe After Effects CC. When a SWF archive is generated, all of the SWF files will be bundled within a ZIP archive that you will find alongside the FLA of your project. Of course, the location and filename can also be explicitly specified in Publish Settings.

Challenge!

As we have designed the animation, it will continue to loop as long as the movie is running. It will never stop, and the ball itself will never adapt to forces like friction or inertia. However, when you're creating a simulation, it's important to consider every aspect of the system you're working in.

As a challenge, why not incorporate these other factors into the project? The bounce would decrease over time and the speed and height would lessen until the ball eventually just stops. Using what you've learned, you can use Animate CC to simulate this progression. Give it a go!

Conclusion

We covered a lot of content in this chapter! We looked at creating and preparing documents; creating shape assets; managing the timeline; animating through frames, keyframes, and tweening; making animation more natural and pleasant; and publishing your project.

CHAPTER OBJECTIVES

Chapter Learning Objectives

- Manage layers in the Timeline.
- Import images to the Stage and library.
- Work with vectors.
- Use masking to hide and reveal objects.
- Create text elements.
- Learn how to export a design in a variety of image formats.

Chapter ACA Objectives

For full descriptions of the objectives, see the table on pages 286–291.

DOMAIN 1.0
WORKING IN THE ANIMATION INDUSTRY
1.4

DOMAIN 2.0
PROJECT SETUP AND INTERFACE
2.1, 2.3, 2.4

DOMAIN 3.0
ORGANIZATION OF DOCUMENTS
3.1, 3.2

DOMAIN 4.0
CREATE AND MODIFY VISUAL ELEMENTS
4.2, 4.3, 4.5

DOMAIN 5.0
PUBLISHING DIGITAL MEDIA
5.2

CHAPTER 3

Construct an Animated Image

You can use the basic tools in Adobe Animate CC to build a wide variety of projects. In this chapter, you'll use them to create an animated meme image. Beyond the vector elements you used in Chapter 2, you'll work with imported bitmaps and text elements. In addition to these topics, you'll explore the Stage and Timeline to see how to arrange and manage assets within your project.

This project is more of a graphic design project than anything else, using three core assets types: bitmap images, vector shapes, and text. You've been tasked by a client to create an Internet meme image (**Figure 3.1**). Apparently, the client expects to get rich off these things—go figure. For an initial image, they've sent over a photo of their cat with some suggested text. The client does mention, however, that if you have anything you think is likely to "go more viral," you can use that instead.

▶ *Video 3.1* *Project Overview*

Figure 3.1 The meme image you'll create in this chapter

Starting the Project

You'll begin by creating a new Animate document. The type of document you choose doesn't matter since any of the supported document types can be used to output a static or animated image like the ones we'll design here. However, if you choose an ActionScript 3.0 document type, you'll have access to all the tools and effects available within the software. So, for this project, you'll use a standard ActionScript 3.0 document.

Don't worry about having to use the same document type for two projects in a row. You'll explore other document types throughout this book. But because the idea with this project is to start off simple and explore core functionality, it makes sense to employ the document type that Animate CC is most comfortable with. What's more, as mentioned previously, this allows you to use any tools you want.

Creating the project document

★ *ACA Objective 2.1*

▶ **Video 3.2** *Setting Up Our Project*

Let's begin.

1   Create a new ActionScript 3.0 document with a Stage resolution of 500px in width and height (**Figure 3.2**). The Stage color is completely up to you. Since we're producing a still image in the first part of this project, the frames per second value (FPS) bears no immediate consequence whatsoever…however, be sure to keep FPS at 24 for use at the end of this chapter.

2   Save the document as a new FLA file. Continue to save your project often.

Animate CC has the ability to autosave documents as well. This setting is on by default, but you can disable it or customize it by using the Preferences dialog box's General tab. Look for the Auto-Recovery option and you'll see it's a simple check box toggle. Also note that you can specify how many minutes you want the application to wait between automatic saves.

Figure 3.2 The Stage Properties panel

CHOOSING A PROJECT TYPE

When selecting a new project document type, opting for ActionScript 3.0 doesn't mean you need to write any code for the project. It simply means that the target platform will be one of the Adobe runtimes, Flash Player or Adobe AIR. It also means that you'll be able to use all the tools in Animate CC for that project.

Setting up your project

★ *ACA Objective 2.3*

In the previous chapter, I went into some detail on snapping and how to modify the settings that go along with it. For this project, enabling rulers and guides will be of even greater importance when laying out the design. Let's take a look at these features before going any further into the project.

Guides and rulers help accurately place objects and identify specific areas of the visible project area. Interactive media applications are typically designed and created using pixels as a ruler unit, so create any preliminary artwork with this in mind.

ENABLING RULERS AND THE GRID

Rulers will not be visible by default. If the rulers are not currently visible in your project, you can enable them by choosing View > Rulers (**Figure 3.3**).

Figure 3.3 Activating rulers

Similarly, you'll need to enable and modify the grid if you wish to use it in a project. The grid will not be enabled by default, but you can activate it by choosing View > Grid > Show Grid.

▶ *Video 3.3* Rulers and Guides

You can also edit grid spacing and other options dealing with the grid by choosing Edit Grid from the Grid submenu instead.

CREATING AND MANAGING GUIDES

NOTE

Settings for rulers, the grid, and guides can (and should!) be managed in individual documents.

Guides are light blue lines that show up only while authoring, and they aren't visible in the final published file. Be sure to enable rulers first if you want to employ guides within your project.

To create a guide, place your cursor in the middle of either the horizontal ruler or the vertical ruler. Drag from the ruler to automatically create a new guide that you can place where needed. As you might imagine, the horizontal ruler produces horizontal guides; the vertical ruler produces vertical guides.

If desired, you can place a horizontal guide around 80px from the top of the stage, and another 80px from the bottom of the stage. We can use these guides later on, but they are not essential.

MODIFYING GUIDES AND GUIDE PROPERTIES

Existing guides can be modified using the View > Guides submenu, which provides commands for showing or hiding guides (**Figure 3.4**). Temporarily hiding the guides lets you view the layout without the light blue lines.

When the Lock Guides command is chosen, it keeps important guides from being accidentally moved and can be used to lock down the design grid for an entire project. To unlock the guides, choose the command again to toggle the setting.

Choose the Edit Guides command (**Figure 3.5**) to open the Guides dialog box. Here you can customize the look and functionality of your guides by providing custom colors and the ability to adjust snapping, locking, and accuracy. It offers many of the same options as the Grid dialog box.

Figure 3.4 Enabling Guides

Figure 3.5 The Guides dialog box

Using External Graphics

Now that you've created your document and set up your project, the first thing you need to do in designing your meme image is to pull in an external bitmap file. Animate CC has support for many types of bitmap images, including PNG, JPG, and GIF. You can also import Photoshop, Illustrator, and even SVG files into your Animate CC project.

★ *ACA Objective 2.4*

Importing a bitmap image

▶ Video 3.4
*Importing a
Bitmap Image*

The primary element in this project is the bitmap image being used as the subject of the project. Animate CC can use both **bitmap** and **vector** images in any project. For this project, you'll be using both types of graphics together, something at which Animate CC excels.

Figure 3.6 Cat photograph "Poe," by Leslie Labrecque

Take some time to choose the image you'd like to use for your meme, keeping in mind the message you want to send. In the example files, I'm using a photograph of a cat provided by the client (**Figure 3.6**). It may not be the most original subject for a meme, but it's certainly time-tested!

1 To bring the image into your project, choose File > Import from the application menu.

2 Then do one of the following:

  ■ Choose File > Import To Library to import the image to the library.

  ■ Choose File > Import To Stage to import the image to the Stage.

Whichever decision you make, the image will be imported to the library. If you do choose to import the image onto the Stage, however, in addition to being placed within the library an instance of the image will be included on the Stage.

★ *ACA Objective 2.4*

THE PROJECT LIBRARY

The project library is an essential feature of Animate CC. Every project includes its own unique library containing any imported assets used within the document, as well as any special objects created within Animate CC, such as movie clip or graphic symbols. The idea is that objects in the library can have many instances created based off them and used within the project. In this project, you'll have a bitmap image in the library and use an instance of it on the visual Stage.

TIP

You can also bring object instances out of the library at runtime via code by using the library items' Linkage ID. You can set the Linkage ID for an object within the Library panel by double-clicking in the Linkage column for the object.

If you choose to import to the Stage, your image will appear directly on the Stage at this point. If you decide to import to the library only, you'll need to bring an instance of the image onto the Stage in order to use it within the project.

Importing from Photoshop or Illustrator

Importing files from Photoshop and Illustrator provides a valuable production tool when creating interactive media content. Animate CC recognizes PSD and AI files and launches an Import dialog box that lets you control how these files load their assets into your project (**Figure 3.7** and **Figure 3.8**).

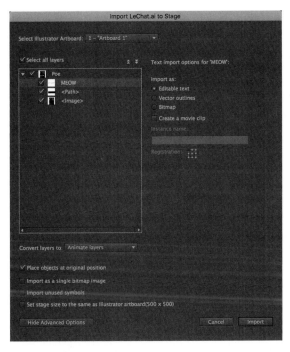

Figure 3.7 Illustrator import options

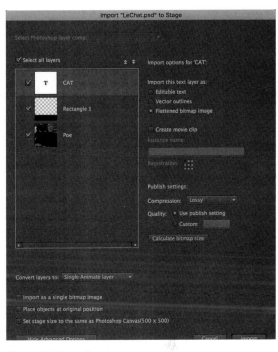

Figure 3.8 Photoshop import options

With some good planning and design work, you can build nearly all of your Animate CC artwork layers just by importing files in either of these formats into your project. For instance, if your entire project uses bitmap images, you can use Photoshop to create and manage them all. If you prefer working with vector objects in Illustrator, then there's no reason you need to even touch the Animate CC drawing tools—just import everything!

▶ *Video 3.5 Using Photoshop and Illustrator Files*

Here are some helpful options available to you when importing from AI and PSD files:

- Collapse all the layers of an Illustrator file to get a clearer view of the basic layer structure.

- Choose specific artboards from documents that contain more than one.

- Place objects at their original positions to preserve the relative positioning of the objects.

- Set the Stage size to the document size to resize the Animate document to match the document being imported. (Just be careful—very few Illustrator documents are sized correctly.)

- Create a movie clip from any selected layer if you'll need to tween your layers or apply interactivity later.

- Preserve text as a text object, render it as vector outlines, or convert it to bitmap data.

If you had imported the image file into your library and not onto the Stage, you must now take an additional step to begin working with it. To create an instance of an object in the library (**Figure 3.9**), do the following:

1 Open the Library panel either by clicking the Library tab, if it is part of your current workspace, or by choosing Window > Library.

2 Drag the image object from the Library panel onto the Stage.

Releasing it onto the Stage will create an instance of the library item. Notice that the library still contains the original object. You can create as many instances as you like in this way.

Figure 3.9 The meme photo in the Library panel

★ *ACA Objective 4.3*

Adjusting the image layout on the Stage

NOTE

With bitmap images especially, it's helpful to create the image in the exact resolution needed for your project. Unnecessary image data will make your project file size bigger than it needs to be.

With the bitmap instance on the Stage selected, be sure to make any desired adjustments to the image so that it appears on the Stage as you like it to. Use the Selection and Transform tools to manage the position and scale of instances on the Stage.

Most Adobe creative software products use two main selection tools. This can be confusing because they look similar, but each serves a unique function. The Selection tool ( ) is used to select entire objects or shape elements like strokes and fills. You can use this tool to move and position your imported image. The Subselection tool ( ) is used to manipulate the control points and Bezier handles of a vector object. When dealing with bitmap images, you'll find this tool fairly useless.

If using the provided cat photograph, I suggest selecting the link icon in the Properties panel to constrain the height and width to each other, and then changing the width to around 540. This will result in a height of 756. Use the Selection tool to adjust the positioning of the image.

Dealing with the Timeline and layers

Now that you have an instance of your imported bitmap image on the Stage, take note of the Timeline. Notice how you have one layer within the Timeline and one frame across time.

★ ACA Objective 3.1

If you were animating anything across time, you'd need to use multiple frames. Since you're not performing any animation in this project, you'll always be working in frame 1. However, you'll be using a number of layers in the project, and taking care to name your layers is a good organizational effort to put forth.

You can use the icons above the layer stack to toggle layer visibility, outline mode, and their locked or unlocked state. Changing the visibility of layers can help you focus on the layers you're currently working with. Viewing layer assets as outlines can help with fast rendering on old machines and, because nothing is obscured, can be useful when you're working with the size and positioning of objects in relation to one another. I suggest playing with these options to familiarize yourself with them.

The next step is to rename your present layer to something more descriptive.

1   Double-click the layer name and type in a new one, such as **Image**.

2   If the layer isn't locked already, you'll have to lock down the layer so you don't accidentally change anything in it (**Figure 3.10**). Do so by clicking the small Lock button (🔒).

TIP

Aside from a setting of visible or invisible, each layer can be assigned a transparency value. Just right-click any layer and choose Properties from the menu that appears. In the Layer Properties dialog box, you can select the Transparent option and set a value of 0–100. The default transparency value is 50.

Figure 3.10 Image layer locked

Managing Bitmap Images

While you won't be dealing directly with any advanced bitmap management concepts in this project, you'll want to know the following commands and techniques. To get the most out of working with bitmap images in Animate CC, you should know what your options are. Go ahead and try some of these options on your imported image instance. Don't worry if you mess up; you can always delete the layer contents and simply drag a fresh instance from the Library panel.

Break apart an image

▶ Video 3.6
Manipulate an Image

A bitmap image, the instance of a symbol, a drawing object, or a group can all be made of multiple individual parts. To see whether any object on the Stage is a complex element of this sort, double-click it. Note that this will only allow us to enter into complex objects and will not actually break them apart. If the object is composed of many different parts, you should be able to go within it to edit those pieces in isolation.

You can also access these individual parts by "breaking apart" the compound graphic using the Modify > Break Apart command (see **Figure 3.11**).

Figure 3.11 An image broken apart

TIP

Try this technique on a block of text. It will first break the words into letters and then break the letters into vector shapes.

If the shape-based artwork or base bitmap is embedded several layers deep, you may need to run the command several times before you see the telltale small dots that indicate you are at the lowest level and can start using the shape tools. Breaking apart the imported image will create a simple vector shape with a bitmap fill.

Bitmap properties

It's worth noting that you cannot edit individual pixels of a bitmap object in Animate CC. If you need to edit the image itself, you can edit it in another application, and then import it again or replace it with a new version. To do this, right-click the image's listing in the Library panel and choose Properties (**Figure 3.12**).

The Bitmap Properties dialog box opens. Use this to update the existing image or import a replacement (**Figure 3.13**).

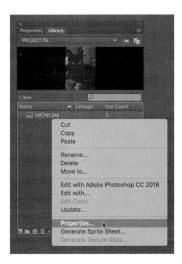

Figure 3.12 Opening the image's Bitmap Properties dialog box

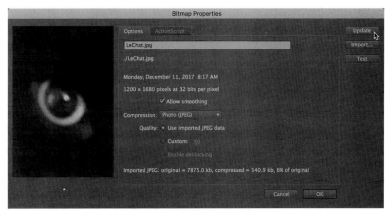

Figure 3.13 The Bitmap Properties dialog box

As mentioned, you cannot make adjustments to a bitmap image within Animate CC, but if you convert the bitmap to vector, then you can do all sorts of things to it! Be sure to close the Bitmap Properties dialog box before moving on. Let's now take a look at how to go about doing that through the Trace Bitmap command.

Using Trace Bitmap

You can also transform an imported bitmap image into vector shapes. Tracing a bitmap involves converting a pixel-based image to a series of vectors. There are many possible reasons for doing this, but it's usually done just because it can look cool (**Figure 3.14**).

★ *ACA Objective 4.5*

Figure 3.14 A vectorized
and recolored photograph

▶ **Video 3.7** *Using Trace Bitmap*

To see this in action, select the photograph on the Stage and choose Modify >
Bitmap > Trace Bitmap. You can use the controls in the Trace Bitmap dialog box
to determine how Animate CC will translate the pixel data into vector assets. You
have control over color threshold, curves, and more (**Figure 3.15**).

Figure 3.15 Trace Bitmap options

- **Color Threshold:** Increasing the threshold value will
  decrease the number of colors in the output.

- **Minimum Area:** The number of surrounding pixels
  that will influence a resulting color adjustment.

- **Curve Fit:** Determines the smoothness of resulting
  outlines.

- **Corner Threshold:** Determines how sharp corners are
  handled as the pixels are translated into vector data.

After you perform a Trace Bitmap command, the image is
noticeably changed. You're no longer dealing with pixel data
but rather a set of vector shapes based on the interpretation
of the original pixels. Just as with any vector shape data in
Animate CC, you can easily modify the paths, change the
colors that are applied, and more.

NOTE

*It's also possible to swap one bitmap image for another by selecting the image
and choosing Modify > Bitmap > Swap Bitmap. This feature is great for creating templates, or even trying out a variety of images in the same project.*

Sharing Library items across projects

By saving an Animate document file that has assets only in the Library panel, you create an external library that can be shared among several Animate CC projects.

To access this external library, you can import it by choosing File > Import > Open External Library. Locate the FLA that holds the previously created assets in the dialog box that appears. The newly opened library can be opened in a new Library panel, and instances can be dragged out and onto the Stage of your current document.

If you're working with a group and anybody in that group changes an asset in an external shared library by changing the assets with a FLA file, the asset will be updated for everyone. Assets will not be updated for any FLA file already using the library, but the library will be changed for any new FLA files created after the edit. Establishing good workflow rules can help minimize problems caused by sharing libraries.

You can also share content between documents that are open in Animate CC. If you have multiple documents opened at the same time, each appears as a tab across the top of the Stage area. From the Library selection menu in the Library panel of one open document, you can easily access the contents of any other open document's project library (**Figure 3.16**).

Figure 3.16 Choosing a library

Hiding content with a mask

★ *ACA Objective 3.2*

▶ **Video 3.8** *Hiding Content with Masking*

Unless the image you imported was exactly the same size as your Stage, you'll probably notice that the large size makes things a little hard to visualize within the project. Unless the Stage borders are enabled, the photo obscures the boundaries of the Stage, leaving you guessing where visual elements end in relation to where the Stage and the pasteboard begin.

> **TIP**
> *You can enable or disable the visible stage borders through the Animate CC Preferences dialog box. Simply select the Hide Stage Border option in Preferences > General.*

A good way to deal with this problem is to use a **mask** and a mask layer. To create a mask, you use one of the shape tools to draw a rectangle or ellipse, or use the Pen or Brush tool to draw something unique.

Masking applies the shape of the mask layer to a single layer or even multiple layers beneath it (**Figure 3.17**).

Setting up a mask is easy:

1 Just put the vector element that will determine the mask shape in one layer and then place the artwork to be masked in a layer directly below that layer.

2 Right-clicking the top layer will allow you to choose the Mask command.

Figure 3.17 The masked image

NOTE

You can mask just about anything. Try masking with videos and animation. You can even animate the mask layer content itself, if you like.

You'll notice in the Timeline that the masking group is indicated with a special icon and a slight indent. You can add several masked layers to a single mask layer group. To see the mask effect in Animate CC, be sure to lock both the mask layer and the masked layers grouped beneath it.

Creating Framing Vector Shapes

Next, you'll create some thick black bars as part of the layout design for your image meme. To do this, you'll use the Rectangle tool and create some vector shapes. Vectors are described by equations represented by Bezier curves and rendered on the screen at runtime. Working with these curves can be challenging, but because of their mathematical nature, they can be scaled without any loss of quality. They're also usually much smaller in file size than imported bitmaps, assuming they are not overly complex.

Creating shape elements

You'll now create the upper and lower framing bars to place behind your text. This text and the associated bars will overlay the image file you've already imported and should help the text elements you have in mind to stand out in the design.

▶ **Video 3.9** *Drawing Vector Framing Bars*

First, you'll need to create a new layer on the Timeline to hold your black bars. It's always preferable to place distinct objects on their own layers for organization and clarity.

1 To create the new layer, click the New Layer button beneath the Timeline.

2 Double-click the layer name, and rename it **Bars** since it will contain both upper and lower bars (**Figure 3.18**).

Figure 3.18 Creating the Bars layer

3 Select the Rectangle tool ( ) from the Tools panel and change the fill color to pure black.

As you draw these elements, they'll automatically be colored black.

4 Draw two rectangle shapes, each 500px wide and 80px high. You may need to guess at first, but it's easy enough to modify the width and height after you create the shapes to match these specific settings.

5 Place the first rectangle at 0px on the x-axis and 0px on the y-axis.

This is the upper-left corner of the Stage; this element is now aligned perfectly to the top.

Figure 3.19 The bars can be aligned against the guides and mask.

6 Place the second rectangle at 0px on the x-axis and 420px on the y-axis (**Figure 3.19**).

Because the rectangle is 80px high, it will align precisely to the bottom of the Stage. Now lock this layer so that you can't change anything by mistake.

NOTE

You could also use the Align panel with Align To Stage selected to easily align either vector shape to the top left or bottom left. There are a lot of different ways to accomplish the same task.

Working with Text Elements

★ *ACA Objective 4.2*

Now you'll add the text to your design as requested by the client. To create text elements in Animate CC, you'll use the Text tool and modify text properties like font, color, size, and so on.

Creating text elements

▶ *Video 3.10
Creating our
Text Message*

Before you start working with the Text tool, you should lock all the currently existing layers to avoid making any unintended adjustments to content that you've already worked with.

1 Select each existing layer and click the Lock icon if the layer is not already locked.

2 Create a new layer, double-click the layer name, and rename it **Text** (**Figure 3.20**).

All of your text elements will exist within this single layer.

Figure 3.20 The new Text layer

You can define the properties of a text element even before you lay out any text on the Stage. These properties include font and typographic information; color; anti-alias settings; superscript and subscript options; alignment; box behaviors, such as single line and multiline; link information; and the ability to apply filters to a text block.

For this project, you want the text to be big and white in contrast to the black bars already established.

1   Choose the Text tool from the Tools panel and take a look at the information and settings displayed in the Properties panel (**Figure 3.21**).

2   You'll be using static text for this project, so choose Static from the Text Type menu.

3   Choose a big font such as Impact for your text and change the Size value to 68.

4   Change Color to white if it isn't already set to that value.

5   To create a text block, drag across the upper bar on top of the Stage.

6   Release the mouse; then type the text you want to display. Type the first part of the text you saw in the final image shown at the beginning of the chapter: **WHATCHA**.

7   To create the second text block, drag across the lower bar. Release the mouse, and then type the text **LOOKIN' AT?**.

8   Use the Selection tool or the Align panel to move your text blocks to the appropriate places in the design (**Figure 3.22**). Center each of them horizontally and vertically on their respective black bar shapes.

Figure 3.21 The Text Tool Properties panel

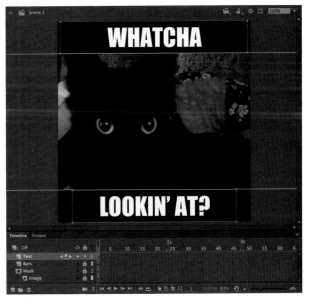

Figure 3.22 Text completed

NOTE

Text blocks appear on the screen with anchor points on each corner. You use these points to adjust the height and width of the text block. You can resize the block, set margins and spacing, and choose the behavior type from the Properties panel.

Additional information about text

Your text elements for this project are now set up, but there's a lot more to learn about text in Animate CC. Let's take a look at the various types of text elements you can create, the differences between them, and how to employ fonts, effects, and more.

TEXT TYPES

Available text types in Animate CC depend on your project's target platform. The different text types available can include static, dynamic, and input text (**Figure 3.23**).

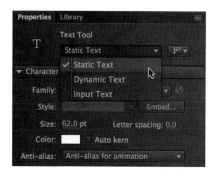

Figure 3.23 Text types

Static text is the simplest of all the text types: text that's created during authoring and that can't be changed at runtime. Even though it's the simplest text type, you can still choose numerous settings for static text through the Properties panel. One of the great things about static text is that you're not required to embed fonts for final publishing.

You can input dynamic text during authoring and change it with ActionScript or JavaScript during runtime. This makes dynamic text ideal for interactive projects where you need to provide user feedback in some way through textual data. Unlike the static text type, dynamic text has an option that lets you assign an instance name to the text element. This makes it possible to interact with the element through code. When using dynamic text it's most always necessary to embed character sets from the chosen font to properly display any characters that were not input during authoring.

Input text has all the functionality and configuration options of the dynamic text type but adds the ability for the end user to enter and edit text information. You can also specify a maximum number of input characters and select an option to apply a border around the Input text field to indicate that it's editable by the user.

EMBEDDING FONTS

Animate CC has the ability to embed fonts into an interactive media application, which expands a designer's type options.

Static text doesn't require font embedding, but creating dynamic text blocks for which the content or properties might be changed usually requires that at least a portion of the font character set be embedded into the file.

You can embed fonts by clicking the Embed button in the Character section of the Properties panel. The Font Embedding dialog box provides options for the process (**Figure 3.24**). Pay particular attention to the Character Ranges menu as this is the area within which you make selections regarding the range of characters you want to embed.

Notice the glyph count as you embed portions of a font. There's a huge difference in the glyph count when you embed the entire font, as opposed to just the Latin I subset and punctuation. The Latin I and punctuation subsets cover the characters needed for Western European languages. To keep file sizes small, embed only the glyphs or character sets required for the particular application.

NOTE

You'll notice that subtle changes in options available appear as you change the text block type from Static to Dynamic to Input. These changes are necessary to let you properly set the properties of these various text types.

NOTE

Embedding fonts is available only in ActionScript 3.0 document types. HTML5 Canvas documents can make use of web fonts from Adobe Typekit and Google Web Fonts to accomplish similar tasks.

Figure 3.24 The Font Embedding dialog box

TEXT ALIGNMENT

Most text-handling programs let you set the alignment or justification of text. In text blocks in Animate CC, text can be set flush left (ragged right), flush right (ragged left), centered, or justified (flush left and right). In addition to justification, line spacing and letter spacing can also be controlled through the Properties panel.

ANTI-ALIAS PROPERTIES

Regardless which type of text is selected, you can choose the anti-aliasing options for a text block from the Properties panel. Anti-aliasing refers to how the edges of the vector-based type characters will be rendered as pixels. This process involves feathering the edge of the type to create the appearance of a smooth edge even though it's created out of square screen pixels.

Video 3.11 Using Text Effects

You can specify how Animate CC anti-aliases these edges by choosing a font-rendering method from the Anti-alias menu:

- **Use Device Fonts:** This option uses fonts on the end user's system.
- **Bitmap Text:** This option will not anti-alias at all and will produce rough, jagged type.
- **Anti-alias for Animation:** This option creates a smooth and rapidly rendered edge that will animate more smoothly with less processing.
- **Anti-alias for Readability:** This option creates a crisp anti-alias edge that enhances readability.
- **Custom Anti-alias:** This option lets you select the exact anti-alias parameters.

BREAKING TEXT APART

Text blocks can be broken apart using the Modify > Break Apart command. This provides some interesting animation possibilities. The Break Apart command splits words into individual letters. Choosing the command twice will break down the individual letters into shapes that can be edited using Animate CC's standard drawing tools.

Generating a Static Image

★ ACA Objective 1.4

★ ACA Objective 5.2

Animate CC will generate any single frame of your project timeline as a static image file. This is useful for generating concept stills for a larger project or for generating fallback images for animated ads. To export our image, we don't need to select a frame at all, because right now we have only one frame to this project.

▶ Video 3.12
Exporting a Static Image

To perform an export, choose File > Export > Export Image, and then you'll have to choose one of the image format presets to render the output. You also have the ability to adjust the size of your exported image by absolute pixel dimensions or by percentage value. You'll also have the opportunity to choose whether you want to clip the image to the stage or to include content outside of the Stage as well. Let's take a look at each of these and how they handle our design.

> **NOTE**
> *You can also choose File > Export > Export Image (Legacy) for a simplified method of exporting images from an Animate CC project.*

Exporting as JPEG

JPG (or JPEG) stands for Joint Photographic Experts Group. This is a great format for representing photographic content for the web. It is a highly compressed, lossy file format for image data.

The main options when exporting a JPEG from an Animate CC project are as follows (**Figure 3.25**):

- **Quality** deals with compression (the higher the setting, the less the image is compressed) and is specified on a scale of 0–100.
- **Blur** applies some blur to the image in an effort to remove any compression artifacts.
- **Progressive** indicates whether portions of the image will be revealed as it is being downloaded.
- **ICC Profile** will include an ICC profile based on color settings. An ICC profile characterizes a color input or output device, or a color space, according to standards promulgated by the International Color Consortium.

Figure 3.25 JPEG export options

Figure 3.26 GIF export options

Export Image as GIF

The Graphics Interchange Format (GIF) is a compressed bitmap image format originally created by CompuServe way back in 1987. It's often used on the Internet today to display both static and animated content. Something important to keep in mind about the GIF format is that it is quite limited in the colors it can display.

The main options when exporting a GIF are as follows (**Figure 3.26**):

- **Lossy** controls the amount of compression the image will be subjected to. (More compression translates to greater loss of image data.)
- **Colors** allows you to restrict the number of colors available to the GIF image.

- **Dither** specifies whether to dither the image to create the illusion of greater color depth and by what percentage.

- **Transparency** will allow parts of the exported GIF image to be transparent, though as with GIF, transparency is quite limited as pixels can only be fully transparent or fully opaque—no partial transparency.

- **Interlaced** specifies whether the resulting image can be downloaded in multiple passes.

Export Image as PNG

Portable Network Graphics (PNG) is a bitmap file format with lossless data compression, unlike JPEG. PNG was created as a non-patented replacement for GIF files. Although PNG is a great format, PNG files can be much larger than JPEGs or GIFs, depending on the settings you use.

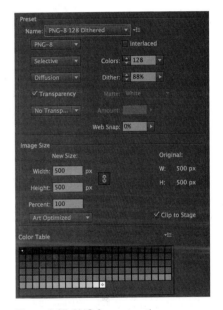

The primary options when exporting a PNG-8 are as follows (**Figure 3.27**):

- **Interlaced** specifies whether the resulting image can be downloaded in multiple passes or not.

- **Colors** allows you to restrict the number of colors available to the GIF image.

- **Dither** specifies whether to dither the image to create the illusion of greater color depth and by what percentage.

- **Transparency** will allow parts of the exported image to be transparent—though with PNG-8, transparency is quite limited.

Figure 3.27 PNG-8 export options

PNG-8 is very similar to what you might expect from a GIF. You also have the option of exporting as PNG-24. This is where the real power of the PNG image format lies… yet you may be surprised that the number of options you have when exporting are actually much fewer.

The options when exporting a PNG-24 are as follows (**Figure 3.28**):

- **Interlaced** specifies whether the resulting image can be downloaded in multiple passes.

- **Transparency** will allow parts of the exported PNG image to be transparent.

With a PNG-24 image, the image has the capability of full transparency and multiple levels of transparency across the image. This is a great choice for image overlays and complex user interface elements because it provides the ability to create complex images with complete control over transparency settings.

Figure 3.28 PNG-24 export options

Export Image as SVG

Scalable Vector Graphics (SVG) is an XML-based vector image format for two-dimensional graphics. SVG files cannot be generated through the normal image export dialog box we used earlier. You must use the older method of exporting images to export an SVG file. The dialog box can be accessed through File > Export > Export Image (Legacy).

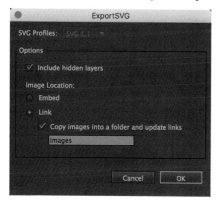

Figure 3.29 SVG export options

The options when exporting an SVG are as follows (**Figure 3.29**):

- **SVG Profiles** is grayed out and disabled, defaulting to SVG 1.1.

- **Include Hidden Layers** allows layers hidden in the Timeline to be rendered in the final image.

- **Image Location** can be set to either Embed or Link. When you choose Link, you can also specify a folder to keep the images in.

It's important to stress that there are many ways of exporting images from Animate CC documents. We've seen a sampling of both the modern and legacy export choices here, but you can also automatically publish static image formats from the Publish Settings dialog box, though you get much less control.

Generating an Animated GIF Image

★ *ACA Objective 5.2*

Let's add a smidgen of animation to our static project and export that as an animated GIF image. We'll have our cat give a wink to let us know he's just messing around.

Adjusting the Timeline

★ *ACA Objective 3.1*

Since our project consists of only a single frame, we'll need to add in some additional frames and an extra layer to create the opportunity for motion. The second markers above the Timeline will assist us in planning this.

▶ **Video 3.13** *Prepare the Timeline for Animation*

1   Select frame 120 (at the 5-second mark) across all four layers.

2   Press the F5 key to insert frames across the Timeline to that chosen point (**Figure 3.30**).

Figure 3.30 Adding frames to the Timeline

The playhead can now run across a full 5 seconds of the Timeline, but since nothing changes across these frames, we have no animation.

3   Click the New Layer button below the Timeline to insert a new layer.

4   Position the new layer anywhere above the Mask layer and double-click the layer name to rename it **Wink**. This layer will hold our simple animation.

5   Select the frame at the 4-second mark (frame 96) in the Wink layer and press the F6 key to insert a new keyframe.

6   Select frame 108 on that same layer and click either F6 or F7 (**Figure 3.31**).

Figure 3.31 The Wink layer

It doesn't matter which key you press. A blank keyframe will be inserted either way, since no content exists within the layer.

Making the cat wink

We will now alter the visual content and produce some simple frame-by-frame animation.

▶ *Video 3.14*
Animating the Image

To make the cat wink, we'll create some vector content over his left eye to make it appear to close across the span of frames designated for this purpose.

1 Be sure the Wink layer is selected and move the playhead to the 4-second mark. You can either drag the playhead or use the contextual keyframe navigation buttons next to the layer name.

2 Use whatever tool you like in order to create a closed eyelid. Three of the tools to consider are the Pen tool, the Brush tool, and the Oval tool.

3 Change the fill to a color appropriate for the kitty's closed eyelid. You can use the Eyedropper tool to sample from the cat's fur (**Figure 3.32**).

Figure 3.32 Cat nap vector eyelid

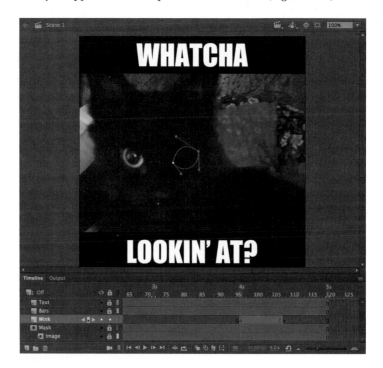

Play the animation by choosing Control > Test or use the playback controls beneath the Timeline. The entire project has no motion at all until the playhead hits the 4-second mark—the kitty winks—and then everything is still once more.

Since the animation is mostly still, with just some additional content appearing at one point in the timeline, we can easily get away with reducing the project's FPS value in order to ensure the animated GIF file we produce is not too large.

1 In the Properties panel, look at the Properties section and select Scale Frame Spans. This will allow the entire animation to adjust relative to changes in the FPS value.

2 Change the FPS value from 24 to 10 (**Figure 3.33**).

Because we enabled the Scale Frame Spans option, everything scales down relative to the time already established (**Figure 3.34**). The animation still takes 5 seconds to execute as before—it just takes fewer frames to do so!

Figure 3.33 Scaling the frame span by changing the FPS value.

Figure 3.34 The completed and adjusted Timeline.

The animated aspect of this project is complete.

> **NOTE**
> *Although there is a change in content across frames, we haven't used any sort of tweening (such as with a Shape Tween) as we did in the previous chapter. This is basically frame-by-frame animation using keyframes.*

Exporting an animated GIF

Now that we have some animation in our project, we can publish and export to a variety of file types and platforms. We might produce an MP4 video file, publish a SWF for Flash Player, or even convert the project for HTML5 Canvas for playback using a web browser.

We will be sticking with image output in this chapter and so will be exporting an animated GIF image. To produce the project as an animated GIF image, follow these steps:

▶ *Video 3.15*
Generate an Animated GIF

1   Choose File > Export > Export Animated GIF. The Export Image dialog box appears with all of the settings configured to produce an animated GIF.

Notice the Animation section in the lower-right corner of the dialog box. It allows you to specify whether the animation loops one time or forever, and it presents some playback controls you can use to test the animation (**Figure 3.35**).

Figure 3.35 Animated GIF export options

To keep the file size down, you will likely want to tweak some of the GIF settings such as the number of colors used. You may even reduce the file resolution to something like 300x300 before saving.

2   Click the Preview button below the image to preview the animation in a web browser (**Figure 3.36**).

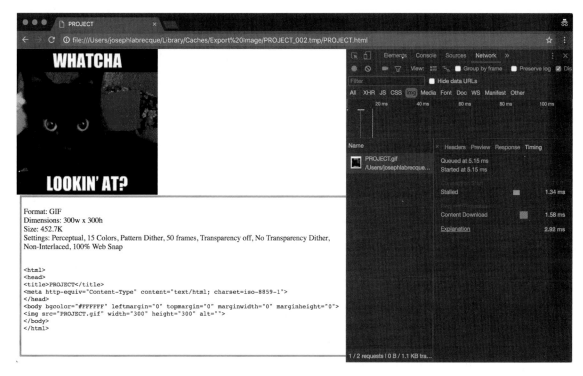

Figure 3.36 Animated GIF preview

3 When ready, click Save to create the animated GIF file.

When you save an optimized file using the Export Animated GIF option, you can generate an HTML file for the image. This file contains all the necessary information to display your image in a web browser.

Challenge!

Import a number of bitmaps into the library and swap them out for a completely different message in the project. Change around the text as well—make this project your own!

Conclusion

This project and the previous included a lot of the fundamental things you need to know when working in Animate CC regardless of project type. Here, you saw the interoperability of Animate CC between other applications in the Adobe Creative Cloud and how even though Animate CC was created as an animation program, you can also create static design content just as easily.

We certainly covered quite a bit of ground with this project! We managed layers in the Timeline, imported images to both the Stage and the library, worked with vectors, used masking to hide and reveal objects, examined a variety of options when creating text elements, and finally had a solid look at exporting our design in a variety of image formats. Well done!

CHAPTER OBJECTIVES

Chapter Learning Objectives

- Work with HTML5 Canvas and WebGL publish targets.

- Access the Brush Library.

- Use the Paint Brush tool.

- Create armatures with the Bone tool.

- Work with movie clip symbols and instances.

- Manage HTML5 Canvas publish settings.

Chapter ACA Objectives

For full descriptions of the objectives, see the table on pages 286–291.

DOMAIN 1.0
WORKING IN THE ANIMATION INDUSTRY
1.4

DOMAIN 2.0
PROJECT SETUP AND INTERFACE
2.1, 2.4, 2.5, 2.6

DOMAIN 3.0
ORGANIZATION OF DOCUMENTS
3.1

DOMAIN 4.0
CREATE AND MODIFY VISUAL ELEMENTS
4.1, 4.2, 4.4, 4.5, 4.7

DOMAIN 5.0
PUBLISHING DIGITAL MEDIA
5.2

CHAPTER 4

Compose an Animated HTML5 Greeting

This chapter will build on everything you've learned so far, but we'll take things in a different direction from previous projects by authoring content that runs natively in the browser without the need for Flash Player. We'll also delve deeper into aspects of the library and symbols while introducing some new tools.

This project involves the traditional web-based greeting card (**Figure 4.1**), but with a twist: the client wants you to design the card in such a way that it can be accessed via a web browser on a desktop, mobile device, or other similar means. In other words, since the browser-based Flash Player is widely available only on desktop browsers, in order to hit mobile targets we'll need to deploy using a native HTML5 target. Luckily, Adobe Animate CC includes a number of target-platform document types suited specifically to this task.

▶ *Video 4.1* *Project Overview*

Figure 4.1 The greeting you'll create in this chapter

Creating a New HTML5 Canvas Document

Content created in Animate CC can be published directly to a number of modern HTML5 formats, including Canvas and WebGL. The primary document type that allows this publish target is HTML5 Canvas. When creating content using this publish target, Animate CC leverages the CreateJS JavaScript libraries to output an entire animation or interactive project for the HTML5 canvas element.

Setting up the project document

The first thing you'll do is create a new document by doing one of the following:

- On the Welcome screen, select HTML5 Canvas as your document type.
- Choose File > New to open the New Document dialog box (**Figure 4.2**). In the Type list, select HTML5 Canvas.

   NOTE

   The HTML5 canvas element is also used to display WebGL content.

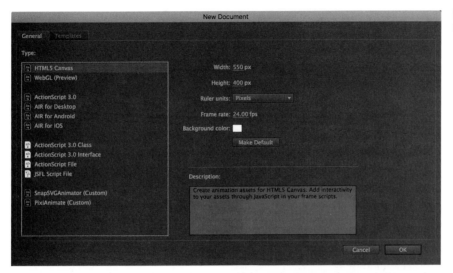

Figure 4.2 The New
Document dialog box

CREATEJS

CreateJS is a suite of modular JavaScript libraries and tools that work together or independently to enable rich interactive content using open web technologies in HTML5. See www.createjs.com to learn more.

Animate CC opens a new document, which initially looks exactly the same as the documents we've already worked with. You should note a number of differences, however:

- First, notice that in the General tab of the New Document dialog box, the name of the file is appended with the (Canvas) qualifier. This lets you know that you're working in that particular document type. ActionScript-based projects have no such qualifier.

- A couple of tools in the Tools panel are disabled: the 3D Rotation tool ( ) and the 3D Translation tool ( ).

- If you select the Text tool (T), you'll notice that you can only choose Static Text or Dynamic Text. Input text Type is disabled.

- When viewing Document Properties, you'll see that a lot of options under the Publish area are disabled because they pertain only to ActionScript-based projects.

NOTE

The HTML5 canvas element is a structure through which bitmap data can be drawn and changed via Java-Script. It also includes the ability to process and respond to various modes of interactivity like mouse clicks and touch events.

Otherwise, creating and animating content targeting HTML5 Canvas should be nearly identical to what you have already encountered.

Preparing the Stage and timeline

Before creating any assets in the greeting card project, you'll do some work on configuring the Stage and other project fundamentals.

1   In the Properties panel (**Figure 4.3**), set the Stage width to 550 pixels and the height to 400 pixels. This is the normal Animate CC default, so there may not be anything to change depending on your preferences.

Figure 4.3 Configuring the Stage in the Properties panel

2   Make sure FPS is set to a value of 24 and choose a background color that suits you. I choose black most of the time, but in this project, I'll select a cheery orange color instead. You'll be drawing a background anyhow, so it doesn't matter all that much.

3   Moving on to the timeline, rename the present layer **BG**. This is where you will draw your project background.

4   Use the New Layer button ( ) to create an additional layer and name it **Frame** (**Figure 4.4**). This layer will contain assets that make up the basic background elements of your project.

Figure 4.4 Frame layer added

5   Save the document in a location that makes sense to you.

Even though you're using a different document type in this project, Animate CC treats the file the same way, even saving it in the same FLA file format.

Laying Out the Background Elements

★ *ACA Objective 4.1*

Now that you have layers for your frame and background assets, you can create these elements using the shape and drawing tools in Animate CC. You'll be using some of the vector tools you're already familiar with, but you'll also be introduced to the concept of variable-width strokes and the super cool Paint Brush tool.

Drawing the background

To draw the background to the greeting card project, you'll use the new Brush Library and the Paint Brush tool in Animate CC.

▶ *Video 4.3 Drawing the Background*

1   To begin, lock the Frame layer to ensure that you don't draw anything in it by mistake.

2   Select the BG layer within the timeline and select either the Rectangle tool (▦) with Object Drawing Mode enabled or the Rectangle Primitive tool (▦).

You're now ready to draw the background.

3   Drag from the top left of the Stage to the bottom right to draw a shape exactly the same size as the Stage: 550x400.

4   You may need to make some adjustments to the size and position of your shape, depending on your snap settings and how steady a hand you have. Do this from the Properties panel with the object selected.

5   If you haven't done so already, choose a background color for your shape. I'm using #FF9933 in the example shown in **Figure 4.5**, but you can choose whatever you like.

Figure 4.5 I'm using an orange-ish background for my shape.

Figure 4.6 No stroke color as represented in the Properties panel

6 You don't need any stroke color for this project, so choose None for the Stroke color. It's represented in the color picker as the white block with the red diagonal line running through it (**Figure 4.6**).

NOTE

You can always turn off stroke or fill by choosing None for either color value.

Decorating with the Paint Brush tool

▶ *Video 4.4*
Decorating with
Art Brushes

Now for some freeform fun! The Paint Brush tool (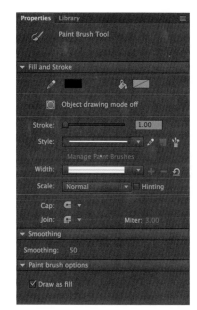) lets you draw out strokes with vector art attached to them. This allows for massive creative possibilities, whether you're using built-in brushes from the Brush Library or using custom brushes you created with the Adobe Capture CC mobile app and shared with Animate CC via the CC Libraries panel.

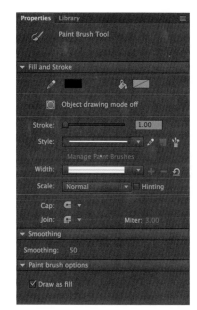

Figure 4.7 The Properties panel with the Paint Brush tool selected

1 To begin, select the Paint Brush tool from the Tools panel. The Paint Brush tool Properties panel opens (**Figure 4.7**). You'll be drawing these decorative assets in the BG layer.

2 Choose Window > Brush Library to open the Brush Library.

In the Brush Library, you'll see a number of categories, which contain a wide variety of prebuilt vector art brushes.

3 Find one you'd like to use and select it.

It should now show up in the Style area of your Properties panel. You can see in **Figure 4.8** that I've chosen the brush named Chalk - Scribble from the Artistic > Chalk Charcoal category in the Brush Library.

Now it's time to get creative!

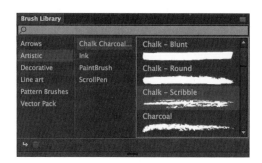

Figure 4.8 The Brush Library

4   Using the Paint Brush tool, drag across the Stage to generate freeform vector artwork. Don't make your art too busy, but don't hold back too much either. Make it interesting.

NOTE

You can also access the Brush Library directly from the Properties panel by clicking the Brush Library icon ( ).

TIP

You may want to select the Draw As Fill option in the Paint Brush Options section of the Properties panel. This will draw out vector art as fill and not strokes. Selecting Draw As Fill will generally be more performant on slower systems since a good part of the rendering is already completed and the appearance does not need to be generated on-the-fly as with stroke-only.

5   Select a Shape color. In **Figure 4.9**, I've chosen to use something a few steps darker than my background (#A35A12), but there's no reason you couldn't use a number of variations in color or even stroke width. You can control all these properties from the Properties panel with the Paint Brush tool selected.

Figure 4.9 An artistic background

6   Once you're happy with the results, lock the BG layer and unlock the Frame layer for the next step in this project.

EDITING AND MANAGING VECTOR ART BRUSHES

You can also edit existing brushes by clicking the Edit Stroke Style icon ( ) in the Properties panel with the Paint Brush Tool selected. This allows even greater variation in how the vector art is mapped to your strokes.

It is also possible to use the Paint Brush Options dialog box to convert vector art brushes into pattern brushes (and vice versa). Pattern brushes are great for things like frames and borders.

To manage all the brushes within your document—or even save custom brushes to your Brush Library—click the Manage Paint Brushes button in the Properties panel with the Paint Brush tool selected.

Drawing the frame with variable-width strokes

Using variable-width strokes in your project is an easy way to impart a bit of controlled chaos to simple strokes. Animate CC will, in place of a linear stroke, impart a stroke whose width varies at certain points. The best way to grasp the concept is to use it. You'll create a nice frame for this project and apply a variable-width profile to the frame stroke.

1 Select the Frame layer so that you can draw the object. You may want to ensure all other layers are locked before proceeding.

2 Choose the Rectangle or Rectangle Primitive tool and draw a vector object the exact size of your Stage: 550px by 400px. Use whatever color you like for the stroke (in **Figure 4.10**, I'm using #336600), and choose a transparent fill.

3 With the object selected, choose a profile from the Width menu in the Fill And Stroke section of the Properties panel. If something doesn't look right, select the Width tool from the Tools panel and tweak existing width points or even create new ones.

4 For an additional creative flourish, apply a vector art brush to the variable-width stroke as well. In **Figure 4.11**, I'm using Artistic > Chalk Charcoal > Chalk - Round from the Brush Library and a stroke value of 26.

Figure 4.10 Drawing Object Properties

Figure 4.11 A little extra creative flourish added with a vector art brush

GROUPING THE LAYERS WITHIN A FOLDER

★ ACA Objective 3.1

▶ **Video 4.6**
Grouping Layers

One of the best things you can do to keep things organized in your timeline is to group layers. You can accomplish this by creating a layer folder for specific sets of layers.

1 Click the New Folder button below the layer stack on the bottom left of the timeline to create a folder to contain your static background elements.

2 Double-click the folder name and change it to **Background**.

3 Drag both the BG and Frame layers into the layer folder you just created (**Figure 4.12**).

Figure 4.12 BG and Frame layers added to the new layer folder

With the folder created, you can now control the lock status, visibility, and outline mode for all layers from the folder itself. You can also collapse and expand the folder by using the small triangle beside the folder icon.

Drawing the Flowerpot

Now that you've defined the static background elements for your greeting, you can begin work on the more complex, animated objects.

▶ **Video 4.7** *Drawing the Flowerpot*

Creating and modifying a vector rectangle shape

You'll begin by drawing a simple flowerpot.

1 Create a new layer and name it **Flower**.

2 With this layer selected, select the Rectangle tool (▢). Don't select the Rectangle Primitive tool because in order for the shape to appear similar to the form of a flowerpot, you'll need to manipulate the shape.

▶ **Video 4.8**
*Shaping with the
Selection Tool*

3   Draw a square about 120px by 120px. It doesn't have to be exact, and the color choices don't matter at this point. You don't have to include any stroke for this square.

4   Select the Selection tool (▷).

5   With nothing selected, hover the cursor along the top edge of your rectangle shape. Notice how the cursor changes to include a small arc. This indicates that you can bend the paths that define your shape by pulling and pushing the edges.

6   Pull down slightly on the top of the square to form a nice dip (**Figure 4.13**). This is the top of your flowerpot.

Figure 4.13 Manipulating the shape

7   You need to create the inside of the flowerpot as well. Select the Oval tool (⬤), activate Object Drawing Mode (▣ Object drawing mode on), and draw an oval that matches the arc and size of the flowerpot top. The color you use should be a dark brown (#4B2500) since this portion of the flowerpot will be in shadow. Don't apply any stroke to this object.

8   Using the Subselection tool (▶), select the bottom-left anchor point of your shape.

9   With the point selected, use the arrow keys on your keyboard to nudge the point over a few pixels, creating a taper in your flowerpot. Perform a similar action on the other side.

10 To finish the flowerpot shape, select the Selection tool again and pull down the bottom of the shape slightly to give a little more perspective to the flowerpot, very similar to the modification you made to the top (**Figure 4.14**).

Figure 4.14 Choose a dark brown for the inside of the flowerpot.

TIP

Selecting Object Drawing Mode will ensure that overlapping shapes do not merge and cut into one another destructively.

Applying colors and gradients

★ ACA Objective 2.5

▶ **Video 4.9** *Using Gradients*

Gradients in Animate CC always start as either centered radial gradients or horizontal linear gradients. You use the Gradient Transform tool (▦) to recenter, rotate, or stretch a gradient. It's very similar to the Free Transform tool, but it affects only how the gradient is displayed. Access the Gradient Transform tool by clicking and holding the Free Transform tool icon (▦) in the Tools panel.

1 Use the Selection tool to select the flowerpot shape.

2 Open the Swatches panel and choose Linear Gradient from the color type menu.

   By default, you'll see a gradient that runs from pure white to complete black.

3 Change this to run from a slightly lighter brown (#824000) to a slightly darker brown (#582C00) (**Figure 4.15**). Gradients often look best when there's a subtle change across the gradient.

If you want to preserve this color definition as a reusable swatch, click the Add To Swatches button to make it selectable from any Swatches panel within Animate CC. You can now select the flowerpot shape and easily apply the recently created swatch to the fill by using the color picker in the Properties panel.

Figure 4.15 The settings you choose in the Color dialog box should match the ones shown here.

Now that the gradient swatch is applied, you can use the Gradient Transform tool to adjust how the linear gradient appears on the flowerpot shape. When an object with a gradient applied is selected using this tool, you can adjust the rotation, center point, width, and more.

ABOUT TAGGED SWATCHES

A recent addition to Animate CC is the concept of tagged swatches. This allows you to choose a swatch from the Swatches panel and transform it into a tagged swatch by clicking the Convert To A Tagged Swatch icon (▣) below the swatches grid. Tagged swatches differ from other swatches in that a small white tag appears in the lower right of a tagged swatch.

When you have a number of shapes using the tagged swatch, you can easily update the swatch and the changes will automatically cascade across all objects using that tagged swatch.

Convert to a graphic symbol

Symbols, at their most basic level, serve as containers for artwork. They come in three varieties, each with unique characteristics that allow them to be used for animation and interaction. Keep in mind that although Animate CC refers to "converting" elements to symbols, you're really wrapping the existing elements into symbols. Using symbols will allow nearly any graphical element to become a button, be animated in specific ways, or even be manipulated by code.

Creating a symbol from an existing set of elements is fairly simple. Here's how.

1   Select everything on the Flower layer of the timeline and choose Modify > Convert To Symbol.

Once the Convert To Symbol dialog box appears, you'll be given the option to type in a name for the symbol, select the symbol type, and specify a registration point alignment (**Figure 4.16**). There's also an area to access advanced options that are used primarily for linkage as a class within ActionScript.

It's a good practice to always name your symbols with no spaces and no special characters and beginning with an uppercase letter. This has to do with how Animate CC views symbols, and it will simplify the process as you explore more advanced topics.

Figure 4.16 The Convert To Symbol dialog box

2   Name the new symbol **Flower** and choose Graphic from the Type selection box. Click OK.

Once you click OK, the symbol is created and stored within the project library. Additionally, an instance of that symbol remains on the Stage, exactly where the conversion occurred.

Types of symbols within Animate CC

You can create three different types of symbols within an Animate CC project: movie clip, graphic, and button. In this project, you've created a graphic symbol. The choice of which symbol type to use isn't always clear, but learning more about each of these symbol types can help you choose the one that will work in your interactive media application.

MOVIE CLIP SYMBOLS

A movie clip symbol has a timeline that behaves like—but is completely independent of—the main Stage and is the primary symbol used when creating custom functionality within Animate CC. We'll see this use of movie clip symbols in greater detail during the later chapters. Movie clip symbols can be controlled with ActionScript or JavaScript as well as through timeline manipulation, making them extremely useful for customizing an interface.

GRAPHIC SYMBOLS

Graphic symbols are fairly simple to create, and the operation of the symbol timeline is exactly the same as that of the main timeline. The main purpose of the graphic symbol is to create reusable graphical elements and simple animations in an efficient package.

BUTTON SYMBOLS

Button symbols provide you with a quick and relatively simple way to create a standard interactive media button. These buttons can be created out of nearly any type of artwork, including other symbol instances, and can support a static or normal state, a rollover state, a down state, and a hit state. You construct the artwork for these states using keyframes, but rather than relying on frame numbers, the interface for construction of a button symbol uses Up, Over, Down, and Hit to identify where the keyframes for these states should be placed (**Figure 4.17**). We'll see this in detail as we work through the project in Chapter 8.

Figure 4.17 The button symbol timeline

The hit state for a button symbol is not visible, but the artwork in the keyframe defines the clickable area of the button symbol. If a button symbol has no hit state, the current keyframe artwork is used to determine the clickable or live area of the button.

> **NOTE**
>
> *If a button symbol has only a hit state, it is an invisible button that will show up in light blue during authortime but will be invisible at runtime.*

Editing the Flower Graphic Symbol

Symbols provide Animate CC projects with reusable elements that can be placed on the Stage as instances multiple times without recreating artwork. This approach can drastically reduce file sizes and can also simplify editing a layout by minimizing the number of graphic elements required to produce an interactive media project.

★ *ACA Objective 2.4*

 Video 4.11
Editing Symbols
and Symbol
Instances

Explaining symbols and instances

When a symbol is created, it resides in the project library. The symbol acts as a blueprint to instruct Animate CC on how to construct an instance of that symbol.

Instances are representations of the symbol that exist on the Stage and timeline. When you drag a symbol from the Library panel to the Stage, you're creating an instance of that symbol. You can have multiple instances of a single symbol on the Stage (**Figure 4.18**). If you edit the symbol, all the instances will change as well.

This feature can be effective for making changes globally in an Animate CC project. However, it can also be frustrating if you want each instance to be slightly different.

Figure 4.18 You can have multiple instances of a symbol on the Stage.

Fortunately, symbol instances can be more than exact copies of the original symbol definition in the Library panel. You can modify the individual properties of each instance using the Properties panel or tools such as the Transformation tool. These property changes affect only the selected instance, not the original symbol definition.

Embedding additional symbols and elements within a symbol definition can also provide a means of customizing each instance using code. A common application is to include a dynamic text field within a symbol definition. With some simple programming, you can alter the content of this text field at the instance level. The nesting can get a bit complicated, but having only a single element in the library can make it worth the trouble if you ever need to make global changes.

Differences between movie clip symbols and graphic symbols

Movie clip and graphic symbols look very similar in the Animate CC authoring environment, but big differences between them exist. The first has to do with the synchronization between the symbol timeline and the main movie timeline.

A graphic symbol is linked to the main timeline, whereas a movie clip symbol is an independent object whose timeline runs independently of the main timeline. If the main timeline is changing frames, so is the graphic symbol. If the main timeline is paused, the graphic symbol (which is linked frame by frame) is paused too. The movie clip timeline isn't bound to the main timeline and runs completely independently.

Another difference involves the use of ActionScript and JavaScript. Using code, you can access and control movie clip instances through the instance name assigned in the Properties panel. The graphic symbol has no option to assign an instance name and is not accessible via code as an object (**Figure 4.19**).

A performance difference exists as well. Graphic symbols require less processing. Even with this advantage, many interactive media developers make nearly every object a movie clip, just to increase the flexibility of the use of the object, though animators often prefer graphic symbols for the ability to specify the presented frame being shown at any time via the Properties panel.

Figure 4.19 The Properties panel with a graphic symbol instance selected

Editing the flower symbol

▶ *Video 4.12*
Preparing the
Symbol

You can edit symbols by double-clicking any instance of the symbol on the Stage or double-clicking the symbol within the Library panel.

1 Double-click the symbol instance you created to edit it in place.

When the symbol opens, notice that a breadcrumb trail showing the hierarchy of the object shows up in the top-left corner of the Stage. You can leave the editing mode by clicking the scene name in this breadcrumb trail (**Figure 4.20**).

Figure 4.20 Clicking Scene 1 in the breadcrumb trail will return you to the main timeline.

Now that you're operating within the symbol, notice that the symbol itself has its own timeline. In an Animate document, each symbol, no matter the type, has its own timeline. This allows for a great range of creative possibilities.

The next thing you'll do is to manage this internal timeline a bit better. Because you already have a number of objects within this symbol, you can place each of them on its own layer.

2 Select all the objects on the Stage either by dragging a selection rectangle around them with the Selection tool or by giving the Stage focus and using the Select All shortcut, Cmd+A (macOS) or Ctrl+A (Windows).

> **NOTE**
>
> *It doesn't matter if you double-click the symbol within the Library panel or use the edit-in-place option of double-clicking an instance on the Stage. You're still editing the base symbol—not the individual instance. This means that any changes you make will be made to all instances of that symbol. This doesn't matter much in this case, since you'll be using only one instance of this symbol.*

3 With all of your elements selected, right-click them and choose Distribute To Layers from the menu (**Figure 4.21**).

This takes each object and creates a new layer for it and then empties the previous layer of all selected content. The original layer is empty, as indicated by a blank keyframe.

4 Delete the original, now empty layer, by selecting it and clicking the Delete Layer icon (🗑) beneath the layer stack in the timeline.

Figure 4.21 Choosing Distribute To Layers

Both the flowerpot shape and the darker, inner pot shape should now be on separate layers.

5 Rename the main pot shape **pot**, and rename the layer representing the inner, backside of the flowerpot **potback**.

6 Ensure the topmost layer is pot and that potback is directly beneath it. Lock these layers before moving on.

Drawing a flower stalk

For the stalk of the flower, you'll create a simple shape with the Brush tool (🖌) so that it isn't completely straight and appears a bit more natural. The Brush tool is a freeform tool that draws shapes composed of fill alone.

▶ *Video 4.13*
Drawing the Stalk

1 Create a new layer and name it **stalk**.

2 Place this layer between the pot and potback layers by dragging the new layer into position (**Figure 4.22**). Now the order from top to bottom should be pot, stalk, and potback.

Figure 4.22 Place the Stalk layer in the middle of the layer stack.

3 Select the Brush tool (🖌) and look at the Properties panel.

4 Choose a nice green color (#32CC32) for your fill and look to the Brush Shape area of the panel to see the brush size and shape options. Select a round brush and bump the size way up to a value of 14 or so for a thick stalk.

5 Keep Object Drawing Mode off for now. Since we are drawing the stalk shapes on their own layer, we do not need to worry about interaction with the other elements.

6 Draw the primary stalk beginning behind the shape on the pot layer and extending up. If you like, you can draw a straight shape by holding down the Shift key as you draw, though it may look more natural if you freehand it. You may wish to adjust the Smoothing value to assist in getting the desired look—a value of 75 works pretty well for this. The stalk, when complete, should measure about 230px in height (**Figure 4.23**).

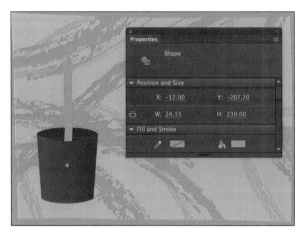

Figure 4.23 Set stalk parameters in the Properties panel.

Before moving on, we need to define some secondary stalks on either side of the primary stalk that was just drawn.

1 Select the Brush tool again and reduce the Size value to 10.

2 Move down a third of the way from the top and draw out a stalk emerging from the left side.

3 Go another third down and draw another stalk emerging from the right.

Figure 4.24 The fully realized stalk shape

You will now have drawn a long, primary stalk for the flower, which includes two branching stalks on either side (**Figure 4.24**). Don't worry if things look unnatural at this point; we'll be able to pose all of the stalk elements more naturally with inverse kinematics!

Animating the Flower Stalk with Inverse Kinematics

Inverse kinematics allows you to animate objects in Animate CC using a series of bones chained into linear or branched armatures in parent-child relationships. This means that when one bone moves during an animation, that connected bones will also move in relation to it. Inverse kinematics is a unique way of animating content to create natural motion.

★ *ACA Objective 4.4*

To animate using inverse kinematics, specify the start and end positions of bones on the timeline. These positions are known as "poses" in Animate CC. The armature will be automatically adjusted to tween positions of the bones in the armature between poses (**Figure 4.25**).

Figure 4.25 Animating an armature using inverse

You can apply inverse kinematics within Animate CC in one of two ways: by drawing bones within a single shape or through the construction of an armature composed of multiple movie clip symbol instances. In this project, you'll create a shape-based armature from the flower stalk you just created.

Animating the flower stalk using an armature layer

▶ **Video 4.14** *Using the Bone Tool*

Your next step is to animate the stalk growing up and out of the flowerpot. To do this, you'll take advantage of the armature you've already created. You don't need to specify any sort of tween when working with armatures; Animate CC will handle all of this automatically once different poses are defined.

TIP

When drawing bone segments, you'll find it helpful to disable all snapping and also zoom the stage for more precise placement. You can also turn off the visibility for layers that may obstruct your view.

1 First, you'll need to extend your frame span to the 6-second marker. To do so, move the playhead to frame 144, select the frames across all layers, and choose Insert > Timeline > Frame.

   These frames will provide enough time to nicely animate the growth of your stalk and will allow for some automated "springiness" once the animation has concluded. Bring the playhead back to frame 1 when finished.

2 Select the Bone tool ( ) from the Tools panel. You'll use this tool to define the bones within your armature.

3 To define a bone, drag a short way from the bottom of the stalk to the first branching stalk (**Figure 4.26**). You will draw subsequent bones across the shape by pressing the mouse button over the end point of the previous bone and dragging out a new segment.

Figure 4.26 Defining the initial bone

4 Draw about three or four bone segments along the central stalk to the top. Try to have each joint (the juncture between each bone) aligned with one of the secondary stalk elements.

5 We will now branch our armature out across the secondary stalk segments. For each joint closest to a secondary segment, pull out more bones to define those segments as part of the armature. Each secondary stalk segment should have about three bones apiece (**Figure 4.27**). The reason for creating many bones is to increase flexibility and refine the range of motion.

Notice how the stalk layer is now empty? A new layer named Armature_1 now exists above it with the frames colored light green, and the icon is a small figure. These changes indicate that this is a new armature layer (**Figure 4.28**).

Figure 4.27 The completed armature extends across all stalk segments.

Figure 4.28 The light green layer color indicates an armature layer.

Because you're using an armature, all you need to do to modify your pose is to drag with the Selection tool. Try it out! Notice how everything naturally moves in relation to any portion of the stalk you click and drag? This is the power of inverse kinematics.

▶ *Video 4.15*
Managing
Armature Poses

Once an armature is assembled, it has a default pose. When you modify a property on any particular frame, it's called a *pose*. Poses can be copied for easy modification and reuse. You want your ending frame to contain a pose with the stalk fully extended.

1 Let's go ahead and delete the existing stalk layer—it is no longer needed. Rename the armature layer to **stalk**, for clarity.

2 Select frame 48 (the 2-second marker) on the armature layer and right-click. Choose Insert Pose from the menu to duplicate the pose from frame 1. The flower stalk will remain completely opened within this second pose.

3 Return to frame 1 and use the Selection tool to modify the initial pose so that the secondary stalk segments are much closer to the main stalk. They will spread out as the main stalk becomes taller.

4 Now, pull the main stalk slightly to the side in order to introduce further differentiation between poses (**Figure 4.29**).

Figure 4.29 The pose for the emerging stalk

5 Use the Selection tool to select the entire plant.

6 Use the arrow keys to reposition the entire stalk down into the flower pot a bit. It's fine to have most of it sticking out, but we want to give the illusion of growth and this will help (**Figure 4.30**).

If you preview the animation between frames 1 and 48, you'll see that Animate CC performs a special armature tween between these two poses. The stalk begins with its branches very close to the main stalk and is seated low in the pot. The secondary stalk branches spread outward as the primary stalk appears to grow taller.

This is nice...but working with inverse kinematics allows us to add in a bit of dynamic animation as well—by applying values of Strength and Damping to each bone segment's Spring property. We have allowed a few extra seconds in the timeline beyond the 2-second mark for this very purpose.

Figure 4.30 The completed pose for the initial stalk

 TIP

You can also use inverse kinematics to construct an armature out of multiple movie clip instances. This is useful when building an armature for a human form or something mechanical in nature. Shape-based armatures are more suited to plants with long swaying stalks or creatures like snakes.

Adding Spring to the armature animation

 Video 4.16
Applying Spring to Your Bones

The stalk animation runs for only two seconds at the moment, but by adjusting the Spring properties for various bones, we are able to dynamically generate additional, subtle movements based on inverse kinematics.

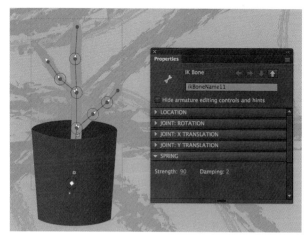

1 Zoom in about 200 percent so that it is easy to manipulate the armature. We'll focus on one of the secondary stalk segments for now.

2 Each secondary segment should have three bones defined across its length. Using the Selection tool, click the bone that is farthest from the main stalk. The bone is now selected and appears highlighted.

3 In the Properties panel, in the Spring section set Strength to 90 and Damping to 2 (**Figure 4.31**).

Figure 4.31 Stalk bones farthest from the main stalk should be very springy.

4 Do a similar thing with the middle bone for this secondary stalk. You can even make it slightly less springy: set Strength to 80 and Damping to 3.

Strength defines the intensity of the springiness of a certain bone, and damping determines the decay of the motion.

5 Now select the bone within the chosen segment that is closest to the primary stalk. Notice the Spring settings are all at the default of 0.

6 For this bone, since it is much closer to the stalk body, the springiness should be less pronounced than the bones that are farther away. Set Strength to around 60 and set Damping at 10 (**Figure 4.32**).

7 Now, switch your focus to the two bones that make up the other secondary stalk. Set the Spring properties values similar to what you've done for the first secondary stalk segment.

Figure 4.32 The less-springy, attached stalk portion

Preview the animation once again. The movement between frames 1 and 48 is nearly identical to what we had achieved before. With the addition of Spring values for Strength and Damping, you'll note that Animate CC also produces some subtle movements in the branches even after the initial animation has completed. This provides a more natural physical movement to the entire armature.

> **NOTE**
>
> *The amount of Spring Strength and Damping applied to each bone may be different for you than it is for anyone else depending on how you've drawn your visual elements, the length of the bones you've defined, and the poses defined for your armature. Play around until you find the best values for your unique armature.*

Designing and Animating the Flower Head

 Video 4.17
*Drawing the
Flower Head*

Now you'll create the head of the flower, which will bloom as the stalk grows. This process is pretty simple—you'll animate the flower head to follow the growth of the stalk and scale accordingly as the stalk rises until you have a fully matured flower.

Drawing the flower head

To draw the head of your flower, you'll use the Oval Primitive tool. But you'll need to do a little setup before you start drawing.

1   Create a new layer directly above the pot layer and name it **flower**.

2   Lock all the other layers and move the playhead to the 1-second mark at frame 24 (**Figure 4.33**).

    This is where your flower will first appear.

Figure 4.33 Playhead
at frame 24

3   Choose Insert > Timeline > Blank Keyframe to create a blank keyframe.

    Now you'll use this new keyframe to contain the vector content that forms your flower head.

4   Select the Oval Primitive tool and draw a small circle by holding Shift as you click and drag. The resulting circle shape should be about 40px to 44px in diameter.

5   Choose the same color for both the fill and the stroke. I'm using #B96D01 in this example.

6   To roughen the stroke a bit, click the Brush Library button with the object still selected and browse the various brushes.

    In this example, I've chosen Artistic > Chalk Charcoal > Charcoal - Tapered as my vector brush and adjusted the stroke width to a value of 8. This is the center of your flower.

7   To draw the petals, once again use the Oval Primitive tool and draw an oval that is roughly 25px wide and 65px tall. Change the color of the fill to something floral, like #FFFF99, and change the stroke to None.

8   Duplicate this petal by making seven copies, resulting in eight complete petals.

9   Using the Free Transform tool, rotate each petal to a different angle around its transform point (**Figure 4.34**). Holding the Shift key will allow you to rotate each petal with mathematical precision.

TIP

You can optionally use the Free Transform tool to shift the transform point (the small white circle) to the end of the petal. This will make it easy to align multiple petals together and allow for rotation around the same point.

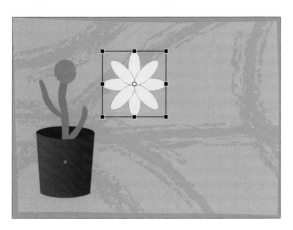

Figure 4.34 Petals arranged

TIP

If you have trouble positioning each petal, be sure that the Snap Align and Snap To Objects options are enabled in the View menu's Edit Snapping settings.

10 Select all the petals and choose Modify > Group. All of the petals are now grouped together, making them easier to manage.

11 Using the Selection tool, position the petals above the center of the flower head atop the stalk. It will obscure the center, but we'll fix this next.

12 Right-click the new group and choose Arrange > Send To Back so that the center shape appears in front. You may need to adjust the portion of the petals a bit so that everything is centered.

TIP

If you need to modify the individual petals in the group, just double-click to enter the group for adjustments.

Animating the flower head along the stalk

Even though the flower head is made entirely out of shapes, you can't use a shape tween to animate it because it is too complex. Instead, you'll create a movie clip symbol and apply a motion tween to the instance that results.

1   Select all the parts of the flower head—the petal group and the center portion—and choose Modify > Convert To Symbol.

 *Video 4.18
Animating the
Flower Head*

2 In the dialog box that appears, name the symbol **Bud**. For the type, choose Movie Clip (**Figure 4.35**).

The movie clip symbol itself will now be in your project library, and an instance of that symbol is added to the Stage.

Now that you have your completed flower head as a movie clip symbol instance on the Stage, all you need to do is tween it along with the growth of your stalk to complete the flower animation. To do this, you'll adjust the scale and position of the instance with a motion tween.

3 Select any frame or span of frames on the Flower layer after the 1-second mark, right-click the frame(s), and choose Create Motion Tween from the menu.

The background of the entire frame span should turn blue, and the layer icon should change to a small box in motion, indicating the motion tween has been created (**Figure 4.36**).

Figure 4.36 A motion tween is created.

Now all you need to do is adjust the scale and position of the movie clip instance on both keyframes.

4 At the 3-second mark, right-click the frame and choose Insert Keyframe > All from the menu that appears. The movie clip instance should be at full size and positioned at the top center of the fully extended stalk.

5   At the 1-second mark, scale down the Bud symbol using the Free Transform tool or the Properties panel so that it measures about the same width as the stalk.

6   Reposition it at the top of the stalk wherever it is at this point in the animation.

That should be it!

DETECTING PROBLEMS WITH TWEENS

Things may not always go as planned when tweening, and errors can occur. The most common tweening errors occur when you try to apply a tween on an incompatible element type.

An example is attempting to apply a motion tween to an object that doesn't support motion tweens. Animate CC tries to help you out by asking if you want to convert the object to a symbol to allow the tween. Although this works, you should have converted your objects to symbols before you apply the motion tween.

Another common error involves attempting to apply a shape tween to a pair of keyframes that don't contain shapes, in which case the option won't even be selectable. You can resolve this issue by using the Modify > Break Apart command to get the artwork to a basic vector level that a shape tween can be applied to.

Having the flower emerge from a bud

If you preview the animation right now, the flower just sort of pops in at the 1-second mark. To make things progress more naturally, we'll create a green bud for the formed flower to emerge from, based on the movie clip we've already created.

▶ *Video 4.19*
Animating an Initial
Flower Bud

1   Create a new layer and name it **flowerbud**.

2   Drag the new layer so that it is directly below the flower layer.

3   Copy the Bud movie clip symbol instance from the keyframe at the 1-second mark of the flower layer.

4   Select the flowerbud layer again, and right-click the Stage. Choose Paste In Place from the menu that appears. A copy of the Bud instance now exists on the flowerbud layer.

Because we are using a copy of the already-created Bud movie clip symbol, we are able to add all sorts of transformations, effects, and filters to the instance. We will be using a simple Tint effect in this case.

Okay, now that we have a copy of the movie clip symbol created on a new layer, we can use some color effects on this instance to turn it as green as the stalk it emerges from.

1 Select the movie clip instance on the flowerbud layer on frame 1 and look at the Properties panel.

2 In the Color Effect section, choose Tint from the Style menu.

3 Click the Tint Color box and choose the green color used for the stalk. You can use the color picker to sample directly from the Stage to match the color perfectly.

4 Bring the Tint value to 100% using the slider (**Figure 4.37**). That is all for the Properties panel.

Figure 4.37 Our Bud instance is now tinted green.

The last thing we need to do to complete our fresh bud is to animate its position across time. We'll use a simple Motion Tween for this.

1 At the 1-second mark of the Bud layer, insert a blank keyframe by selecting the frame and pressing F7.

2 Right-click any frame between frame 1 and frame 23 on the Bud layer and choose Create Motion Tween from the menu that appears.

3 Select frame 23 on the Bud layer and right-click. From the menu, choose Insert Keyframe > All.

4   Move the playhead back to frame 1 and reposition the instance so that it aligns with the top of the stalk at this frame (**Figure 4.38**).

5   Preview the animation once again to see the transition from green bud to full flower.

Figure 4.38 The timeline expressing fresh bud to full flower

All right! That's all for the flower animation. It should look pretty good but feel free to tweak the motion or any visual elements before we move on to the next step in our project.

Create a Personalized Text Message

The final visual element to apply to your animated greeting is the message that the viewer sees after the animation has concluded. We'll create a text object and use the various font properties available to us to relay the personalized message.

★ *ACA Objective 4.2*

Building the text block

In this exercise, you'll build a text message that you'll include on the main timeline.

▶ *Video 4.20*
Creating a Text Greeting

1   If you're still within the Flower graphic symbol instance, click the scene name in the location breadcrumbs above the Stage to return to the main timeline.

2   Extend the main timeline to cover a full 6 seconds of animation to match the nested Flower animation by moving the playhead to the 6-second mark, selecting this frame across all layers, and choosing Insert > Timeline > Frame (**Figure 4.39**).

Figure 4.39 The main timeline is extended.

NOTE

When you select the instance and check the Properties panel, you'll notice the Looping section. This section provides even greater control when using graphic symbols; you can specify the starting frame, how many times the animation loops, and other options. We'll explore these properties in greater depth once we've created our text message.

With the number of frames on the main timeline now matching those in the graphic symbol instance, scrubbing the playhead will reveal one of the strengths of graphic symbols. Notice that for every frame, the animation is completely synchronous!

If you compare this with a movie clip symbol instance, you'll see only the first frame of that animation unless you test or publish. This is one reason graphic symbols are great for animation.

3   Create a new layer above the Flower layer and rename it **Message**.

This layer will hold your text message content. The message won't display until the animation is nearly complete, so you need to create an empty keyframe around the 5-second mark and create your message there.

4   To do so, choose Insert > Timeline > Keyframe.

Notice that it created a blank keyframe even though you didn't choose that option. That's because there was no content in the previous keyframe, and inserting a keyframe simply duplicates the content of the previous keyframe—which, in this case, contained nothing.

5   Select frame 120 (at the 5-second mark) on the Message layer, lock every other layer, and then select the Text tool.

6   Access the Properties panel and notice in the Text Type menu that only Static Text and Dynamic Text are available because you're targeting HTML5 Canvas (**Figure 4.40**). Choose Static Text and select a font that looks nice to you with the Size value set to roughly 60 pt.

NOTE

When using static text, all of the characters of text will be rendered as shape outlines when the HTML5 Canvas document is published. Because of this, you won't need to worry about users having installed your chosen font.

Figure 4.40 Choose Static Text from the Text Type menu.

7   For color, click the color swatch and then use the Eyedropper tool that appears to sample the color from the flower petals on the Stage. You can, of course, color as you desire.

8 With your text properties in place and the Text tool selected, drag out a text block in an empty area of the Stage. Feel free to move the Flower instance to the side if need be.

9 Type in a message. I'm using the generic greeting "A Flower for You!" but as with many choices in this project, it's up to you.

The text should display in the exact font, color, and size you have chosen (**Figure 4.41**).

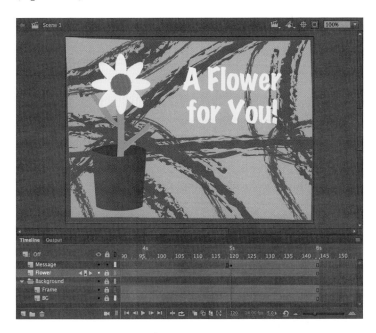

Figure 4.41 Text displayed as intended

10 Because the text is editable, select the text block to modify any of the properties in the Properties panel. You can also adjust the size of the text block itself. Double-click anywhere in the text block to edit the text and change your message, if needed.

Applying text effects

Only the Dynamic Text type accepts filters, whose controls are at the bottom of the Properties panel. Since we are using the Static Text type for this project, we'll need to wrap the text object in a symbol, which can have filters applied to it. You access

▶ **Video 4.21** *Text Effects in HTML5 Canvas*

these filters by selecting the object and then clicking the Add Filters icon in the Filters section.

- Available filters for ActionScript 3.0 documents include Drop Shadow, Blur, Glow, Bevel, Gradient Glow, Gradient Bevel, and Adjust Color.
- Available filters for HTML5 Canvas are restricted to Drop Shadow, Blur, Glow, and Adjust Color.

Let's convert the Static Text object to a movie clip symbol instance in order to apply filters to it.

1 With the text block selected, choose Modify > Convert To Symbol.

2 When the Convert To Symbol dialog box opens, create a movie clip symbol named **Message**.

You now have a movie clip symbol instance that contains a text object on the Stage. Next, you'll add a drop shadow to this instance.

1 Select the instance on the Stage and access the Properties panel.

2 Click the Add Filter button in the Properties panel.

3 Choose Drop Shadow and make the following adjustments: change Blur X and Blur Y to a value of 6, keep Strength at 100%, and choose #000000 for the color (**Figure 4.42**).

   The project is now able to include text with a nice Drop Shadow effect because the text is contained in a movie clip instance (**Figure 4.43**).

Figure 4.42 Choosing Drop Shadow settings

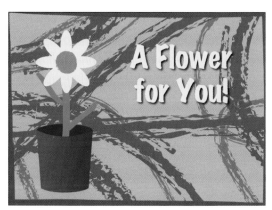

Figure 4.43 Drop Shadow effect applied

Creating multiple messages

We currently have a single message for our greeting. Let's create a set of messages to choose from and make it super simple to switch between them by using a graphic symbol and the Frame Picker.

▶ **Video 4.22** *Using the Frame Picker*

1   Double-click the Message movie clip instance on the Message layer in order to edit it in place.

2   Within the Message symbol, select the text object on the Stage that composes the message itself.

3   With the text selected, choose Modify > Convert To Symbol. The Convert To Symbol dialog appears (**Figure 4.44**).

Figure 4.44 Creating the Messages graphic symbol

4   Provide a name of **Messages** (note this is plural) and choose Graphic from the Type menu. Click OK to close the dialog box and create the graphic symbol.

Now that we have created a new symbol from the text, an instance of the Messages graphic symbol exists on the Stage within our Message movie clip symbol. We have a fair bit of nesting involving different symbol types now! Next we'll enter the new symbol and edit its contents.

1   Enter the new symbol instance on the Stage by double-clicking it. You are now in the Messages graphic symbol.

2   You currently have only a single keyframe containing the original text object. Duplicate this keyframe (F6) three times for a total of four keyframes (**Figure 4.45**).

Figure 4.45 Duplicate the text keyframes.

3 For the content on frames 2–4, change the text messages, color, and font choices to whatever you like. The important thing is to make each one visually unique.

Here are some text suggestions to use: "Springtime Flowers," "Happy Birthday!," and "With Deepest Sympathies."

4 With the four unique text messages in place, click Message above the Stage to move up one level to the Message symbol. Don't go out to Scene 1 just yet!

The last thing we need to do is to use the Frame Picker to select which particular message is displayed to the user. The Frame Picker only works with graphic symbol instances and allows us to choose specific frames along the symbol's internal timeline through a clean visual representation.

1 Go up one level to the Message movie clip symbol instance and use the Selection tool to select the Messages graphic symbol instance on the Stage.

2 Access the Properties panel. In the Looping section, select Single Frame from the Options menu and then click the Use Frame Picker button. The Frame Picker panel will appear.

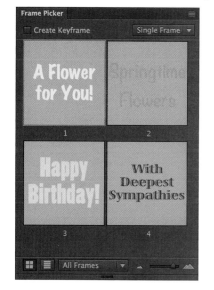

Figure 4.46 Using the Frame Picker

3 In the Frame Picker panel, deselect Create Keyframe and note that the choice of Single Frame looping is still in place. Beneath this you will see a visual representation of each of the four keyframes in the Messages graphic symbol (**Figure 4.46**).

Note that as you select each one, the instance on the Stage changes to display the message chosen in the Frame Picker.

4 Once you are happy with the message chosen in the Frame Picker, close the Frame Picker panel and return to the main timeline by choosing Scene 1 above the Stage.

With that, our animated elements are complete. Before publishing the project, we'll need to be sure to stop the playhead once it reaches the final frame of the timeline. A tiny bit of JavaScript code will do that for us.

TIP

Since the filter we applied before is applied to the Message movie clip symbol instance on the Stage, any of its contents inherit the application of that filter. Note that the single filter is applied dynamically to contents of the parent symbol instance—no matter which particular text message is being displayed.

Using JavaScript Code to Stop the Playhead

If you test the project at this point by choosing Control > Test, you'll see how well everything has come together. But the animation loops continuously and the actual text message blips by too quickly. You need to stop that playhead so the viewer can read the message.

★ ACA Objective 4.7

Working with code in Animate CC

Whether you're working with ActionScript or JavaScript in Animate CC, the initial workflow is basically identical. Code can be placed on the timeline on specific frames to instruct the project to perform instructions in various ways. The two main panels you'll deal with when writing simple code are the Actions panel and the Code Snippets panel. You access both from the Window menu.

ACTIONS PANEL

The Actions panel is a simple code editor where you write all your frame scripts (**Figure 4.47**). It doesn't matter what sort of code you're writing in the Actions panel—both JavaScript and ActionScript are supported.

Figure 4.47 The Actions panel

NOTE
You might also notice a button in the upper right of the Actions panel labeled Add Using Wizard. The Actions Wizard is available only in HTML5 Canvas documents— and we'll take a look at this workflow in Chapter 6.

Of course, you can use ActionScript only in an ActionScript-based project and JavaScript only in an HTML5-based project. Frame scripts are the pieces of code you bind to certain frames along the timeline. On the left side of the panel is a sidebar, which makes it easy to jump around to different pieces of code located on different objects and frames.

Figure 4.48 The Code Snippets panel

CODE SNIPPETS PANEL

Working in the Code Snippets panel (**Figure 4.48**) is a great way for those who are new to working with code to learn how to do some fundamental things in Animate CC projects. The snippets included are divided into three main categories: ActionScript, HTML5 Canvas, and WebGL. These correspond to the target platform you're working with.

Within these three main categories are a number of additional, functional categories. Every target platform represented has snippets for manipulating the playhead: either stopping the timeline from playing or jumping around to different frames.

Using JavaScript to stop your animation

▶ **Video 4.23**
Stopping the Playhead

Next you'll stop that playhead and give your text more screen time with a little JavaScript. The first thing you need to do is decide where to place the code. You'll use frame 144 because that's the frame you need to stop the playhead on—but which layer?

It's best practice in Animate CC to create a layer called Actions where all your frame scripts will be placed. Not only does this make it easy to find any of your code, but it also keeps the code separate from your visual assets that exist in other layers.

1 Create a new layer and name it **Actions**.

2 Insert a blank keyframe on frame 144 (the 6-second marker) by choosing Insert > Timeline > Blank Keyframe.

   The only other thing you have to do is write some code in the last frame of your Actions layer to stop the playhead.

3 With the final frame of the Actions layer selected, open the Actions panel and place the cursor at line 1 (**Figure 4.49**). Type the following code within the panel:

```
this.stop();
```

Figure 4.49 Code entered in the Actions panel

It's important to understand what this does. In the code, `this` refers to the present Stage—the main Stage. The instruction `stop()` tells the playhead on that Stage to stop moving immediately and stay in place, effectively stopping the animation. That's it! You could certainly use the Code Snippets panel to do this, but it is so simple that typing the code is the more direct route.

Notice on frame 144 that the keyframe has changed. In place of the empty circle, the keyframe now bears a stylized lowercase *a* that lets you know there is code on that keyframe.

> **NOTE**
>
> *The syntax for stopping an animation in ActionScript is exactly the same as the syntax used here, in JavaScript. CreateJS was written to be as close to Action-Script as possible. Some major differences exist, however. Using JavaScript, frame numbers begin at 0 instead of 1 as they do when using ActionScript.*

NOTE

In JavaScript parlance, an instruction like `stop()` *is a* **method**—*that is, a code function that's a member of a particular* **class** *(a template or a blueprint for a type of object)—in this case, the* `MovieClip` *class).*

TIP

There is also an option in the Publish Settings for HTML5 Canvas that allows you to stop looping the playhead at the end of the project timeline. This only works for stopping the playhead at the final frame—using code allows you to stop the playhead at a specific frame.

ANIMATING WITH CODE

All of the animation techniques discussed so far in this book involve working with the timeline. This is the easiest way for a new interactive media creator to get something to move on the screen. Using ActionScript or JavaScript code to animate your creations can be challenging, but it provides a level of control and interactivity that can't be achieved using the timeline alone.

Carefully analyze what you're trying to accomplish and determine the best route to getting the results required for the project. Once you get past learning the syntax for whichever platform you're targeting, your animation will be much more flexible and easier to edit once created.

Publishing Your Project for HTML5 Canvas

★ *ACA Objective 1.4*

★ *ACA Objective 5.2*

▶ *Video 4.24*
Publishing for HTML5 Canvas

Publishing for HTML5 Canvas is a bit more straightforward than publishing for Flash Player, simply because you have fewer publish settings to set. When publishing for HTML5 Canvas, in place of a single SWF file, you'll have a number of different files that must all be kept together for the project to run. The number of files you have depends on the file types used in the project and your publish settings. The primary file among these is a JavaScript file (with the .js extension).

Publish Settings

You can access the Publish Settings for HTML5 Canvas in the same manner you do when targeting Flash Player. With nothing in your project selected, the Properties panel displays document properties.

1   In the Publish area of the panel, click the Publish Settings button to open the Publish Settings dialog box.

2   On the left side of the Publish Settings dialog box, you'll see a column where you can select JavaScript/HTML under the Publish heading. Make sure this check box is selected.

Whenever you're ready, click Publish.

WORKING WITH WEBGL

The secondary native HTML5 document type involves the use of WebGL (Web Graphics Library) technology. Interestingly enough, WebGL also makes use of the HTML5 canvas element, but in a different way. WebGL content is actually GPU-accelerated, meaning that it makes direct use of the hardware graphical processing unit (GPU) rather than sharing rendering tasks with everything else running on the central processing unit (CPU). This makes for a much more effective and powerful rendering target.

Although WebGL can be rendered in an accelerated way, it's more difficult to work with than HTML5 Canvas documents. Adobe has created a specialized WebGL runtime to make things easier, but it's still not as robust and direct in use as CreateJS. If you're considering WebGL, be sure that your project will benefit from being GPU-accelerated.

The settings for the JavaScript/HTML Publish option are separated into four tabs. We'll look at each one individually.

BASIC

The basic options mainly have to do with where the files are saved and how the presentation is configured (**Figure 4.50**).

- **Output Name:** This first section allows customization of the output file, asking you to specify the filename and directory for the output.

- **Loop Timeline:** You have the option of looping the timeline or stopping it at the final frame.

Figure 4.50 The Publish Settings Basic tab

- **Include Hidden Layers:** This incorporates any hidden layers into the published content.

- **Center Stage:** Centers the stage in the HTML view horizontally, vertically, or both.

- **Make Responsive:** Will scale the project down by width, height, or both, if the HTML **viewport** (the portion of the browser where HTML is rendered) is too small.

- **Scale To Fill Visible Area:** This option becomes available if you select Make Responsive. It also allows the presentation to scale up in order to fit the HTML viewport if it is larger than the project. You can choose Fit In View or Stretch To Fit, but the latter can distort the proportions of the project.

- **Include Preloader:** Allows the use of a default animated loader to display as the project content is loaded. You can also browse to choose your own animated GIF to use as a preloader if you do not like the default.

- **Export Assets:** If you use any images or sounds in your project, choose the folders where you want them to be saved. You can also specify the folder for the published CreateJS files if you don't select the Hosted Libraries option on the Advanced tab.

Figure 4.51 The Publish Settings > Advanced tab

Figure 4.52 The Publish Settings > Spritesheet tab

Figure 4.53 The Publish Settings > Web Fonts tab

ADVANCED

The Advanced tab includes template controls and deals mostly with JavaScript handling in your project (**Figure 4.51**). Many of these settings are beyond the scope of this book, but here are the ones that are important to know:

- **Overwrite HTML File On Publish:** This option will allow you to manage whether or not any previously published HTML file for the project is overwritten by subsequent publish actions. If you edit the HTML outside of Animate CC, you probably want to deselect this option or you'll lose your customizations.

- **Include JavaScript In HTML:** When this option is selected, the JavaScript produced will be written within your HTML file instead of being written to a standalone JavaScript file. One less file to deal with.

SPRITESHEET

If you're including bitmap images in your project, you can also export them all to a single spritesheet and modify the spritesheet settings using this tab (**Figure 4.52**).

- **Combine Image Assets Into Spritesheets:** If this is deselected, images will not be packaged into spritesheets.

- **Format:** You can choose the formats you'd like to export any spritesheets as: PNG, JPEG, or BOTH.

- **Format Settings:** These become available depending on your format selection. They allow you to define compression and other format-specific file properties for these image types.

WEB FONTS

This is only needed when using Typekit web fonts and dynamic text fields. When using Typekit, you need to let the service know which web domain name (josephlabrecque.com, for example) to allow the font delivery. This tab provides the mechanism to do that (**Figure 4.53**). If you're using Google web fonts, that step is not necessary.

Challenge!

Right now, your message text just pops in. But it could transition into the card in a subtler way. Find a way to tween the text in as a fade, scale it in, or use some other mechanism for performing an advanced reveal. The next chapter will give you good ideas for accomplishing this.

Conclusion

Wow…that was a lot of content we just covered! You used a large variety of tools and techniques to build an animated greeting that can be run in your web browser without the need for Flash Player to be installed. That means your greeting will also run on mobile devices like Android phones and iPads. Of course, even if you do have Flash Player installed on your desktop, this project doesn't rely on or use it.

While working on this project, you've seen how easily some of the tools and concepts we already covered when targeting Flash Player are adapted to new publish targets. You've also explored new tools and techniques such as vector art brushes, the Paint Brush tool, variable-width strokes, the Width tool, armature layers, the Bones tool, graphic and movie clip symbols and instances, text effects, and HTML5 Canvas and WebGL publish targets.

CHAPTER OBJECTIVES

Chapter Learning Objectives

- Import bitmap images.
- Work with animated masks.
- Use the PolyStar tool.
- Design with 3D tools for animation.
- Work with variable-width motion guides.
- Use blend modes and filters.
- Create animated text.
- Perform raw video export and encoding with Adobe Media Encoder.

Chapter ACA Objectives

For full descriptions of the objectives, see the table on pages 286–291.

DOMAIN 1.0
WORKING IN THE ANIMATION INDUSTRY
1.4

DOMAIN 2.0
PROJECT SETUP AND INTERFACE
2.1, 2.4, 2.6

DOMAIN 3.0
ORGANIZATION OF DOCUMENTS
3.2

DOMAIN 4.0
CREATE AND MODIFY VISUAL ELEMENTS
4.2, 4.4, 4.5, 4.6, 4.7

DOMAIN 5.0
PUBLISHING DIGITAL MEDIA
5.2

CHAPTER 5

Generate a Promotional Video

Animate CC, due to its rich and engaging history, is a great choice for producing flashy, animated content. This project will be a no-holds-barred example of this! You'll be targeting video for this project, so you don't have to worry about the limitations of certain platforms—you'll just make an awesome little video. One of the major uses of Animate CC is to animate and produce content for television and film, so you're in good company.

In this project, you'll animate a demo reel intro video using imported images, animated masks, blend modes, and effects (**Figure 5.1**). You'll employ all sorts of tools like 3D Rotation and variable-width motion guides to build a real eye-catcher. Generating video content from Animate CC is easy, and it can be used in a variety of other applications.

▶ *Video 5.1*
Project Overview

Figure 5.1 The animated video project you'll create

★ *ACA Objective 2.1*

Video Project Setup

▶ **Video 5.2** *Video Project Setup*

The first thing you'll need to do, as always, is to create a new document in Animate CC and prepare it for your project assets. At this point, you should know that if you're not targeting the web browser, an ActionScript-based document type is generally the best choice simply due to the number of extra tools and filters available. In this project, you'll render a video from our animation, so you want to use as much of Animate CC as possible.

Figure 5.2 Setting properties for this project

1   To begin, create a new ActionScript 3.0 document and save it to your computer.

2   In the Properties panel (**Figure 5.2**), set the Stage width to 1280px and the height to 720px.

    This is a 16:9 aspect ratio, which is perfect for HD video. Leave FPS at a value of 24 as this is standard for film. Black always makes for a solid Stage background color.

3 Click frame 240 (the 10-second marker) in the Timeline (you'll have to scroll a bit) and fill this expanse with frames by choosing Insert > Timeline > Frame (**Figure 5.3**). If you look down below all layers in the Timeline, you'll see that 240 frames at 24fps will total 10 seconds of video. That's the target duration for your promo video.

Figure 5.3 Setting 240 frames as the target duration for this promo

Importing the backgrounds

★ *ACA Objective 2.4*

▶ *Video 5.3*
Importing Background Images

For the background content, you'll animate between two static images. These images were created in Adobe Photoshop and measure 1280px in width by 720px in height—the same resolution as your project Stage.

1 Rename the existing layer to **Background**.

2 Import a prepared background image by selecting File > Import > Import To Stage.

   You're using the provided image bg.png (**Figure 5.4**). Since the image is the same size as the Stage, it should be placed automatically in the correct position.

Figure 5.4 The provided background image on the Stage

3 Lock the layer.

4 Create another new layer directly above the previous one and name it **Foreground**.

5 Import an additional background image, fg.png, into this layer.

   This new image completely obscures the previous one (**Figure 5.5**).

6 Lock the layer to ensure the contents are not accidentally moved.

   Both background layers are now in place and ready to be composited against one another with the addition of an animated mask.

Figure 5.5 Background and Foreground layers on the Stage

★ ACA Objective 3.2

Creating Dynamic Backgrounds with Animated Shape Masking

You saw a simple example of masking when creating your meme image in Chapter 3. Now you'll create a mask to animate your background content images. However, the images themselves won't be animated at all—only the mask will be.

Drawing the mask shape

To draw the mask, you'll need a new layer.

▶ **Video 5.4** *Create a Star Mask*

1 Create an additional layer directly above the Foreground layer and name it **BGMask**.

   In this layer, you'll draw a shape to serve as your mask.

2 Select the PolyStar tool (⬡).

   The PolyStar tool is a shape tool (not unlike Rectangle or Oval) that will create either a star or a polygon.

3 To set the number of sides your shape will have, click the Options button in the Tool Settings section of the Properties panel with the PolyStar tool selected. The Tool Settings dialog box opens.

4 Choose Star from the Style menu. The default number of sides is 5, and that should be fine for this mask.

5 Draw a star shape by dragging on the Stage with the BGMask layer selected (**Figure 5.6**). The size doesn't matter much since you'll be scaling the shape across your animation, so just make it as large or as small as you want while still retaining manageability.

Figure 5.6 Star shape against the background

6   To make this layer a mask layer, right-click the layer itself and choose Mask.

The layer icon changes its appearance to look like a rectangle with a circle punched out of it. This indicates a mask layer. The layer directly beneath the mask layer automatically becomes masked by this layer and changes its appearance as well. The layer icon changes to resemble the Mask Layer icon but altered slightly in that it looks more like a turned-up page with a circle punched out of it (**Figure 5.7**). It also becomes nested and indented beneath the mask layer.

Figure 5.7 The BGMask layer is now easily recognizable as a mask layer by its layer icon.

Animating the mask

Now you'll create a shape tween for the BGMask layer.

1   Right-click the frame span and choose Create Shape Tween.

The frame span turns green, but you should also see a broken line across the frames. This happens because you have only a single keyframe at frame 1.

2   Move the playhead to the very end—frame 240—and choose Insert > Timeline > Keyframe to insert an additional keyframe.

The broken line now appears solid, indicating a working shape tween (**Figure 5.8**).

Figure 5.8 Broken line now solid

3   Move the playhead to the 3-second mark (frame 72) and insert an additional keyframe. This is where your animated mask will first appear.

4   Select the star shape and resize it to around 30px in width or height—you don't need to be exact. Use the Align panel to align the shape to the center of the Stage.

5   You don't want your mask to appear until frame 72, so move the playhead
     to frame 1, select the star shape with the Selection tool, and in the Properties
     panel, make the width and height of this object both a value of 1. In order for
     the mask to work, there needs to be a shape on the Stage at all times. Be sure
     to align the shape to the center of the Stage.

6   Additionally, you don't want the star to animate from 1px to 30px from frame
     1 to frame 72, so right-click anywhere along that frame span and choose
     Remove Shape Tween from the menu.

     With your mask at 1px in total diameter across frames 1–71, you won't see
     any noticeable masking until you want to—at frame 72.

     Here's the part where you can get really creative. What you need to do now
     is animate the shape, scale, position, or rotation of this shape using a num-
     ber of additional keyframes between frame 72 and frame 240. You can insert
     an additional keyframe at every second or two and use the Transform tool to
     modify scale and rotation as you see fit.

     The idea is to make it engaging and to provide constant motion. To accom-
     plish this, you'll simply scale the star shape up and down between staggered
     keyframes along the Timeline (**Figure 5.9**).

Figure 5.9 Animating the shape with additional key-frames in the Timeline

7 Next, preview the animated mask by locking both layers and scrubbing the playhead across the Timeline. Alternatively, you can choose Control > Test to compile and view the animation (**Figure 5.10**).

You should see the mask you've just created and animated revealing portions of the foreground image against the background image.

USING SHAPE HINTS

If you're doing complex shape tweens in your animation, you may find it helpful to employ *shape hints*. You can add shape hints to a tween by selecting a keyframe containing your shape and choosing Modify > Shape > Add Shape Hint. You can add as many shape hints as you like (up to 26) to guide the shape tween more precisely between keyframes. Simply adjust the position of the hint circles from keyframe to keyframe on corresponding shape edges.

Design a 3D Rotating Headshot

The next step in your little promotional video is to import a nice headshot and then perform some 3D transforms on it. Additionally, you'll employ some blend modes and filters to make things interesting. These are some great techniques that will make your content come to life.

Creating the headshot movie clip   ★ *ACA Objective 4.6*

The first thing you'll do is import your headshot image. If you don't have a nice headshot, you should go get one. At the very least, take a selfie with your mobile device and use that. This technique works best with a 1:1 ratio (a square), but if you don't have a square shot, just use what you have on hand.

1   Create a new layer in the Timeline and name it **Headshot** (**Figure 5.11**). This layer should be positioned above every other layer, and those layers beneath it should be locked so that you do not mistakenly modify their contents.

Figure 5.11 The Headshot layer at the top of the layer stack

> ▶ **Video 5.6**
> *Importing the headshot*

Now you need to import the headshot image into your project.

2   Choose File > Import > Import To Stage.

3   Browse to your headshot bitmap image and select it for import. Once it's on the Stage, depending on how large your image is, you may need to adjust its size. I've made mine measure 420px by 420px. Be sure and re-center the photo, if need be.

> ▶ **Video 5.7** *Stylize the Headshot*

Now you'll stylize the image a bit by giving it a nice border. The best way to do something like this in Animate CC is through the use of a stroke, but how can you add a stroke to a bitmap image with no stroke or fill? The solution is to break the image apart. Breaking apart a bitmap image will render it as a simple shape object with a bitmap fill using the bitmap it previously was. Because it's a shape, you can easily apply a stroke using the Ink Bottle tool.

> **NOTE**
> *You could also apply a pattern brush from the Brush Library to your stroke. Pattern brushes can make great frames!*

4   Select the bitmap image on the Stage.

5   Choose Modify > Break Apart to convert the bitmap to a shape.

6   Select the Ink Bottle tool (🖋) and, using the Properties panel, choose a color for your stroke.

Clicking any of the four edges of your new shape will apply a stroke of that same color to the already present fill. Using the Properties panel, you can also change the stroke size, cap, and join properties. I'm using a size value of 14 with a square cap and join miter of 3 in order to simulate a nice, thick border (**Figure 5.12**).

Figure 5.12 Stylizing the image with a border

Now that you've changed your image to represent the visual you desire, it's time to transform the shape into a movie clip symbol.

▶ *Video 5.8* Prepare the Headshot for Animation

7   Make sure the Headshot image is still selected, and choose Modify > Convert To Symbol.

8   Choose Movie Clip as the symbol type and name it **RotatingHeadshot** (**Figure 5.13**) since this instance of the headshot will have rotations applied to it. Additionally, be sure that the registration point is at the center of the movie clip symbol and click OK.

Figure 5.13 Customizing movie clip symbol settings in the Convert To Symbol dialog box

You now have a movie clip symbol instance on the Stage, but you want to perform 3D transformations on this instance while retaining control over this instance on the main Timeline. To do this, you'll have to wrap this instance within yet another movie clip symbol.

9 Select the existing instance and choose Modify > Convert To Symbol once again. This time, name it **Headshot** (**Figure 5.14**).

10 Double-click the Headshot movie clip instance on the Stage to enter it. The hierarchical relationship from the Stage through the movie clip wrapped in another movie clip is now *Stage > Headshot > RotatingHeadshot > Shape*. This type of hierarchy is known as nesting in Animate CC.

This Headshot movie clip will contain within its timeline the actual 3D transformations and associated tweens that will be applied to the existing RotatingHeadshot instance.

Figure 5.14 The Stage (signified by "Scene 1" here) contains Headshot, which itself contains RotatingHeadshot.

Using the 3D Rotation tool to rotate your Headshot movie clip

▶ *Video 5.9*
Introduction to
3D Tools

To focus this promotional introduction video on yourself, you'll have the head-shot appear in the center of the Stage and begin rotating, keeping it constantly in motion while visible on the screen. You'll perform this effect by using the 3D tools native to Animate CC. First, we'll go over some of the tools and concepts you'll use for this portion of the project.

THE 3D ROTATION AND 3D TRANSLATION TOOLS

★ *ACA Objective 4.5*

Animate CC offers two dedicated 3D transformation tools. The first is the 3D Rotation tool ( ) that allows you to rotate a 2D movie clip symbol instance around the x-axis, y-axis, or z-axis. When you use this tool to select the instance, a special graphical interface appears as an overlay.

NOTE

Notice the effect of the vanishing point, which is used to provide perspective to the artwork as it's moved through the simulated 3D environment.

To use this tool, just begin dragging the outermost circle of the graphical overlay to rotate around either the x-axis or the y-axis. The inner circle lets you rotate around the z-axis (**Figure 5.15**). It takes some practice, but it's a quick way to simulate 3D using a 2D medium.

The 3D Translation tool ( ) lets you move a movie clip in simulated 3D space. The red horizontal arrow allows the element to be moved along the x-axis; the green vertical arrow moves the element about the y-axis (**Figure 5.16**). Dragging the blue dot will move the element along the z-axis.

Figure 5.15 Adding simulated 3D rotation

Figure 5.16 Adding movement along the x- and y-axes

CREATING THE ROTATION EFFECT FOR YOUR HEADSHOT

For this effect, make sure you're editing the Headshot symbol Timeline.

1   To access the symbol Timeline, either double-click the instance on the Stage to edit in place or double-click on the symbol in the project library to edit in isolation (**Figure 5.17**).

▶ **Video 5.10**
Creating the
Rotation Effect

Figure 5.17 Editing the symbol

Whichever method you choose, the results will be the same.

To perform the rotation animation, we'll first extend the frames in your movie clip Timeline to 2 seconds.

2 Select frame 48 at the 2-second marker within the Headshot symbol and choose Insert > Timeline > Frame to create a full-frame span across all 48 frames.

3 Right-click any of these frames and choose Create Motion Tween.

   The background of the entire frame span turns blue, indicating a motion tween.

4 Rename the present layer **Animation**.

5 Select the 3D Rotation tool ( ). You'll be rotating the RotatingHeadshot instance along the y-axis and have it flip vertically over and over again, making a continuous loop. The y-axis is indicated by the horizontal yellow line in the 3D overlay controls. If you click and drag from this line, notice that a portion of the 360-degree circle overlay becomes shaded. This indicates the change in rotation from the present state.

6 Move the playhead to frame 12 and click and drag along the y-axis until just shy of a quarter of the circle is indicated through visual shading (**Figure 5.18**). This indicates that we will rotate this object slightly less than 90 degrees along the y-axis.

TIP

When rotating your headshot in this manner, if you happen to rotate too far, the animation may reverse. If that happens, adjust your rotation so it isn't quite 90 degrees.

Figure 5.18 The shaded area in the overlay indicates a change in rotation.

7 Move the playhead up 12 additional frames to frame 24 and do the same thing, a bit less than ~90 degrees; again at frame 36; and a final time at frame 48 to complete a nearly 360-degree, complete rotation (**Figure 5.19**).

A good way to visualize the rotation of our object is to use the Motion Editor.

1   Double-click the motion tween you've been working on to open the Motion Editor in the Timeline itself. This allows you to adjust aspects of each property change across time.

Here, you can see how the Transform > Rotation > Y Value changes by a value of ~90° across each keyframe, eventually ending as a complete 360-degree rotation (**Figure 5.20**). In addition to helping you visualize individual properties of an animation, the Motion Editor allows the use of advanced easing through manipulation of the adjustment curves and even automated easing through a set of presets.

2   Testing the animation in the Timeline should show a smooth rotation, consigned to the y-axis and moving in one direction only. If your animation is jerky or moves in the wrong direction, you can continue to tweak the rotation or even clear the keyframes and start again until everything animates exactly as you intend.

> **NOTE**
>
> *This is just one suggested approach to 3D rotation. You can choose to animate along any axis you wish, or even try out the 3D Translation tool as well to completely change perspective.*

NOTE

Not all filters and blend modes are available for all project document types. One of the primary reasons you're using an ActionScript 3.0 document type for this project is so you have access to so many effects.

▶ *Video 5.11
*Employing Blur Filter Effects***

Applying filters and color effects

Filters can be applied to movie clip symbol instances and text blocks within your project, whereas color effects and blend modes are properties on only movie clip symbol instances. You'll use both of these effects to enhance perspective during the animation and to provide some interesting visual interaction between elements in your video.

USING BLUR FILTERS TO ADD PERSPECTIVE MOTION TO YOUR ROTATING HEADSHOT

All movie clip symbol instances accept filters, which can be applied from the bottom of the Properties panel. You access these filters by selecting the instance on the Stage and then opening the Add Filter menu in the Filters area of the Properties panel. Available filters include Drop Shadow, Blur, Glow, Bevel, Gradient Glow, Gradient Bevel, and Adjust Color. You'll be using a Blur filter for this animation.

You'll apply the blur to those times when the headshot is rotated in such a way that you see only the thin-side view. Adding a blur to these frames will increase the perception of motion and perspective in 3D space.

1 Move the playhead to frame 18 and then select the object on the Stage with the Selection tool.

2 In the Filters area of the Properties panel, click the Add Filter icon and choose Blur as your filter.

3 Unlink the Blur X and Blur Y properties by clicking the linkage icon so that it appears broken. Now you can adjust each value independent of the other.

4 Set the Blur X value to 200 and Blur Y to 0 and set Quality to High (**Figure 5.21**).

Figure 5.21 Setting blur properties.

5   Move the playhead to frame 42 and right-click that frame.

6   Choose Insert Keyframe > Filter from the menu that appears.

This will duplicate the current filter properties on this frame. If you play back the animation or scrub through the Timeline, you'll notice that far too many frames are blurred. You want to blur only a couple of frames before and after frames 18 and 42. To do this, you need to take your filter settings down to 0 values on certain frames.

7   Move the playhead to frame 15 and select the object on the Stage.

8   In the Properties panel, dial the Blur X value back down to 0. Do the same on frames 21, 39, and 45 (or whatever frames might look good to you).

9   Move the playhead back to frame 1 and select the object. Note that the default blur values are still present on this frame.

10 Take both Blur X and Blur Y down to a value of 0 and choose High for a Quality setting to match the rest of your filter settings (**Figure 5.22**).

Figure 5.22 Blurring additional frames in the Timeline

If you open the Motion Editor now, you can see exactly how your Blur filter is plotted along the graph (**Figure 5.23**). Notice that you can select from all of the tweened properties in the left-hand column. You are blurring only along the x-axis, so you can select Blur X to highlight that line in the graph. You should see plainly through the spikes how your filter is applied to the instance and at which points it drops off completely.

Figure 5.23 The Blur filter plotted in the Motion Editor

ANIMATING THE COMPLETED HEADSHOT WITH A FADE-IN

Video 5.12 *Fade In the Headshot*

Now you'll go back out to your main Timeline and focus on the Headshot layer. With all of the internal animation and effects properly designed, you can focus on creating a subtle fade-in for the complete headshot in your video. Since you're using a movie clip symbol instance and the timeline of a movie clip runs completely independent of the main timeline, you don't have to worry at all about syncing frames and can treat this instance independent of anything going on internally.

Figure 5.24 For Style, choose Alpha in the Properties panel.

1   Return to the main Timeline.

2   To achieve a fade-in effect, first right-click the Headshot layer and choose Create Motion Tween.

3   Move the playhead to the 3 second marker at frame 72 and use the Selection tool to select the object on the Stage.

4   In the Properties panel, go to the Color Effect area and choose Alpha from the Style menu (**Figure 5.24**).

Since you have your playhead at frame 72, any changes you make to this value slider will be recorded as a new keyframe along the Timeline.

Notice how the object disappears completely if you pull the value slider down to 0? Pull it all the way back up to 100 to make your object completely visible again. The keyframe is preserved.

5   Move the playhead back to the 1-second marker at frame 24, select the object, and again pull the Alpha slider down to 0, keeping it there.

6   Do the same thing on frame 1 to ensure the headshot never becomes visible until you hit frame 24 (**Figure 5.25**).

From frame 24 until frame 72, the Headshot object will fade in to a value of 100 and be completely visible for the remainder of the animation.

Figure 5.25 The Headshot object set to fade in from frames 24 to 72

I've chosen not to use any blend modes on my animation, since it would be rather distracting. But it might enable some interesting effects between different layers in your animation, especially if you have different assets or have changed things up a bit. At the very least, take a look at the various blend modes available to you by selecting the RotatingHeadshot movie clip symbol instance on the Stage and checking the Display area of the Properties panel. You'll find a number of blend modes on the Blending menu to choose from, including Normal, Layer, Darken, Multiply, Lighten, Screen, Overlay, Hard Light, Add, Subtract, Difference, Invert, Alpha, and Erase.

Blend modes cannot be animated from one to another, so whichever one you choose is applied to the entire animation.

Video 5.13 *Using Blend Modes*

Animating Your Name with Motion Presets

Since this is a personal promotional spot, your name is a pretty important part of it. Animate CC comes with a number of motion presets that enable some common animations through an easy-to-use mechanism. Now you'll create some text and then animate it using one of these presets.

Creating your name as a movie clip

This part is pretty straightforward.

1   Create a new layer and name it **Name**.

2   Your animation will start after 2 seconds have elapsed at frame 48, so click frame 48 and choose Insert > Timeline > Blank Keyframe. You could also choose Insert > Timeline > Keyframe, since there is no content in this layer yet.

★ *ACA Objective 4.2*

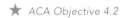
Video 5.14 *Creating the Headline Text*

3 Select the Text tool (T) and set some text properties in the Properties panel (**Figure 5.26**).

Figure 5.26 Setting text properties

I've chosen to Static Text using a 96-point Futura typeface. Futura is a nice, thick font, so it will have some real presence at 96 points. I've also chosen pure white for my text color so that the name stands out against the darker background elements.

4 Be sure frame 48 is selected on the Name layer and create a new text block by clicking the Stage and typing in your name.

5 Open the Align panel. With Align To Stage selected, choose to align the text block to the Stage center (**Figure 5.27**).

Figure 5.27 My name typed into the text block and aligned to Stage center

6   In the Properties panel, set the Y position to 120 pixels.

    With your text block created and positioned correctly, there's one more thing you need to do before applying a motion preset: you must convert the text into a movie clip symbol instance so that it can have a motion tween applied to it.

7   With the text selected, choose Modify > Convert To Symbol.

8   Name it **Name** and be sure to set the registration point to the center. Click OK to create your movie clip symbol.

Animating with motion presets

Next, you'll apply a motion preset to your Name movie clip symbol instance.

1   With the object on frame 48 of the Name layer selected, open the Motion Presets panel by choosing Window > Motion Presets.

    In the panel, check out the Default Presets category. You can choose among a number of existing motion presets, and the preview window above the selection area allows you to see how each preset will appear applied to a simple red ball or square object.

2   Select the zoom-in-2D preset and click the Apply button at the very bottom of this panel (**Figure 5.28**).

Figure 5.28 Applying the zoom-in-2D preset

The motion preset is then applied directly to the instance selected, and a number of additional keyframes are produced (**Figure 5.29**).

★ ACA Objective 2.6

▶ Video 5.15
Animating with
Motion Presets

TIP
If you'd like to take a closer look at which properties are being tweened across the frame span, double-clicking the new motion tween that has been created along that frame span will open the Motion Editor.

Figure 5.29 Additional keyframes created

TIP

You can also save your own motion presets, as well as load and export motion presets, by opening the Motion Presets panel menu (in the upper-right corner of the panel) and choosing a command. This makes it easy to create animations that you can apply to many objects and even share with the community.

You can adjust any of the properties across the Timeline and even further modify the motion tween by adjusting other properties if desired.

Additionally, use the Transform tool or the Properties panel to scale down the headshot and position it below the name text. We don't want things to get too crowded!

You'll also want your name to remain on the screen for the duration of the entire animation, so you will need to extend the frames in this layer all the way to the 10-second marker at the end.

Dynamic Animation with Variable-Width Motion Guides

One of the most creative enhancements to Animate CC in the past few years has been a rather nifty extension of the classic motion guide. For this portion of the project, we'll put these enhancements to use when animating three descriptive, text-based movie clips across your animation.

Before moving on, you'll need to think of three words that best describe you or your work. You'll animate these words across the screen, and they'll be very prominent—so make them count!

Building the descriptor text movie clips

▶ *Video 5.16*
Creating
Descriptor Text

The approach you'll take with these objects is to build one of them completely and then duplicate and edit the copies as unique symbols.

1   To begin, lock down all the current layers in your project.

2   Create a new layer and name it **Flying Text 1**.

3   Using the Text tool, create a text block using the first of your chosen words.

I'm using the Impact font at 38 points, colored with a medium gray value of #999999. I recommend this gray color because, later on, you'll apply a color tint to these objects in your animation and they show up best on a neutral color like gray.

4   Select the Selection tool and click the text you just created to select it. Convert it to a movie clip symbol by choosing Modify > Convert To Symbol.

5 Choose Movie Clip as the symbol type, assign the registration point to the center, and name this symbol **Text1** (**Figure 5.30**).

You now have a movie clip symbol that you can duplicate and edit to create the remaining two words for your animation.

Figure 5.30 Text named, registration point set

6 In the Library panel, right-click the Text1 symbol and choose Duplicate (**Figure 5.31**).

▶ *Video 5.17*
Duplicate and Edit Symbols

Figure 5.31 Duplicating the Text1 symbol

7 You'll be prompted to give the duplicated movie clip a new name, so name it **Text2**. Perform these same actions to create a third symbol and name this one **Text3**.

8 With these two additional symbols created, double-click each one and edit the text blocks contained within to display your two additional words.

The words I've used for myself, and the corresponding movie clip names, are represented here. Note that I'm using all caps to give each word the maximum impact.

AUTHOR = "Text1" movie clip symbol

DESIGNER = "Text2" movie clip symbol

DEVELOPER = "Text3" movie clip symbol

When this has been completed to your satisfaction, return to the main Timeline.

Animating the descriptors with classic motion guides

▶ *Video 5.18*
Animating with Classic Motion Guides

NOTE

A classic motion guide layer is created to work alongside a classic tween. You can't use a classic motion guide on a motion tween. Motion tweens have their own motion guides built in.

With your movie clip symbols created and ready to go, you need to create some additional layers to contain their instances. Similar to how you created these symbols, the most efficient way to create additional layers—since the content is so very similar—is to duplicate them. But first, you'll create a parent layer, along with our classic motion guide layer.

1 First, for the classic motion guide layer, right-click the existing Flying Text 1 layer and choose Add Classic Motion Guide from the menu that appears (**Figure 5.32**).

Figure 5.32 Adding the classic motion guide

This automatically creates a new layer that will serve as your classic motion guide and nests the selected layer within it, applying whatever guide you eventually draw on the Stage. Notice how the appearance of each affected layer changes to reflect all of this.

Within your newly created guide layer, you need to create an element that will serve as your classic motion guide.

2 Select the Line tool (▱); a line will serve the purpose of a classic motion guide.

3 Draw a line that measures 2000 pixels across and is positioned –360 pixels on the x-axis and 500 pixels on the y-axis (**Figure 5.33**).

This effectively centers the shape vertically on the Stage.

4 Select the Flying Text 1 layer, and on frame 1, move the Text1 instance so that the transform point locks up with the line you just created. You may need to adjust your snapping options if it isn't aligning correctly.

I've aligned it to a Y position of 500 and an X position of 1600. This places the text on the pasteboard, initially (**Figure 5.34**).

5 Move the playhead to frame 52 and select that frame in the Flying Text 1 layer. Choose Insert > Timeline > Keyframe to create a keyframe.

6   Select the instance at frame 52 and modify the X position to –300 so that it appears on the opposite side of the Stage.

Since you're using a classic motion guide, the instance will tween across this guide, even if the guide object is curved or similarly complicated in structure.

7   Right-click anywhere on that layer between these two keyframes and choose Create Classic Tween from the menu that appears.

The frame-span background turns purple, indicating a classic tween has been created (**Figure 5.35**). Classic tweens are very similar to motion tweens but do certain things in slightly different ways.

Figure 5.35 The purple frame span indicates a classic tween has been created.

TIP

Since classic motion guides require classic tweens and classic tweens require that keyframes be created in this way, you have to create additional keyframes like this manually.

8   Test the animation to be sure the transform point of the movie clip symbol instance on both frame 1 and frame 52 are properly aligned and that the animation follows the guide we have established. If it doesn't, you'll need to adjust the positioning of these elements because the transform point of the instance on each frame must come in contact with the guide element for it to be effective.

You've already created a Flying Text 1 layer tween that contains your movie clip symbol instance named Text1 and that animates nicely in accordance with the established classic motion guide. Why go through all that trouble two additional times when you can simply duplicate the layer and swap out symbols?

▶ *Video 5.19*
Duplicating Layers and Swapping Symbols

9   Right-click the Flying Text 1 layer and choose Duplicate Layers from the menu that appears.

Animate CC creates an exact copy of that layer.

10 Rename the layer to **Flying Text 2** and then swap out its Text1 instances on both frame 1 and frame 52 for Text2 instances. To do this, select the instance in question and, in the Properties panel, click the Swap button.

Note that it may be very useful to lock any layers you do not want to select content from!

11 In the Swap Symbol dialog box that appears, choose Text2 and click OK (**Figure 5.36**).

Figure 5.36 The Swap Symbol dialog box

12 Perform this same operation to create a third layer, naming it **Flying Text 3** and swapping its instances of frames 1 and 52 for Text3 (**Figure 5.37**).

Figure 5.37 Flying Text layers duplicated in the Timeline

Now, you'll stagger your animated text instances to flow in one after the other accordingly.

13 Drag across all 52 frames of the Flying Text 1 layer, and then with that entire span of frames highlighted, drag it along the Timeline so that the initial keyframe lands at frame 70 and the last keyframe at frame 121.

14 Perform the same action on the Flying Text 2 layer but drag it so that the initial keyframe lands at frame 121 and the last keyframe at frame 172.

15 Finally, perform this same set of actions on the Flying Text 3 layer so that the initial keyframe lands at frame 172 and the last keyframe at frame 223.

All three layers should be nicely staggered (**Figure 5.38**).

> **NOTE**
>
> *You can swap out any movie clip in the current project library without having to change position, scale, color effects, or anything else applied to a symbol instance.*

Figure 5.38 All Flying Text layers are now staggered in the Timeline.

★ *ACA Objective 4.5*

▶ **Video 5.20**
*Variable Width
Motion Guides*

Employing variable-width stroke options

Variable-width strokes can do more than simply adopt and adapt width profiles. When used as classic motion guides, they can also influence the scale and color of the objects they are guiding. You'll convert your simple line guide to one that employs a variable width and use it to add more dynamic characteristics to our animation.

1   Select the line in your classic motion guide layer and increase the stroke size in the Properties panel to a value of 77.

2   For the stroke color, choose the default rainbow-colored linear gradient swatch. Strokes can have gradients applied to them just like fills (**Figure 5.39**).

Figure 5.39 Setting stroke properties in the Properties panel

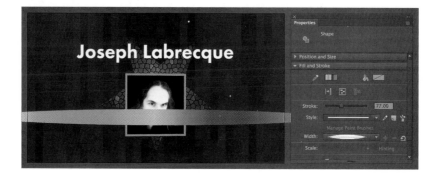

TIP

Feel free to change both the width profile and color of your guide stroke to adjust things to your liking. Experiment and have fun!

3   Take a look at the variable width profiles on the Width menu. Choose Width Profile 1.

Your guide line should now look sort of like a rainbow-colored flying saucer. You'll modify this with the Width tool.

4   Select the Width tool and then pinch down two new width points so that the stroke is thick in the center but thin everywhere else (**Figure 5.40**).

Figure 5.40 Shaping the guide stroke

5　Click the first text layer nested beneath the classic motion guide layer.

This will select the classic tween itself and allow you to manipulate some of its attributes in the Properties panel.

6　In the Tweening section, select both Color Along Path and Scale Along Path (**Figure 5.41**). Do the same to the remaining two classic tweens so that all of the text behaves similarly.

Figure 5.41 Setting Tweening properties

These options are peculiar to classic tweens and work only in conjunction with a classic motion guide like the one you created here. Test your project and watch as the scale and color shifts across the entire tween. Note that the line serving as our classic motion asset does not appear in the published animation.

Rendering and Converting the Raw Video

Now that you have completed the animation for your video, it's time to convert it to actual video data. Right now, the project is just data wrapped in an FLA. If you publish this project, it will be compiled to SWF for playback in Flash Player. You're going to do something different, though: render this project to a **raw** HD video file.

★ *ACA Objective 5.2*

Exporting Video from Animate CC

When your animation is complete and you're ready to render it all to a video file, select File > Export > Export Video. The Export Video dialog box appears, allowing you to specify a number of settings before rendering the video file to disk (**Figure 5.42**).

Video 5.21
Rendering the Video

Figure 5.42 The Export Video dialog box

Among these settings are the render width and height, the path you want to export to, and whether to open the resulting video in Adobe Media Encoder for further transcoding. Once the file is in Adobe Media Encoder, you can apply a wide variety of settings to create as many derivative video files as needed.

Adobe Media Encoder

▶ **Video 5.22** *Using Adobe Media Encoder*

Even without considering digital rights management (**DRM**) issues, the sheer variety of video file formats available can be overwhelming. Adobe Media Encoder is a dedicated video transcoding application that is included in the Adobe Creative Cloud and provides an efficient interface for converting media file formats for all sorts of purposes (**Figure 5.43**).

The software has an elegant interface that lets you convert one file at a time using presets. You can even set up a drop folder to process your media automatically using a custom compression setting as soon as it is copied into that directory.

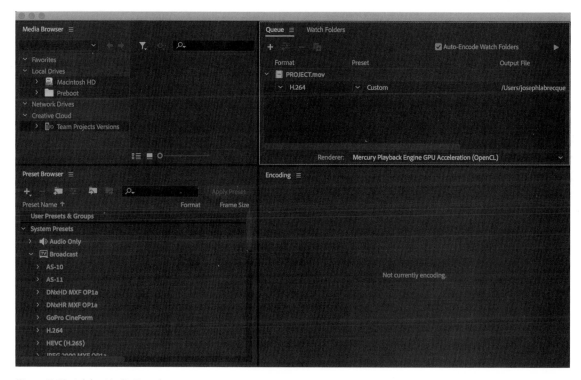

Figure 5.43 Adobe Media Encoder

TRANSCODING THE VIDEO

Now that you've rendered your animation to a video, you have one more step before you can use it on the web. You'll need to **transcode** the raw render to a compatible format for your target. You'll use Adobe Media Encoder to convert this video for the web using presets.

1 Start Adobe Media Encoder and drag and drop your rendered video into the Queue panel of the interface. If you selected the "Convert video in Adobe Media Encoder" option in Animate, you can skip this part since it should already be added. (You'll see a message in the middle of the panel that reads "To add items to the queue, drag files here," so it's pretty hard to miss.)

2 Once the video has been added to the queue, select a preset from the Preset Browser panel (**Figure 5.44**). You could also use the menus under the Format and Preset columns. For this project, choose H.264 for Format and YouTube 720p HD for Preset.

These selections will produce a video file that is playable on the vast majority of web browsers and is optimized for upload to YouTube.

Figure 5.44 Adobe Media Encoder's Preset Browser

3 When ready, click the Start Queue button that appears as a small green arrow.

Any items within the queue will then be transcoded and output to their specified destinations.

Using the video

TIP

You can also use an MP4 file with additional playback options— both HTML5 and JavaScript players and those based on Adobe Flash Player. It's a truly versatile video format.

With a standard **H.264**-encoded MP4 file in your possession, you can now distribute your video to the world! It's simple enough to upload your video to a service like YouTube or Vimeo, and if you've chosen to export an MP4 file, you can integrate it into a web page and deliver the video yourself.

To embed the video for playback in a web browser, you can use the native HTML5 video element. Here's a simple example:

```
<video width="1280" height="720" controls
src="myRenderedVideo.mp4"></video>
```

Video in Animate CC

ACA Objective 1.4

ACA Objective 5.2

Animate CC (or Flash Professional) and video playback have been closely related for a considerable span of time. For years, web browsers had no way of implementing video playback natively. Instead, browsers needed to leverage some sort of plugin to play back video. Before Flash Player became the de facto standard for web video, an assortment of additional plugins were used, including Real Player, Windows Media Player, and QuickTime.

With the advent of YouTube in 2007 and thanks to a number of video playback and streaming advancements in the Flash Player runtime, Flash Player took over the video scene very quickly, becoming the primary method of video playback on the web for years. Recently, web browsers have begun to support native video playback using the HTML5 video element. With Animate CC, there are ways of using video files across both ActionScript 3.0 and HTML5 Canvas project types.

Supported video file types

Animate CC projects targeting ActionScript 3.0 support a number of video file types. These range from those file types with unique, specific qualities that can be used only in ActionScript-based projects to the most widely used video file type on the web today: MP4.

- **FLV:** The FLV format is usually presented in a smaller, standard-definition resolution and can be embedded directly into an Animate CC FLA project. However, you probably don't want to do that unless the video is very small. One unique feature of an FLV is that it can include a full alpha channel, meaning that you can use video with transparent backgrounds in your Animate CC project. No other video format on the web today can do this. Note that this format can no longer be output using Adobe Media Encoder.

- **MP4:** The MP4 file format, or H.264, is the standard for web video and is supported by many mobile devices. It allows for high-resolution video delivery and includes a number of different profiles, nearly all of which are supported by the Adobe Flash runtimes. This allows Flash Player or an Adobe AIR-based playback to play videos that are also compatible with tablet devices and smartphones that don't support the Adobe Flash runtimes through alternate means, such as the HTML5 video element.

- **F4V:** The F4V format also supports high-definition resolution and has much more metadata associated with the file. F4V is based on the MP4 specification, but it includes additional metadata to work specifically with Animate CC projects.

Embedding video files

Video can be added to an ActionScript 3.0 Animate CC project either by placing an FLVPlayback component on the Stage and configuring the properties through the Properties panel or by using the File > Import > Import Video command. The latter will take you to a wizard that will walk you through the steps to configure the FLVPlayback component to play the selected FLV, F4V, or MP4 file. When you have finished those steps, you'll be set up with the very same components that you would have had if you had done it manually.

> **NOTE**
> *As mentioned, video embedding is available only for use in the ActionScript 3.0 document type. Embedded video works best for smaller video clips, with a playback time of less than 10 seconds. If you're using video clips with longer playback times, consider using progressively downloaded video or streaming video using a dedicated streaming server.*

VIDEO PLAYBACK IN HTML5 CANVAS PROJECTS

When targeting HTML5 Canvas in Animate CC, you cannot embed video files... but it is possible to play them through use of the dedicated HTML5 Video component. Within your project, open the Components panel by choosing Window > Components and locate the Video component in the Video folder. Dragging an instance of this component onto the Stage allows you to specify an MP4 video file to play back once the project has been published. You'll learn more about the use of components in Chapter 6.

NOTE

Since ActionScript 3.0 documents do not support rendering embedded MP4 videos, they are not published. Importing MP4 video files for animation guides in this manner is a design-time-only feature.

ADDING MP4 VIDEO AS A GUIDE

With the most recent releases of Animate CC, you can also import video to be used as a guide for your animated content. To do this, choose the File > Import > Import Video command and select "Embed H.264 video in the Timeline." When an MP4 video is embedded, the frames of the video are rendered on the Stage as you scrub along the Timeline. This feature enables you to use videos as a guide to synchronize your animation on the Stage.

Working with published video

Whether the video content originates from an Animate CC project—as is the case with the project you produced in this chapter—or from some other source, you have a few options for playing back that video either through the Adobe Flash run-times or through the native HTML5 video element in the browser. Whatever your source, be sure to encode the video file as an H.264-compliant MP4 file to ensure the broadest amount of compatible playback options.

PLAYBACK USING PROGRESSIVE DOWNLOAD

Progressive download is a simple form of video playback that involves the download of an entire MP4 file for playback through either Flash Player or the HTML5 video element. All it takes to enable this sort of playback is for the video files to be served via HTTP from a web server. This is the only widely supported delivery mechanism for the HTML5 video element.

The positive aspect of progressive download delivery is that it's easy to implement. Just place the video file on a web server and point your playback to the file.

The downsides of this method of video delivery are that the user can't skip around to various parts of the video until those portions have been downloaded. This is quite problematic for long videos; the entire video must be downloaded before the user can view later portions. What's more, with progressive download, there is generally no security or DRM protection enabled on the video. Because this is basically a direct download, the entire video is copied from the web server to the client machine.

PLAYBACK USING VIDEO STREAMING

Deploying the videos through use of a video streaming service will not only allow true streaming but can also automatically adapt the quality of the video based on the end user's bandwidth. All of this happens on the fly, meaning the quality can be throttled even as the video is playing.

The positive aspects of streaming delivery are that the user can easily skip around to various parts of the video as soon as a connection to the server is made and the stream is initiated. They never have to wait for the video to download—just for the stream to buffer a little.

Streaming a video is the most secure method of delivery since the actual video file never touches the client machines. Instead, small chunks of video content are delivered in a stream and removed from memory as soon as they are consumed.

The downsides of this method of video delivery are that streaming is complicated, and it involves an additional, specialized streaming server. You must also take into account the streaming protocols you want to use and whether a specific playback mechanism supports those protocols.

Challenge!

What good is video if you can't play it back? Try taking the video file you've created and working with it in some other capacity. Take it into an Adobe Premiere Pro or Adobe After Effects project, build a simple player in Animate CC, or even just try for simple playback through the HTML5 video element by using Adobe Dreamweaver.

Conclusion

You should come away from this chapter thinking primarily about the various ways of working with video in relation to Animate CC—whether through content creation, ingest, or playback. Video is such a huge part of Animate CC and the wider Adobe Flash platform story that it deserves much attention.

We've covered a lot of great visual effects and techniques in this chapter: image import, animated masks, the PolyStar tool, 3D animation tools, variable-width motion guides, blend modes, effects and filters, animated text, raw video export, and the use of Adobe Media Encoder. Additionally, we've explored other video playback and streaming concepts that should provide a solid base for determining playback methodologies.

CHAPTER OBJECTIVES

Chapter Learning Objectives

- Use HTML5 Components.
- Use the Virtual Camera.
- Use the Actions Wizard.
- Understand Advanced Layers mode.
- Work with Web fonts and dynamic text.

Chapter ACA Objectives

For full descriptions of the objectives, see the table on pages 286–291.

DOMAIN 1.0
WORKING IN THE ANIMATION INDUSTRY
1.4

DOMAIN 2.0
PROJECT SETUP AND INTERFACE
2.1, 2.5, 2.6

DOMAIN 3.0
ORGANIZATION OF DOCUMENTS
3.1

DOMAIN 4.0
CREATE AND MODIFY VISUAL ELEMENTS
4.1, 4.2, 4.3, 4.5, 4.6, 4.7

DOMAIN 5.0
PUBLISHING DIGITAL MEDIA
5.1, 5.2

CHAPTER 6

Build a Poem Generator

In this chapter, we'll swing back to using the HTML5 Canvas document type but this time with an emphasis on dynamic content and interactivity. We'll take a look at some of the newer tools at our disposal when working in HTML5 Canvas projects. These include the virtual camera, Advanced Layers mode, dynamic web fonts, HTML5 components, and more.

The project we will build is a poem generator (**Figure 6.1**) that allows the user to input certain key words, which will then get compiled into a completed poem and displayed to the user. Most of us have a time in life where we write sad poetry, right? Let's make this a *sad* poem generator!

▶ *Video 6.1* *Project Overview*

Figure 6.1 The completed poem generator

Create a New HTML5 Canvas Document

We already had a look at using the HTML5 Canvas document type when we designed our animated greeting card a few chapters ago. The basic document creation and setup remains similar across these projects.

Document and Stage properties

★ ACA Objective 2.1

▶ **Video 6.2** *Create a New HTML5 Canvas Document*

As with any project, we must first create a new document. On the Welcome screen, or via File > New in the application menu, choose HTML5 Canvas as your document type.

Figure 6.2 Document properties for this project

Animate CC opens a new document for us to begin working with. Let's take a look at our document properties (**Figure 6.2**). Set the following values in the Properties panel:

- FPS: **24**
- Stage Width: **500px**
- Stage Height: **500px**
- Stage Background Color: **#000000**

Once you've set the properties accordingly, be sure to save your project with a name that makes sense to you.

Organizing the Timeline

★ ACA Objective 3.1

▶ **Video 6.3** *Creating Timeline Layers*

We'll be dealing with some advanced concepts in the Timeline itself, so it is best to go ahead and set this all up before getting too far into the project. As with any new document, we have a default layer already present that we can now rename.

1. Double-click the layer name and type **Background** to rename the existing layer.
2. Click the New Layer button beneath the timeline to create another layer. Name this layer **Content**.
3. Create four additional layers, naming them **Base**, **Navigation**, **Labels**, and **Actions** (**Figure 6.3**).

Figure 6.3 Layers in the project timeline

4   Lock all the layers before proceeding so that you do not accidentally work within an incorrect layer moving forward.

▶ **Video 6.4** Adding frame labels

With our Timeline layers established and locked down, we'll now extend our frame span across all layers and add label markers to define the various portions of our Timeline. Six seconds should be more than enough for this project.

1   At the 6-second mark, click-drag across all six layers to highlight this frame across all layers. If you set your project FPS to 24, this will be frame 144.

2   Choose Insert > Timeline > Frame. A new span of frames will be created up to the 6-second mark on every single frame (**Figure 6.4**). This allows any content we create to be ever-present across our timeline.

Figure 6.4 A frame span of 6 seconds

Now let's focus on the Labels layer. We need to establish a set of text labels across the Timeline that we can then address through JavaScript later on. This will allow us to jump to different positions on the Timeline without needing to know specific frame numbers.

1   Select frame 10 on the Labels layer and choose Insert > Timeline > Keyframe. An empty keyframe is inserted at the selected frame.

2   Access the Properties panel. In the Label section, type **beginagain** as the Name value. Make sure the default value Name is chosen from the Type menu.

3   Select frame 24 (the 1-second mark) and insert a new keyframe once more.

NOTE

Frame labels also assist in diminishing potential problems with frame numbering across different document types, since HTML5 Canvas frame numbers begin at 0 and **ActionScript** *3.0 frame numbers begin at 1.*

4 Perform the same actions in the Properties panel, this time using a Name value of **moveforward**.

5 Select the frame at the 4-second mark. Insert a new keyframe and provide a frame label of **goback** (**Figure 6.5**).

So, what are all of these labels for? They specify a set of positions within the overall timeline that we will use to navigate the project based on various user interactions. You'll learn more about this once we start writing the JavaScript code to perform these actions.

Figure 6.5 Labels created on the timeline

With our labels now in place along the timeline, it's time to focus on designing some content.

★ ACA Objective 2.5

★ ACA Objective 4.1

Designing layout elements

▶ **Video 6.5** Design the Background

A couple of design elements are needed at this point; a scrolling background and some framing elements for our navigation to rest within. We'll also add a title to our application using static text.

★ ACA Objective 4.5

First, we'll deal with the background elements:

1 Unlock the Background layer and select it.

2 Select the Rectangle tool and choose a stroke of None. Use a fill color of #DFC3AE.

3 Draw out a new shape with a height of 500px and a width of 1500px. The width is three times that of the Stage because we will be panning the camera across the Stage in that way.

4 Using the Selection tool, select the shape you just created to ensure it is the correct width and height. Align it to the top left of the Stage (**Figure 6.6**).

Figure 6.6 The back-
ground shape properly
drawn and aligned

This next part is a bit tricky, but your result doesn't have to match exactly what is
shown here. The idea is to have a transition from one color to another across the
entire shape so that when the camera pans by, the user will notice the change taking place.

Video 6.6 Enhance
the Background

1   Using the Lasso tool, draw an angled selection across the height of the shape,
    and include in the selection everything to the right (**Figure 6.7**).

★ *ACA Objective 4.3*

Figure 6.7 An irregular,
angled selection is made
with the Lasso tool.

2   Open the Color panel and choose Linear Gradient from the Color Type menu.

3 Have the gradient go from pure black (#000000) to a light gray (#CACACA).
See **Figure 6.8.**

Figure 6.8 A portion of the background shape is given a gradient fill.

4 With this portion of the shape still selected, using the Gradient Transform tool, make any adjustment necessary to make the transition appear as desired (**Figure 6.9**).

Figure 6.9 Use the Gradient Transform tool to shift the gradient edge at an angle.

We'll now add a bit of texture to the shape by applying some **vector** art to it.

1 Select the Ink Bottle tool and click between the two shapes to add a stroke between them.

2 With the Selection tool, double-click the new stroke to ensure it is completely selected.

3   In the Properties panel, in the Stroke And Fill section, set the stroke color to black and the stroke size to around 48.

4   Click the icon that looks like a can of paintbrushes to open the Brush Library panel.

★ *ACA Objective 2.6*

5   From here, you can choose a vector art brush from the set of categories. Choose Artistic > Paint Brush > Dry Brush 3 for a ragged effect (**Figure 6.10**).

Figure 6.10 A vector art brush is applied to the stroke.

Dismiss the Brush library when finished.

Okay, that should be all for the background. We'll now design some overlaying base elements to hold our title and navigation:

★ *ACA Objective 4.2*

▶ **Video 6.7**
Designing Base Elements

1   Make sure all layers are locked; then unlock and select the Base layer.

2   Select the Rectangle tool and set it with a stroke of None and a fill of pure black.

3   Draw a shape along the top of the Stage that measures 500x70.

4   Draw a second shape along the bottom of the Stage measuring 500x90 and position it on the y-axis at 410px.

5   Select the Text tool and draw out a static text element across the topmost shape. Type the application title, **Sad Poem Generator**.

6   For Character properties, choose a family that is solid and bold. I am choosing Expo Sans Pro Bold, but you can use whatever you wish. I'm using a 48pt font size and a dull orange (#CC6633) as the color. Text alignment is centered within the text block.

7 The text should also be centered against the topmost shape. Reposition with the following properties: X: **8**, Y: **4**, W: **484**. See **Figure 6.11**.

We now have our basic background and layout elements designed and positioned appropriately. Be sure to lock all of your layers before proceeding.

Advanced Layers mode

As mentioned previously, we are going to be using the virtual camera (new in Animate CC 2017 release) to animate across different views within this small application. The camera allows us to easily pan across all of the contents of the Stage without any fuss. However, we want certain layers of our content to stay in place as the camera shifts, including everything within our Base layer.

The ability to switch from Basic Layers mode to Advanced Layers mode will enable us to attach certain layers to the camera. This will effectively lock them in place, and any of the camera movements that change our perspective across the rest of the Stage will not affect any attached layers whatsoever.

Although we aren't going to be dealing with the camera for a little bit, it's a good idea to begin working in whichever layers mode you require for the project as soon as possible, so we'll do so next.

1 Look at the left end of the timeline and you'll see a small icon there with the word Off next to it. This lets you know that you are now working in

Basic Layers mode. Click this toggle to switch to Advanced Layers mode (**Figure 6.12**).

Figure 6.12 Toggling between Basic and Advanced Layers modes

2 A dialog box appears (**Figure 6.13**), letting you know that switching between layer modes can affect certain aspects of your project. It also requires that you confirm that you do want to enable Advanced Layers mode.

Figure 6.13 The Advanced Layers mode confirmation dialog

3 Click Use Advanced Layers to dismiss the dialog box and confirm your choice (**Figure 6.14**).

Figure 6.14 Advanced Layers mode has been activated.

Advanced Layers mode is now enabled for our project. You can always switch back to Basic Layers mode, if you wish, but we'll need to keep this enabled for the remainder of our project.

NOTE

With Advanced Layers mode activated, we can also make use of the powerful Layer Depth panel. Although we won't be using this functionality in this project, we will discuss it a bit further on.

★ *ACA Objective 4.1*

Using HTML5 Components

▶ *Video 6.9*
Adding Button Components

Figure 6.15 HTML5 components in the Components panel

Components in Animate CC (**Figure 6.15**) are prepackaged functional objects that, similar to symbols, can be instantiated upon the Stage, given instance names, and interacted with in much the same way. One of the major differences between components and symbols is that components will have a more generic look in Animate CC because any **skin** that you apply is viewable only at runtime.

Each component generally represents a common user interface element like a button, a check box, or list. Of course, there are exceptions—you can even play video files by using the Video component!

Creating navigation buttons

We already have a nice black overlay at the bottom of the Stage that is ready to serve as a backdrop for a couple of Button component instances. All we need to do is pull some components onto the Stage and tweak some parameters to make them unique.

1 Select and unlock the Navigation layer.

2 Open the Components panel by choosing Window > Components. You'll see a number of categories to choose from, including User Interface, Video, and jQuery UI.

NOTE

A skin is a collection of graphics or CSS rules that defines the appearance of a component.

3 Expand the User Interface category and locate the Button component.

4 Drag a Button component instance onto the Stage (**Figure 6.16**).

NOTE

Components in HTML5 Canvas are not even part of the Canvas element. They are overlaid atop the Canvas in a separate layer and are composed of HTML elements.

Figure 6.16 A Button component in the Library panel and an instance on the Stage

Now that we have a Button component instance on the Stage, if you take a peek within the Library panel, you will see the component definition is now included there. Unlike symbols, which can be edited directly from the Library panel, components must be manipulated on a per-instance basis through the Component Parameters panel.

★ ACA Objective 1.4

NOTE

ActionScript 3.0 document types also have their own distinct set of components. They are accessed and instantiated the same way as you see here, but you interact with them via ActionScript instead of JavaScript.

We'll next adjust some of the properties of our component instance, customize specific parameters, and duplicate the instance in order to have a mechanism for the user to move back and forth through the experience.

1. Using the Selection tool, choose the Button component instance on the Stage.

2. In the Properties panel, set the following values: X: **20**, Y: **432**, W: **180**, H: **48**. This will size and position the instance appropriately.

3. Next, provide an instance name of `back_btn`. Instance names allow you to manipulate and interact with the project through code. See **Figure 6.17**.

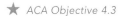
★ ACA Objective 4.3

NOTE

A class in CSS is different from a class in JavaScript or ActionScript. You can think of a class in CSS as a way to target certain elements by referring to a certain class name.

Figure 6.17 Button instance properties

4. Look below the instance name and click the Show Parameters button to open the Component Parameters panel (**Figure 6.18**).

5. Enter **Back** as the Label value and note that there is a class value of `ui-button` already assigned. We will use this later to skin the component.

Figure 6.18 The Component Parameters panel

Now we will duplicate the existing Button component instance and give it its own unique property and parameter values.

1. Alt-click/Option-click the existing Button component instance and drag a duplicate to the other side of the Stage. It will retain the same width and height.

▶ *Video 6.10*
Duplicating Components

2 Select the instance you just created and provide an Instance name of `next_btn`.

3 You may want to reposition the new Button component instance using these values: X: **300** and Y: **432** (**Figure 6.19**).

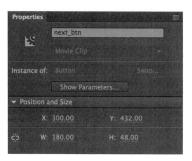

Figure 6.19 Properties of the second Button component instance

4 Look at the Component Parameters panel again and set the Label value to **Next**. Keep every other parameter at the default.

You now have a set of Button component instances on the Stage (**Figure 6.20**), ready to be wired up with JavaScript. We'll now explore the use of an additional component that allows the user to input data into our application: TextInput.

Figure 6.20 The completed Button component instances on the Stage

Creating text inputs

Our next task is to create a form. I know that sounds pretty much like the most boring thing we could possibly do, but the results will be worth it.

▶ **Video 6.11**
Adding Text Input Components

First, we'll create four static text labels, one for each of our TextInput component instances, that will prompt the user to enter a certain value.

1   Unlock the Content layer and select it. We'll create all of our static text and component instances in this layer.

2   Select the Text tool from the Tools panel.

3   Select Static Text as your Text type and provide the following properties: Family: **Expo Sans Pro** (or whatever you used for the title text), Size: **24pt**, and Black (**#000000**) for the Color.

4   You'll be creating four pieces of text on the Stage. Click in the upper left (but underneath the title text) and type **Name:**; then click beneath that and type **Concept:**. Continuing beneath the existing text, create a third text block with the value **Animal:** and another with the value **Color:**.

5   Now, arrange them in a stack from top to bottom (**Figure 6.21**). You can use the Align panel if you wish.

Figure 6.21 The arranged text in the Content layer

You now should have a column of text labels along the left-hand side of the Stage. We'll next create a TextInput component instance to match each of these labels.

1   Open the Components panel by choosing Window > Components.

2   Expand the User Interface category and locate the TextInput component.

3   Drag a TextInput component instance onto the Stage (**Figure 6.22**) and align it beside the Name: label.

4   Use the Selection tool to select the component instance you just created and look at the Properties panel.

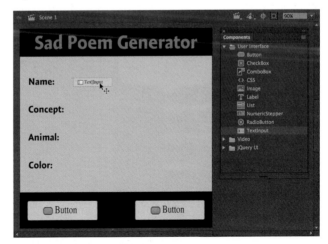

Figure 6.22 Dragging a TextInput component instance onto the Stage

5 In the Properties panel, assign this instance the name `name_input`. Giving this component a unique name allows us to read values entered into this component instance by the user via JavaScript.

6 Change the width to **320** and the height to **44** (**Figure 6.23**).

If you click the Show Parameters button, the Component Parameters panel appears. We will not be changing any of these parameters, but it is important to note that there is a class value of `ui-textinput` already assigned. This will come in handy later on when we skin these components with CSS rules.

7 Now, duplicate the TextInput component instance you just created three times, aligning each instance to one of the existing text labels.

8 Select each instance to modify its instance name in the Properties panel. Aside from the existing `name_input` instance, we should have a `concept_input` instance, an `animal_input` instance, and finally a `color_input` instance.

9 Again, make sure that each instance is aligned to the appropriate text label (**Figure 6.24**). If you have trouble, you can always use the Align panel.

Both the TextInput and Button component instances in Animate CC are simple placeholder previews. Testing or publishing will allow you to see how the components are visually rendered in the web browser.

10 Choose Control > Test to see how everything looks (**Figure 6.25**).

Figure 6.25 The project as it now appears when published

Yikes! Those Button instances could certainly look better. Let's fix them with a little CSS.

Using CSS to style your components

★ ACA Objective 4.6

 Video 6.12 Adding CSS to Your Project

Defining custom CSS style rules and then using the CSS component in a project will allow you to target and effectively skin other components on the Stage. This allows you to radically alter each component's default appearance when viewed in a web browser.

The first thing to do is to create a CSS component instance for our project.

1 Open the Components panel by choosing Window > Components.

2 Expand the User Interface category and locate the CSS component (**Figure 6.26**).

3 Drag a CSS component instance and place it somewhere out of the way—on the pasteboard will work (**Figure 6.27**). The CSS component instance, once published, has no visual presence.

Figure 6.26 The CSS component in the User Interface category

Figure 6.27 A CSS component instance is placed on the pasteboard.

Make sure that you have the pasteboard visible and that the Clip Content Outside The Stage button is not activated; otherwise, you won't see your instance on the pasteboard.

4   With the CSS component instance selected, access the Component Parameters panel and notice it has a single parameter: Source (**Figure 6.28**).

Figure 6.28 Source is the only parameter for a CSS component instance.

Source refers to the external CSS file used by the component. Its value is blank because no file has been associated with it. Click the pencil icon to browse for a CSS file (the source file) to be included in our project and published along with everything else. Before we can browse for such a file, we have to first create it.

1   To create a custom CSS file, open your text editor of choice. I'm quite fond of Visual Studio Code, but you could also use Dreamweaver CC, Brackets, or even Notepad.

2   Create a new file called **custom.css** and save it to your Animate CC project directory (**Figure 6.29**).

With this new CSS file created and opened in your editor, insert some CSS rules targeting both the `ui-button` and `ui-textinput` classes. These are the classes already assigned to our Button and TextInput component instances in use.

3   Type the following into the CSS file to set properties like colors, fonts, and size values (**Figure 6.30**):

Figure 6.29 A newly created CSS file for our project (which may look different on your computer)

```
.ui-button {
    font-size: 3.2rem;
    color: #3a0000;
    background-color: #CC6633;
    font-weight: 900;
}
.ui-textinput {
    font-size: 2.4rem;
    padding:8px;
}
```

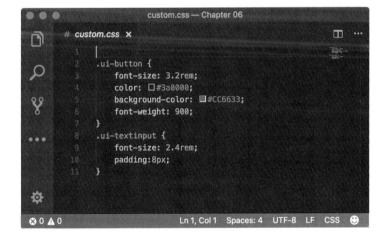

Figure 6.30 The completed custom CSS file

4   Save the CSS file and pop back over to Animate CC.

5   In the Component Parameters panel, with the CSS component instance selected click the pencil icon to open the Content Path dialog box.

6   Click the folder icon to browse for and select the CSS file you just created (**Figure 6.31**).

7   Choose Control > Test to see how everything has changed with the addition of this CSS (**Figure 6.32**).

Figure 6.31 The modified CSS component instance parameters

Figure 6.32 The published project with custom CSS applied to component instances

All right! Those Buttons look a lot better now, and the TextInputs are improved as well.

Camera Movement

 Video 6.13
Camera Overview

Before we get into some of the more technical, code-centric aspects of this project, we'll put to use one of the coolest new features Animate now offers: the virtual camera.

About the virtual camera

The Animate CC camera functionality allows animators to simulate the use of a real-life camera. Previously, animators relied on third-party extensions of varying quality and compatibility, or they modified their animations to mimic a camera's movement.

Animators can use the following camera features:

- Panning with the subject of the frame
- Zooming in the object of interest for dramatic effect
- Zooming out of a frame to remind the viewer of a larger picture

- Modifying the focal point to shift the attention between subjects.
- Rotating the camera view.
- Applying color effects and tint to an entire scene.
- Attaching layers to the camera in Advanced Layers mode.
- Creating expressive parallax effects using the Layer Depth panel in Advanced Layers mode.

To use the camera, you must first select the Camera tool from the Tools panel or click the Camera toggle button at the bottom of the Timeline panel (**Figure 6.33**).

Figure 6.33 Our project with the Camera tool selected and the camera enabled

Either of these actions will enable the camera for your project, displaying a special Camera layer in the timeline and camera control overlays on the Stage. With the Camera tool selected, you'll also have access to Camera properties in the Properties panel (**Figure 6.34**).

When you set a camera view for your composition, you look at the layers as though you were looking through that camera. The Camera layer behaves like a regular object; you can add tweens or keyframes to it, as well as animate it like other objects in the document.

Figure 6.34 Default Camera properties

With the camera enabled for our document, we will be able to create animated camera movements across the entire Stage. For this project, we'll pan the camera across different areas of the project based on user interaction.

★ ACA Objective 3.1

▶ Video 6.14
Setting Camera
Properties

Changing the view with Camera Motion

Let's employ the camera in order to animate a pan transition across our project, moving from the input area to what will eventually display our poem text.

1 Select the Camera tool from the Tools panel.

You'll immediately notice a number of changes occur across the project: a set of camera controls appear floating across the Stage, a new Camera layer appears in the Timeline, and the Properties panel changes to display Camera properties (**Figure 6.35**).

Figure 6.35 The Camera layer and HUD overlay

2 Move the playhead to the 1-second marker and insert a new keyframe on the Camera layer.

3 Move the playhead to the 3-second marker and insert a second keyframe (**Figure 6.36**).

Figure 6.36 The Camera layer with keyframes at the 1- and 3-second markers

4 Using the camera controls, press Shift and drag across the Stage so that the camera pans across and to the right. Keep an eye on the Camera properties and stop panning once the Camera X position is at about –1000, or the very right edge of the background content (**Figure 6.37**).

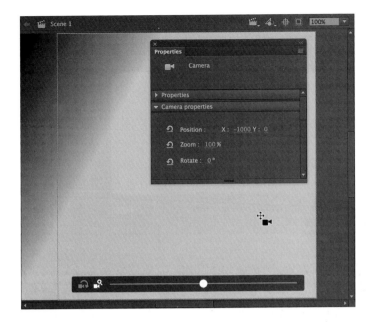

Figure 6.37 The initial camera pan at the 3-second marker keyframe

5 Right-click anywhere between the two keyframes and choose Create Classic Tween from the menu. Generally, using classic tweens is recommended for animating the camera because they provide smoother performance than motion tweens. This first tween will create the camera motion that pans from left to right.

6 Move the playhead to the 4-second marker and insert a third keyframe. This effectively places a hold on the camera from the 3-second marker until the 4-second marker.

7 Insert a final keyframe at the 6-second mark.

8 With the Camera tool selected and with the playhead at the 6-second mark, examine the Properties panel. Reset the camera position by clicking the Reset Camera Position button (**Figure 6.38**). You could also change the value of X to 0.

9 Right-click anywhere between the two keyframes you just created and choose Create Classic Tween once again. This second tween will create the camera motion that pans back from right to left.

Figure 6.38 Resetting the Camera position

▶ **Video 6.15** *Easing the Camera Motion*

★ *ACA Objective 2.6*

10 Select any frame of each classic tween in the Camera layer and apply some easing presets to the tweens through the Properties panel (**Figure 6.39**). I recommend using either Quart > Ease In Out or Quint > Ease In Out.

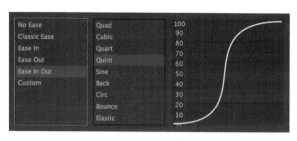

Figure 6.39 Apply some easing presets to the two tweens on the Camera layer.

NOTE

Using eases on camera tweens is a good way to add realism and finesse to any movement established using the camera.

If we now scrub the playhead across the Timeline, we'll see how adding movement to the camera is effective at creating a nice transition between two different states of an application. Right now, the overlays, title, and navigation all go away when the initial transition occurs. We'll remedy that next.

Attaching layers to the camera

★ *ACA Objective 4.6*

Using Advanced Layers mode in a project allows us to attach specific layers to the camera. This ability can enable advanced features such as text overlays, design elements, and user interface objects that appear to be completely unaffected by the movement, effects, and other properties of the camera.

▶ **Video 6.16** *Attaching Layers to the Camera*

Let's attach the Base and Navigation layers to our camera so they no longer move when the camera does. Since we enabled Advanced Layers mode earlier in this project, you may have noticed something different about the Timeline. There is an additional column aside from the lock and visibility controls column that allows us to attach and detach layers from the camera.

1 Click the black dot aligned with the Navigation layer under the Attach Layer To Camera column. The column is represented by a camera icon with a chain link overlaying it.

2 Do the same for the Base layer. Both layers will now be attached to the camera (**Figure 6.40**).

Figure 6.40 Two layers are now attached to the camera.

Once both layers have been attached to the camera, each will display a chain link icon. Scrub through the Timeline again to see that these two layers are no longer affected by the camera movement, yet all the other layers are.

About layer depth

Although we are not using the Layer Depth features made available through activation of Advanced Layer mode, you should be aware these options.

The Layer Depth panel enables you to specify z-depth for each layer (and even folders) in your project. You can access this panel from an icon that appears next to the Advanced Layer mode toggle button (**Figure 6.41**) or by choosing Window > Layer Depth.

NOTE

Not only are all these neat camera and layer depth features part of the Animate CC user interface, but you can hand control of the camera over to the user or perform programmatic effects with the powerful VirtualCamera API! This API is available in ActionScript 3.0, HTML5 Canvas, and WebGL, and it even has functionality built into the new Actions Wizard for HTML5 Canvas!

Figure 6.41 The Invoke Layer Depth Panel button in the Timeline panel

This feature presents a major new set of capabilities in Animate CC. It allows you to specify how near or far any specific layer is in front of or behind the camera. You can create dynamic parallax effects when animating the camera as the layer content at varying depths shifts differently in relation to the camera view depending on each layer's z-depth (**Figure 6.42**).

In addition, layer depth is completely tweenable and allows objects to move closer and farther away from the view as an animation progresses. We are using the camera for this project, but you can employ z-depth changes without even touching the camera; there are lots of possibilities!

Using layer depth along with the camera lets you create depth and parallax effects easily by using the camera against layers of varying depth.

We won't modify the z-depth of any layers for the current project. We are only mentioning this as a function of Advanced Layers mode, to get you thinking of other creative ways to use these tools. If you do choose to play with layer depth for this project, just be sure to reset all of the layers to a depth of 0 when you finish.

Figure 6.42 The Layer Depth panel showing layers at varying z-depth

Using Dynamic Text and Web Fonts

The set of user-entered values will have to be concatenated, or merged together, with additional text data to form a complete poem for display. In an Animate CC project, we can display such string data through a dynamic text field.

★ *ACA Objective 4.7*

 Video 6.17 Create Dynamic Text

Creating the dynamic text

The first thing we need to do is establish a text object on the Stage that will accept instructions from JavaScript. This object will need to be a text field defined as dynamic text, and it also requires an instance name.

1 We'll create this text object in the Content layer, so be sure to lock all the other layers.

2 Move the playhead between the 3- and 4-second markers (**Figure 6.43**). This will bring the other side of the Background layer content into focus through movement of the camera.

Figure 6.43 The layers that are attached to the camera remain fixed as the others pan aside.

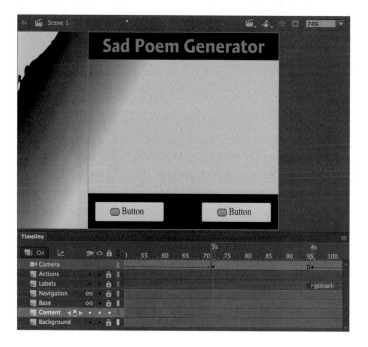

3 With the Content layer selected, choose the Text tool from the Tools panel and create a new text object on the Stage.

4   Type the following string in the text field you just created: "My sad poem will appear here!" (**Figure 6.44**).

5   Select the text object with the Selection tool and look to the Properties panel to adjust the object's properties.

6   In the top area of the Properties panel, choose Dynamic Text from the Text Type menu and provide an instance name of **poem_text**. These changes will allow you to manipulate certain text properties through JavaScript.

7   In the Position And Size section of the Properties panel, set the following properties: X: **1015**, Y: **94**, W: **470**, and H: **296**. This will size and position the text object properly (**Figure 6.45**).

Figure 6.44 The poem text is created on the Stage.

We now have our text object nearly configured. Since we are using dynamic text in an HTML5 Canvas document, we will need to specify a particular web font to use in our project.

Figure 6.45 The Properties panel showing properties for a dynamic text object

Choosing a web font

★ *ACA Objective 4.2*

▶ *Video 6.18 Select a web font*

The use of dynamic text in an HTML5 Canvas document requires a web font. We will now choose an appropriate font family from a web service and choose the size and color to apply to the content of our dynamic text field.

1   Be sure that the poem_text text object is selected and access the Properties panel.

2 In the Character section, set Size to **32** and Color to **#414141**.

3 Click the small icon to the right of the Family menu that looks like a globe. Doing so allows you to add web fonts from either Typekit or Google Fonts.

Both Typekit and Google Fonts are services that allow us to choose and use web fonts in an Animate CC project (**Figure 6.46**).

Figure 6.46 Choosing a web font service

Typekit fonts require a bit more work to use, though some spectacular fonts are available through that service. The Typekit option is a feature of most Creative Cloud subscriptions since Typekit is an Adobe service.

Google Fonts are simpler to implement and available for use no matter what level of Creative Cloud subscription you might have, so that is what we'll choose for our project.

4 Choose Google Fonts from the Add Web Fonts menu. The Google Fonts dialog box opens (**Figure 6.47**).

Figure 6.47 The Google Fonts dialog box

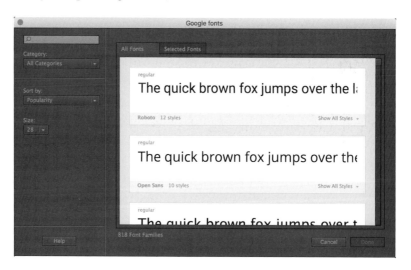

5   You can use search terms and filters in this dialog box, but we know exactly what we want, so type **Shadow** in the Search box.

6   A number of fonts appear. Click Shadows Into Light and a blue check mark will appear in the upper right, signifying that this font has been selected (**Figure 6.48**).

Figure 6.48 A web font has been chosen.

7   Click Done to dismiss the Google Fonts dialog box and you'll see a message appear in the Output panel: "1 web font family is added to the Text->Font menu." See **Figure 6.49**.

Figure 6.49 Check the Text > Font menu to verify that the chosen web font has been added.

You now need to apply the chosen font to your text object. Web fonts are always moved to the very top of the Family menu.

8   Ensure that the poem_text text object is selected, and in the Character section of the Properties panel, open the Family menu and scroll to the top to locate the Shadows Into Light web font.

The web font is now being used to render text in your text object (**Figure 6.50**). Since this is a dynamic text field, whenever you change the text contents, the same web font will apply...which is exactly what we want.

Making It Interactive with JavaScript

All of the assets and animation are now completely present and in their final form. The last thing we need to do to make all of this work is to write some JavaScript code.

Dealing with timeline navigation

If we test the project as it is right now, we see the view transition animation loop endlessly. That isn't quite the experience we are shooting for. The first thing we have to do to correct this is to stop the playhead at appropriate points along the timeline.

The first thing we'll do is employ the Actions layer to hold any code and add in some keyframes at the appropriate points. If any of the existing layers are currently unlocked, be sure to lock them all before we continue.

1   Lock the Actions layer if not already locked. This layer exists only to keep the JavaScript code separate from any visual assets, so locking it prevents us from adding visual content in error.

2   Insert new keyframes on frame 2, frame 96, and frame 144 (**Figure 6.51**).

Figure 6.51 The Actions layer with empty keyframes across it

The keyboard shortcut to insert a new keyframe is F6. Pressing F7 will insert a blank keyframe, but in this case, both shortcuts will do the same thing since there is no content in the layer.

3   Select the keyframe at frame 2 and open the Actions panel by choosing Window > Actions.

4   In the Actions panel, type `this.stop();` to stop the playhead when it hits the current frame.

5   Select the keyframe at frame 96 and enter the same code in the Actions panel: `this.stop();`.

6   Select the final keyframe at frame 144. We'll enter something a bit different in the Actions panel for this frame: `this.gotoAndStop("beginagain");`.

Instead of stopping the timeline at frame 144, we are instructing the playhead to jump to and stop at the frame with the label beginagain. We do this so that the JavaScript code present at frame 2 will run only once—we will be setting up a lot of code on that frame that should be configured only upon initialization of the project.

Setting global variables

JavaScript variables defined in certain objects or on certain frames will not necessarily be available to other object or nested symbol timelines. To get around this, we have the concept of global variables. When defining variables globally, we must ensure that they are easily accessible across the entire project, no matter where the code resides.

With the Actions panel open, and any frame selected, you will notice that we also have access to a Global designator above Scene 1. Previous to this point in the

▶ *Video 6.20* Setting *global variables*

project, all of the code written has been done so on specific frames as part of the Scene 1 Timeline designation (**Figure 6.52**).

NOTE

Variables are simply containers of data (text, numbers, and so forth) that are given an identifier to be read or even changed through code.

Figure 6.52 The Actions panel with the Global section expanded

We are going to set a number of global variables for this project.

1 Expand the Global designator in the Actions panel. You will see two options nested in it.

2 Select Global > Script. Any variables declared with this selected are designated as global variables and can be accessed across all aspects of a project.

NOTE

You also have the option to include additional JavaScript code and even entire libraries by using the Include feature, which is also nested in the Global designator. Although we do not use Include for this project, you should understand that you will be able to include external JavaScript code by referencing it using this mechanism.

3 Enter the following four variable declarations:

```
var name = "";
var concept = "";
var animal = "";
var color = "";
```

You've now established each of these variables as having global scope (**Figure 6.53**).

Figure 6.53 Our Global variables are defined.

With our global variables defined, we can move on to wiring up the Button component instances with event listeners.

Writing the next and back functions

We'll now return our attention to the Button component instances that allow navigation from one state to the other—or at least, they will soon. As a reminder, we have one instance with the name of `back_btn` and another with the instance name `next_btn`. We are able to write JavaScript to create event listeners (instructions that tell your interactive objects to react to user interactions like mouse clicks) because of these identifiers.

You may not know how to write the code that allows each Button component instance to respond to clicks from the user. That's just fine, because we don't really need to. We're going to make use of the Actions Wizard to write the initial code for us!

We'll now access the Actions Wizard and tell it what we need:

1   Open the Actions panel and select frame 2 on the Actions layer.

2   In the Actions panel, you will see a button in the upper-right of the panel labeled Add Using Wizard. Click this button to switch to the Actions Wizard (**Figure 6.54**).

3   Portions of the Actions panel change as the Actions Wizard interface takes command. You must now choose from the list of possible actions. Since we need to perform the animation to the next state, we will choose Go To Frame Label And Play.

4   Once the action has been chosen, a new prompt appears asking which timeline we want to manipulate. Select This Timeline.

5   The code preview above will display a snippet (**Figure 6.55**) and the label will be highlighted for you, indicating that you should enter a frame label. Replace the highlighted text with `moveforward`.

6   Click the Next button below the actions lists in order to select a triggering event.

▶ *Video 6.21 Using the Actions Wizard*

NOTE

The Actions Wizard is only available for HTML5 Canvas document types as of this writing. Similar helpers do exist across all document types through the Code Snippets panel.

Figure 6.54 Click Add Using Wizard to reveal the Actions Wizard.

Figure 6.55 A snippet is being generated by the Actions Wizard.

7 From the actions list, select On Mouse Click. A second list will appear that prompts you to select which object you'd like to bind this event to. Notice that since you provided instance names to both of your Button component instances, they both appear as options to choose from. See **Figure 6.56**.

Figure 6.56 Assigning an object to trigger the event

8 Select the next_btn option from the objects presented and click Finish And Add.

The Actions Wizard will now revert back to the normal Actions panel editor (**Figure 6.57**), and we can continue to edit the code that was generated.

Figure 6.57 The Actions Wizard goes away once the code is generated.

```
1   this.stop();
2   var _this = this;
3
4   /*
5   Clicking on the specified symbol instance executes a functio
6   */
7   $('#dom_overlay_container').on('click', '#next_btn', functio
8   /*
9   Moves the playhead to the specified frame label in the timel
10  Can be used on the main timeline or on movie clip timelines.
11  */
12  _this.gotoAndPlay('moveforward');
13  }.bind(_this));
14
15
```

Line 11 of 15, Col 3

As of now, you will see the following code in the Actions panel:

```
$('#dom_overlay_container').on('click', '#next_btn',
→ function() {
  this.gotoAndPlay('moveforward');
}.bind(this));
```

Before you do anything else, copy this entire code block and paste it into the Actions panel below the previous code so you can manipulate it for use with the `back_btn` component instance.

Change the copied function so it targets `back_btn` and the playhead is sent to the `goback` label on the timeline:

```
$('#dom_overlay_container').on('click', '#back_btn',
→ function() {
  this.gotoAndPlay('goback');
}.bind(this));
```

We now have functions that are triggered by a mouse click for each of our Button component instances. We do not want the user to be able to click the Back button if they're already positioned at the first state of the animation or click the Next button while at the second. We can leverage jQuery to disable or enable either button depending on our needs.

Add the following lines of code in the body of the `next_btn` function:

```
$('#next_btn').attr("disabled", true);
$('#back_btn').removeAttr("disabled");
```

This bit of code will look slightly familiar. It uses the same jQuery syntax as the event listener assignments to target the `back_btn` and `next_btn` component instances, setting their `disabled` attribute to `true` or removing that attribute altogether, thus enabling the instance.

We will add similar code to the body of the `back_btn` function:

```
$('#back_btn').attr("disabled", true);
$('#next_btn').removeAttr("disabled");
```

One more thing: since we do not want the user to be able to click the Back button after initialization, let's make sure that it is disabled by default:

1 Open the Actions panel if it isn't already open and select frame 2 on the Actions layer.

▶ **Video 6.22**
Manipulating generated code

NOTE
When we refer to the body of a function, we mean the code between the opening and closing curly braces, { }. This is true for both JavaScript and ActionScript.

2 Add the following bit of code at line 3 of the code in frame 2 in the Actions panel: `$('#back_btn').attr("disabled", true);`

This will effectively disable the Back button until `next_btn` is clicked, reenabling it.

The code on frame 2 will now read as follows:

```
this.stop();
var _this = this;
$('#back_btn').attr("disabled", true);
$('#dom_overlay_container').on('click', '#next_btn',
→ function() {
  $('#next_btn').attr("disabled", true);
  $('#back_btn').removeAttr("disabled");
  _this.gotoAndPlay('moveforward');
}.bind(_this));
$('#dom_overlay_container').on('click', '#back_btn',
→ function() {
  $('#back_btn').attr("disabled", true);
  $('#next_btn').removeAttr("disabled");
  this.gotoAndPlay('goback');
}.bind(this));
```

The user will now be able to move from one state view to the next and back—but will never be allowed to click a button that goes nowhere.

JavaScript comments

TIP

You can also comment out pieces of code that might be causing JavaScript errors. This is a good trouble-shooting technique!

Using JavaScript can be difficult depending on what you are programming. Help yourself out by commenting your code. Commenting involves putting notes in your code to help you find your way around at a later date. You can see from this project that the Actions Wizard makes extensive use of comments to explain the code it has written.

There are two main ways of commenting: single-line and block comments.

You create single-line comments by starting a line with double slashes:

```
// this is just a short, single-line comment!
```

Block comments start with /* and end with */. This will let you block off larger blocks of text like this:

```
/*
This is a multi-line
comment. Use it to comment
out big chunks of code
or to make lengthy notes
to reference later
*/
```

NOTE

It's fine to remove any comments in the code. Code in comments never executed and is designated by // or / */.*

To keep things clean, I've removed all of them from the generated code in this lesson.

Building and displaying the poem

★ *ACA Objective 4.7*

▶ *Video 6.23*
Reading from the TextInput Components

To combine the user values from our TextInput component instances with some predefined string values, we'll need to modify the function attached to our `next_btn` instance.

Let's add some instructions that will gather the values from the four TextInput component instances we created earlier and save those values to our global variables. Add the following lines of code directly after the opening curly brace:

```
name = $("#name_input").val();
concept = $("#concept_input").val();
animal = $("#animal_input").val();
color = $("#color_input").val();
```

All we need to do in order to complete the code is to write the function that pulls it all together and displays the results in our visual project:

▶ *Video 6.24*
Building the Poem

1   Ensure that frame 2 of the Actions layer is selected and open the Actions panel, if necessary.

2   We will now write a custom function. Add the following code below all existing code in the panel:

```
function generatePoem() {}
```

3   In the body of the `generatePoem` function, we need to create a variable named **poetry** that will hold our poem in its entirety:

```
var poetry = "Fallen is my sad " + animal + "\r" +
→ concept + " no longer has meaning\ras the " + color +
→ " smiles fade\rdripping from hollow teeth\r" + name +
→ " speaks to ghosts.";
```

We use string fragments along with the stored values present in our global variables, concatenating them together with the + operator. The \r text signifies a line return that forces a new line in our text display.

4 Finally, set the text value of **poem_text** to the local poetry variable value:

```
exportRoot.poem_text.text = poetry;
```

We use **exportRoot** to refer to the main timeline in this case. This is a special global variable you can always use in an HTML5 Canvas document to refer to the main timeline.

5 Insert the following function invocation before moving the playhead in the **next_btn** function block:

```
generatePoem();
```

We need to invoke the newly created function before switching to the poem view so that everything will be in place once it becomes visible.

The code on frame 2 should read:

```
this.stop();
var _this = this;
$('#back_btn').attr("disabled", true);
function generatePoem() {
  var poetry = "Fallen is my sad " + animal + "\r" + concept +
  ⟶ " no longer has meaning\ras the " + color + " smiles
  ⟶ fade\rdripping from hollow teeth\r" + name + " speaks
  ⟶ to ghosts.";
  exportRoot.poem_text.text = poetry;
}
$('#dom_overlay_container').on('click', '#next_btn',
⟶ function() {
  name = $("#name_input").val();
  concept = $("#concept_input").val();
  animal = $("#animal_input").val();
  color = $("#color_input").val();
  generatePoem();
  $('#next_btn').attr("disabled", true);
  $('#back_btn').removeAttr("disabled");
  _this.gotoAndPlay('moveforward');
```

```
}.bind(_this));
$('#dom_overlay_container').on('click', '#back_btn',
→ function() {
  $('#back_btn').attr("disabled", true);
  $('#next_btn').removeAttr("disabled");
  _this.gotoAndPlay('goback');
}.bind(this));
```

The code is now complete and we can either test or publish the project. See
Figure 6.58.

Figure 6.58 The completed
poem generator

Advanced HTML5 Publish Options

Although it is true that ActionScript 3.0 document types publish HTML as a wrap-
per and that you can specify certain properties of that HTML document, when
targeting HTML5 Canvas we are really talking a whole other level as the project is
completely web native. As you might imagine, projects targeting HTML5 Canvas
have a number of advanced options to consider when publishing. Let's take a look
at a simple example of what can be done.

ACA Objective 5.1

▶ **Video 6.25**
*Publishing the
poem generator*

Centering the published content

Sometimes the publish customization you desire exists right in front of you. This is certainly the case with a lot of options that you would've previously had to edit an HTML5 Canvas template to accomplish. But now you can do so directly through the Animate CC user interface.

Such an example is centering the Stage in an HTML document. Here's how to do it:

1 Open the Publish Settings dialog box from the Document properties.

2 On the Basic tab, toggle the Center Stage check box. You can choose how you want it centered: Horizontally, Vertically, or Both (**Figure 6.59**).

Figure 6.59 Centering the project from Publish Settings

3 Choose Both and click OK to close the Publish Settings dialog box.

★ *ACA Objective 5.2* The compiled HTML5 Canvas project will appear in a new browser window and the changes will become obvious with the content itself perfectly centered in the browser viewport.

Challenge!

As the project exists right now, a user can generate the poem without entering any values for the custom prompts. This would make a *truly* sad poem! The challenge is to write some JavaScript that doesn't allow the user to click the next button unless he or she has filled out all the requested information.

Conclusion

In this chapter, we've seen some rather advanced stuff all working together in a tight, focused, and fun project. Concepts such as the camera, Advanced Layers mode, and layer depth are going to play a huge role in the future of Animate CC. Of course, you can use all of these features across document types as well.

In addition to those features, we had a look at using some HTML5 Canvas necessities like JavaScript, web fonts, dynamic text, components, and the Actions Wizard. This project has covered a lot of angles and also allows for a great deal of personalization, so feel free to experiment according to your own interests.

CHAPTER OBJECTIVES

Chapter Learning Objectives

- A brief introduction to ActionScript.

- Work with Adobe AIR for Desktop.

- Build nested, interactive Movie Clip symbols.

- Manipulate visual assets through code.

- Implement basic ActionScript concepts like variables, functions, and event listeners.

- Import sound files and use them on the timeline.

- Control sound from ActionScript code.

- Publish an Adobe AIR for Desktop project.

Chapter ACA Objectives

For full descriptions of the objectives, see the table on pages 286–291.

DOMAIN 1.0
WORKING IN THE ANIMATION INDUSTRY
1.4

DOMAIN 2.0
PROJECT SETUP AND INTERFACE
2.1, 2.4

DOMAIN 4.0
CREATE AND MODIFY VISUAL ELEMENTS
4.1, 4.2, 4.4, 4.5, 4.6, 4.7

DOMAIN 5.0
PUBLISHING DIGITAL MEDIA
5.1, 5.2

CHAPTER 7

Tick-Tock…
Build a Virtual Clock

In previous chapters, you've seen how you can use Adobe Animate CC to create static and animated content for various target platforms. In this chapter, you'll break free from the web browser and move into the realm of merging design and development in order to target the desktop operating system.

In this project, you'll build a functional, animated clock application (**Figure 7.1**) that can be installed on either the Windows or macOS desktop. To do this, you'll employ Adobe AIR and a nice bit of ActionScript code to get everything wired up. Don't think you won't be designing and animating, though! One of the strengths of Animate CC is the tight integration between design and development. This project aims to be a true showcase of this fact.

▶ **Video 7.1** *Project Overview*

Figure 7.1 Our virtual clock desktop project

Working with ActionScript 3.0

ActionScript is a programming language originally developed for the manipulation of 2D graphics. It has gone through many iterations and has evolved into a powerful interactive media development environment. It can control and create a wide variety of interactive media objects, including images, type, sound, and video.

ActionScript uses standard syntax, making it accessible to programmers familiar with JavaScript. The included libraries simplify the control of many advanced interactive media interactions.

Versions of ActionScript

ActionScript has been through three major revisions. Previous versions of Animate CC allowed authors to select which version of ActionScript they wanted to use for authoring. Adobe Animate CC now requires all documents to be authored in ActionScript 3.0 if an ActionScript-based target platform is selected. ActionScript 3.0 is much more powerful, flexible, and efficient than previous versions.

The only downside to the deprecation of previous ActionScript versions is the maintenance of older code that should have been updated long ago for security and performance reasons. If you need to update or publish ActionScript 2.0 projects, you'll have to use Adobe Flash Professional CS6 to do so.

ActionScript vs. JavaScript

Although ActionScript may seem quite different from JavaScript, the truth is that both languages have a lot more in common than is readily apparent. Both are based on the **ECMAScript** specification or, rather, different versions of that specification. When Adobe (and ActionScript's originator Macromedia) was developing ActionScript 3.0, developers made a great deal of effort to align the language with the upcoming ECMAScript 4 specification, which would form the basis of the next version of JavaScript. The idea was that ActionScript and JavaScript being nearly identical in their implementation of the ECMAScript specification would be the best thing for everyone.

This plan would've worked out wonderfully if ECMAScript 4 hadn't been declared dead before it could be implemented in JavaScript. Unfortunately, JavaScript would never see all the goodies in ECMAScript 4 like packages, classes, strong typing, and the rest. But ActionScript 3.0 would see these things since it was (and remains) based on this abandoned specification. Not only can you use the advanced programming concepts described here, but you've been able to do so for nearly a decade while these capabilities remain unavailable in JavaScript.

So, although ActionScript and JavaScript do share a lot of syntax and are based on similar specifications, just enough differences exist to make the relationship confusing to newcomers. In this project, you'll be using ActionScript, which means you can use all the extra features you want!

ACTIONSCRIPT 4.0

A few years ago, Adobe began researching what it referred to as "Action-Script Next," which was intended to be the next iteration of the ActionScript programming language. Adobe eventually decided that the direction the new version was taking would be too drastic a difference, especially considering the number of frameworks and libraries being written for Action-Script 3.0 that would be rendered unusable in this new version.

Adobe announced in January 2013 that the company would abandon further research into this new version of ActionScript and instead focus on adding planned features to the current version of the language.

Actions panel

You encountered the Actions panel (**Figure 7.2**) earlier in this book, and you'll spend quite a bit of time there in this project. To open the Actions panel, choose Window > Actions, or press F9. The code you write can be stored externally or attached to a frame known as a frame script and be completely contained along with all assets and animations with a single FLA file.

Figure 7.2 The Actions panel

When you're working with frame scripts, it is best practice to start by creating a dedicated layer named **Actions** for your code on the timeline. Any code that is bound to a specific frame in that layer will be executed when the playhead reaches it. You'll write a good amount of ActionScript in this panel as you work through this chapter.

Creating an Adobe AIR for Desktop Document

As with most projects designed using Animate CC, the first thing to do is create a new document and prepare for the work ahead. For this project, forget the web! You're building a desktop application with Adobe AIR.

About Adobe AIR for Desktop

If Flash Player can be considered the primary Adobe runtime, then the secondary Adobe runtime is Adobe AIR (**Figure 7.3**). AIR is an acronym for Adobe Integrated Runtime and allows programs written in ActionScript to run directly on the operating system as an installable application, completely bypassing the browser environment. Depending on the version of Adobe AIR in use, you can target Windows, macOS, and certain Linux-based operating systems.

Adobe AIR programs can be packaged in two different ways. The primary method of program distribution is to package the program as an AIR file and install it on a system that already has the Adobe AIR runtime installed separately. The drawback of this approach is that the user must install both your program and the runtime on which it relies. The benefit is that you're choosing a completely cross-platform method of distribution: both Windows and macOS users can share and install the same AIR file.

The second (and recommended) way of distributing Adobe AIR programs on desktop operating systems involves packaging the actual AIR runtime itself along with your program within a single-installer package. Not only does this strategy remove the reliance on a separate runtime install, it also ties your program to a specific, tested version of Adobe AIR. It allows for extended native desktop capabilities such as the powerful Native Process API, enabling you to tap into additional executable code and processes that are either bundled along with your application or native to the operating system. The downside is that you must produce separate packages for each operating system you're targeting. What's more, it will result in a much larger package of files.

Setting up the Adobe AIR project document

To create an Animate CC document that targets Adobe AIR for Desktop, you'll make choices similar to those you've made when beginning other projects in this book.

1 From the Welcome Screen, select Create New > AIR For Desktop. Alternatively, choose File > New > AIR For Desktop (**Figure 7.4**).

However you've gone about creating your document, it should now be open and ready for you to start working.

Figure 7.3 Adobe AIR Logo

★ ACA Objective 1.4

NOTE

Linux is supported only for Adobe AIR versions up to and including 2.5. Later versions are no longer supported due to the smaller general user base on Linux systems.

★ ACA Objective 2.1

▶ *Video 7.2 Creating a New AIR for Desktop Document*

For this project, you'll be building a small clock application that can tell time in both analog and digital formats. The application Stage does not need to be very large for this, but neither do you want it to be too small.

2 Choose a width and height of 500 pixels to form a completely square Stage.

3 Set the background to whatever color you want. (I'm choosing black again.) Set the FPS value to 12.

You won't have a lot of animated content on the timeline for this project, so keeping the FPS down a bit will save resources for the end user.

Once the project document is created and open in Animate CC, notice that AIR 26.0 for Desktop is the chosen runtime version in the Target menu.

UPDATING ADOBE AIR

Animate CC includes a simple mechanism to update Adobe AIR to the latest version, in case your software is a version or two behind.

Adobe delivers major, numbered releases of AIR every quarter, and security and bug updates as needed between quarters. Animate CC generally has only a couple of updates a year, and so it may be necessary to update your internal AIR SDK more frequently than you update Animate CC.

There are a number of places where you can download AIR SDK versions, but the safest is directly from Adobe: www.adobe.com/devnet/air/air-sdk-download.html (**Figure 7.5**).

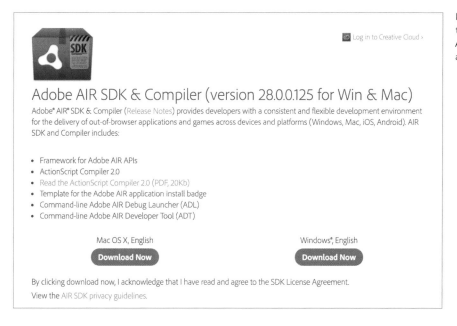

You will not need to update your AIR SDK for this project, but it's good to know how to go about it.

1   To update or add versions of Adobe AIR to Animate CC, choose Help > Manage Adobe AIR SDK.

The Manage Adobe AIR SDK dialog box (**Figure 7.6**) appears, prompting you to locate a downloaded AIR SDK via your system file browser.

2   Click the Add New SDK button in the upper left of the dialog box to open a file browser.

Figure 7.6 The Manage Adobe AIR SDK dialog box

3   Use the file browser to locate the SDK you have downloaded to your local file system and click OK.

Animate CC will add it to the list of available AIR versions in both the Manage Adobe AIR SDK dialog box and the Publish Target menu.

★ ACA Objective 2.4

▶ **Video 7.3** *Import the Background Texture*

Creating the application background

Now you'll add a background to the Stage using an image I've prepared that looks very much like an old wall texture.

1 Rename the Layer 1 layer that is created by default to **Background** by double-clicking the current name and typing in the new one.

2 Choose File > Import > Import To Stage and choose the provided wall.png image or use your own background image if you like.

   The bitmap image is imported into the project library, and an instance of the bitmap is placed perfectly on the Stage (**Figure 7.7**).

Figure 7.7 The time-line and Stage with Background

NOTE

When using Adobe AIR as a publish target, you can create an application with a transparent background, if you wish. You can even completely disable all visual elements of the application window system chrome (the visual elements of a window frame and associated controls). You'll learn more about this topic later in this chapter.

3 Lock this layer and save your document when finished.

Building the Basic Clock Visual Elements

★ ACA Objective 4.1

Before you get into any sort of development for this project, you'll want to design a number of visual elements. Some of these elements will remain static, whereas others will have their properties manipulated through the ActionScript code you will write.

Building the clock body

You have your application background already established, so now you'll build the main body of your clock. The body will consist of a main cabinet, and you can also create the visual effect of having a recessed space to house the clock pendulum.

▶ **Video 7.4** *Build the Clock Body*

1   Create a new layer to hold the clock body visual assets and name it **ClockBody**.

2   With that done, select the Rectangle tool (▢) and draw a shape that measures 340px in width and 500px in height.

3   Be sure that Object Drawing mode is enabled, or select the Rectangle Primitive tool (▢) instead.

4   For the visual properties to your shape, use the Selection tool (▷) to select it and then have a peek at the Properties panel.

5   The shape should have no stroke whatsoever, so get rid of the stroke if your shape currently includes one.

For the fill, you'll be using a bitmap fill, which is generated from an imported bitmap image file. You can select this special fill type from the Color panel, but first you need to import the bitmap image to the project library.

6   Choose File > Import > Import To Library and find the woodgrain.png image. Click OK to import it. The bitmap will exist in the library and will be visible in the Library panel (**Figure 7.8**) but not on the Stage.

7   With the shape selected, open the Color panel and choose Bitmap Fill, specifying the image just imported as the fill (**Figure 7.9**).

Figure 7.8 The imported image in the Library panel

Figure 7.9 Using a bitmap image for the fill of a shape

8 Use the Align panel to center this shape both vertically and horizontally to the Stage.

This completes the main clock body, but you still need to create a nook for the pendulum to reside in.

9 In the same ClockBody layer, with the Rectangle tool selected, click the Fill Color box in the Properties panel to open the Color Picker. Choose black and set Alpha to 40%.

10 Draw a rectangle measuring 140px wide and 290px tall using these settings. Using the Align panel, center this object vertically on the Stage and align it horizontally to the Stage bottom (**Figure 7.10**).

Figure 7.10 The clock body with a nook

Drawing the clock face

▶ **Video 7.5** *Build the Clock Face*

The clock face is probably the most recognizable portion of the application; this visual asset contains numerals that indicate the current time in hours, minutes, and seconds. It also serves as the main interactive element of our application. Before you begin, be sure all additional layers have been locked.

1 Lock all the current layers.

2 Create a new layer and name it **ClockFace** (**Figure 7.11**). Select the Oval tool (⬤) with Object Drawing mode enabled, or select the Oval Primitive tool (⬤).

Figure 7.11 The ClockFace layer is added and selected.

3   In the Properties panel, set the stroke to black and the fill to #E0CDB0. Draw a circle measuring 266px in diameter by dragging across the Stage with the Shift key held down.

With this shape created, you'll position it on the Stage with help from the Align panel.

4   Center the object to the Stage along the x-axis and shift the object to 80px along the y-axis. This is the proper positioning for the clock face; it allows a bit of room for the digital display above and for the pendulum below (**Figure 7.12**).

Figure 7.12 The ClockFace shape on the Stage

LAYING OUT THE CLOCK FACE NUMERALS

The numerals on the clock face will range from 1 to 12. They'll be arranged in a traditional way around the entire clock face, using the round portion you've already created as a guide and a backdrop.

★ *ACA Objective 4.2*

▶ *Video 7.6*
Creating Clock
Face Numerals

1 Select the Text tool (T). In the Properties panel, select Static Text from the text menu and choose your font (I chose Trajan Sans Pro 3 at 44pt). The font color will be a nice, dark brown such as #663300 (**Figure 7.13**).

2 Create 12 separate text blocks, each displaying numerals 1–12 using these same settings. Position all of these numerals as they would appear on a traditional clock face. You may want to place guides along the clock face to assist in placement.

3 When you're done positioning the numerals, select all the individual text blocks with the Selection tool and group them together by choosing Modify > Group.

You can now move all the numerals around as a single group (**Figure 7.14**).

Figure 7.13 Numeral text properties

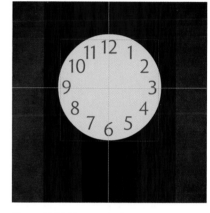

Figure 7.14 The numeral group

Working with dynamic text

▶ **Video 7.7** *Create a Digital Readout*

Next, you'll create a dynamic text block that will display the current time in a digital format directly above the analog clock face. This portion of your clock doesn't work directly with any of the other visual assets you've built so far. It's only a supplementary addition through which you'll output a digital readout of the current time.

1 Create a new layer for your dynamic text block and name it **Digital**.

2 Select the Text tool once again and change the text type to Dynamic Text.

3 For your font selection, choose a monospaced font so that the shifting digits don't cause any visual aberration. I've chosen Source Code Pro as my typeface at 44pt.

4 Using the Text tool, create a text block on the Stage directly between the top of the clock face and the top of the Stage itself (**Figure 7.15**). It's a good idea to put some placeholder text in the text block so that you can see how it will appear when you run the application. I've entered **12:00**.

Figure 7.15 Dynamic text object

5 Select the newly created text block using the Selection tool and look at the Properties panel. Notice that since you're using the dynamic text type, you can enter an instance name in the panel. This instance name is what allows you to target the specific dynamic text block for manipulation through ActionScript code.

6 Click in the empty input field and provide the instance name of `timeDisplay` (**Figure 7.16**). You'll use this later to change the text that's displayed in our text field to the current time.

Figure 7.16 `timeDisplay` instance properties

WARNING

Now that all text is in place, and since we are using dynamic text in a number of areas for this project, we must be sure to embed the font characters to be used. Click the Embed button next to the Style menu in the Character section of the Properties panel to create an embedded font and then use that newly created font for any dynamic text.

Designing the Clock's Animated Movie Clip Assets

You'll be using two different methods of animation for this application. You're already familiar with one of them: timeline animation through the Animate CC tweening engine. The other is something we haven't touched on yet: dynamic animation through the manipulation of visual assets with code.

★ ACA Objective 4.6

▶ Video 7.8 Create a Clock Face Movie Clip Symbol

Building the clock face movie clip

One of the most powerful structures used in Animate CC is the concept of a nested movie clip symbol. Not only can you achieve multiple layers of independent animation in this way, but when working in ActionScript, you also have full control over the nested hierarchy of instances, as long as you provide appropriate identifiers.

1 Using the Selection tool, select both the round clock face and the group of numerals you've established.

2 Choose Modify > Convert To Symbol to open the Convert To Symbol dialog box.

3 Create a movie clip symbol and name it **ClockFace**.

   Before you edit the ClockFace symbol, you need to provide the instance you now have on the Stage with a name, just as you did with the dynamic text block.

NOTE

Instance names are case-sensitive, so be sure you remember both spelling and case as you continue.

4 Select the instance on the Stage and locate the Instance Name field in the Properties panel. Click in the empty input field and type the instance name `clockFace` (**Figure 7.17**).

Figure 7.17 Type `clockFace` as the instance name.

Now you'll be able to directly target this symbol instance through use of ActionScript code.

5   Double-click the symbol instance on the Stage to enter it.

6   In the ClockFace symbol timeline, select both the clock face shape and the group of numerals. Right-click and choose Distribute To Layers from the menu.

7   Don't delete the empty layer yet; you'll use this in the next step. But do rename the two new layers to **Face** and **Numbers** accordingly (**Figure 7.18**).

Figure 7.18 Established ClockFace symbol layers

Creating the clock hands

★ ACA Objective 4.5

You will be using three rotating clock hands in order to display the current hours, minutes, and seconds based on the time gathered through ActionScript. You must build each one to be visually unique so that the user can easily distinguish between the three different values indicated.

▶ **Video 7.9** Building Vector Art Clock Hands

The first thing you'll do is create the hour hand of the clock in the empty layer left over from the last step in the previous exercise. The new Brush Library contains some neat arrow brushes that are perfect for building clocks.

1   Select the Line tool ( ) and click the Brush Library button in the Properties panel to access the Brush Library.

2   Choose Arrows > Arrows Standard and select Arrow 1.29 by double-clicking it.

    This brush will now appear in the Properties panel as your selected stroke style.

3   Change the stroke value to 18 and the stroke color to #333333 (**Figure 7.19**).

4   With that set, draw out a straight vertical line on the Stage measuring 80px tall. Select this new shape object with the Selection tool and choose Modify > Convert To Symbol.

    You'll make this a movie clip symbol with its registration point anchored to the bottom of the symbol.

Figure 7.19 Properties for the Line tool

Figure 7.20 MinuteHand properties

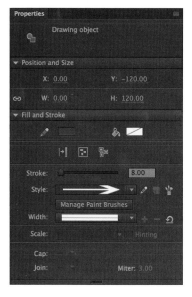

Figure 7.21 SecondHand properties

5 Name this symbol **HourHand**. With the instance of this symbol selected on the Stage, go to the Properties panel and assign it an instance name of `hourHand`.

You'll now do something very similar for the creation of the minute hand.

6 Select the Line tool and click the Brush Library button in the Properties panel to access the Brush Library.

7 Select a different brush located in the same category: Arrows > Arrows Standard. This one is called Arrow 1.09. With this new brush assigned to the Line tool stroke style, change the stroke value to 12 and the stroke color to #333333.

8 Draw a straight vertical line on the Stage measuring 126px tall. Convert this shape to a movie clip symbol with its registration point anchored to the bottom.

9 Name this symbol **MinuteHand**, and with the symbol instance selected on the Stage, in the Properties panel assign it an instance name of `minuteHand` (**Figure 7.20**).

Now for the final movie clip symbol of the whole set: the seconds hand.

10 With the Line tool chosen and the Brush Library open, select the Arrow 1.11 brush from the Arrows > Arrows Standard category. This one is nice and thin—perfect for a seconds hand.

11 In the Properties panel, change the stroke value to 8 and the stroke color to #990000.

12 Draw a straight vertical line on the Stage measuring 120px tall. Convert this shape to a third movie clip symbol with its registration point anchored to the bottom in the same way as before.

13 Name this symbol **SecondHand**, and with the symbol instance selected on the Stage, in the Properties panel assign it an instance name of `secondHand` (**Figure 7.21**).

You could just leave all three of these instances in the same layer; changing object properties through ActionScript does not require everything to be in single, unique layers like motion tween and shape tween animation. But to be as organized as possible, you'll place each on a new layer.

14 To automate this process, select all three instances, right-click, and choose Distribute To Layers.

Animate CC creates a new layer for each instance, and even names them properly for you.

15 Delete the empty layer (**Figure 7.22**).

Figure 7.22 The completed ClockFace symbol

 Video 7.10 Modify Art Brushes

Having assigned each of your clock hand instances specific instance names, you can now target them in your `clockFace` instance in order to manipulate various properties such as rotation. With the clock hands' registration points all aligned to the bottom, they will all rotate around this point, just like a real clock.

> **TIP**
>
> *While having the registration points aligned to the bottom is fine, you may wish to take the extra time to shift the contents of each shape asset down slightly in each movie clip symbol in order to have a bit of each hand protrude below the registration point as well (**Figure 7.23**). This can add a bit more realism to the clock.*

Figure 7.23 Shifting past the registration point

Building the clock pendulum

This portion of your project is the only piece that is animated along the timeline; everything else is driven by ActionScript code. Now you'll create a perpetual swinging motion for your clock pendulum to show that time is indeed flowing.

▶ **Video 7.11** Construct a Pendulum

Figure 7.24 Pendulum layer

Figure 7.25 Centered pendulum assets

Figure 7.26 Pendulum movie clip symbol

1 If you're not there already, go back out to the main timeline and create a new layer named **Pendulum**.

2 Lock all other layers so you don't mistakenly draw assets where they don't belong (**Figure 7.24**).

3 Select the Rectangle tool and set the fill color to #B0A795 and the stroke color to None.

4 Enable Object Drawing mode so that you do not create destructive shapes. Draw a rectangle on the Stage that measures 200px high and 9px in width.

   This will serve as the rod of your pendulum.

5 To build the weight, select the Oval tool with Object Drawing mode enabled. Holding down the Shift key, drag a circle measuring 44px in diameter. The stroke should be set to None with a fill color of #B0A795, just as you did when drawing the rod.

6 Move the weight shape to the bottom of the rod shape until both are vertically centered (**Figure 7.25**). Optionally, you can use the Align panel to perform this action.

   Now you have a set of pendulum assets that you can animate, but you'll want to animate them as a unified whole.

7 Select both the rod and weight shapes and choose Modify > Convert To Symbol.

8 Name the new movie clip symbol **Pendulum** and set the registration point to the top center, which should be the top end of the rod opposite the weight (**Figure 7.26**).

9 With this movie clip symbol created and an instance sitting on the Stage, select the instance and once again choose to convert that instance to a movie clip symbol, this time named **SwingingPendulum**.

Doing this effectively nests an instance of the symbol you just created in an additional symbol. This new symbol is where the repeating pendulum animation will take place since the timeline of a movie clip symbol will continue playing and looping, regardless of how many frames it occupies in a parent timeline.

The next few steps involve some organization of the timeline.

10 Move the Pendulum layer beneath the ClockFace layer so that it is more obscured.

11 On the main timeline, create a new layer group and name it **Analog**.

All of the elements of your analog clock face will be nested in this new layer group.

12 Drag the ClockBody, Pendulum, and ClockFace layers into the Analog layer group (**Figure 7.27**). Lock everything but the Pendulum layer before moving on.

Figure 7.27 The Analog timeline folder

ANIMATING THE CLOCK PENDULUM

Now that you have the assets for the pendulum created and formed as a single movie clip symbol, you need to animate it swinging back and forth in the body of the clock. You'll use a motion tween to accomplish this.

1 Double-click the movie clip symbol instance in the Pendulum layer on your main timeline to edit the SwingingPendulum symbol in place.

You should now be in the symbol itself and able to modify the symbol timeline (**Figure 7.28**).

★ *ACA Objective 4.4*

▶ *Video 7.12*
Animating the Pendulum

Figure 7.28 Movie clip nesting navigation and properties

Figure 7.29 Transform point

2   Extend the frame span to the 2-second mark at frame 24 by selecting frame 24 in this layer and choosing Insert > Timeline > Frame.

3   Right-click the frame span and choose Create Motion Tween from the menu.

Now you're almost ready to animate the clock pendulum.

4   Before you begin animating, select the Free Transform tool and select the instance of the pendulum on the Stage in order to shift the transform point to the top center of the object (**Figure 7.29**).

5   On frame 1, hover the cursor just outside any of the bounding box corners until the cursor appears as a circle of arrows. Click and drag to rotate to the left and stop the rotation when the weight of the pendulum touches the side of the indentation you created earlier.

6   On frame 12, perform the same rotation action, but rotate to the right until the weight again touches the indentation asset edge. Finally, on frame 24 duplicate the rotation that exists on frame 1. It doesn't have to be exact, but it should be close (**Figure 7.30**).

Figure 7.30 Keyframed pendulum animation visualized through onion skinning

TIP

Animating the back-and-forth swing of the pendulum offers a good opportunity for playing around with the easing presets. Think of the way a pendulum moves in space and try to replicate that movement by applying one of the Ease In and Ease Out presets or by experimenting with the Motion Editor.

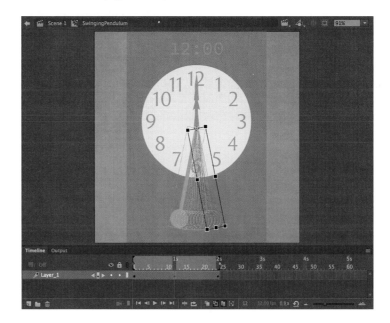

Using Imported Audio in an ActionScript Project

Audio has numerous uses in interactive media, and those uses are growing every day. In Animate CC, you can use ActionScript to bring audio into the timeline, bind sounds to specific keyframes, or play audio from the project library. It's also possible to play external audio files with a little ActionScript.

★ ACA Objective 2.4

Audio file types

Before importing a sound file into your project, you need to make sure it is in a compatible format. Animate CC currently supports the following audio file types when working in an ActionScript-based project:

- AIFF
- WAV
- MP3
- Adobe Sound Document
- Sun AU
- Sound Designer II
- Ogg Vorbis
- FLACC

Fortunately, Animate CC installations include another Creative Cloud application called Adobe Media Encoder, a software package that converts other file formats to those compatible with Animate CC and other applications. If you need to deliver the audio files in both an ActionScript and an HTML5-compatible format, you'll most likely want to stick with MP3. Animate CC will automatically convert any audio format to MPEG Audio Layer III (MP3) for playback in the Flash Player or Adobe AIR on project compilation.

NOTE

You can convert only media that doesn't have DRM encoded into the file.

Audio file import

An audio file is imported just like a bitmap file, using the File > Import > Import To Library command. Once the sound file is in the project library, you can set it up to be called by ActionScript or place it manually on the timeline.

NOTE

It doesn't matter if you choose Import To Stage or Import To Library; Animate CC imports all audio to the project library regardless of the command.

▶ *Video 7.13*
Importing Audio

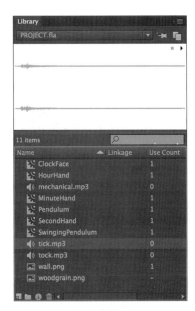

Figure 7.31 Audio in the Library panel

Figure 7.32 Your Mech linkage ID

Placing audio on the timeline isn't quite the same as it is with a graphic or an image. It's usually done by selecting a frame on the timeline and choosing an audio file from the Properties panel. The sound will be attached to the keyframe and is not visible on the Stage; however, you should see a waveform displayed in the layer itself on those frames that are affected.

We've prepared three audio files for use in this project:

- **tick.mp3**: You'll use this file as part of the swinging pendulum.
- **tock.mp3**: You'll also use this file as part of the swinging pendulum.
- **mechanical.mp3**: You'll use this file as a constant, looping background sound.

1   To import these files to the project library, choose File > Import > Import To Library. In the file browser that appears, select all three MP3 files and click Open.

Animate CC will bring the MP3s into the library as audio files.

2   In the Library panel, take a look at the files you've just imported (**Figure 7.31**).

You'll use the files tick.mp3 and tock.mp3 in the Pendulum movie clip symbol timeline as sound effects in synchronization with the pendulum animation. You'll invoke the other file, mechanical.mp3, from the project library with ActionScript code when your application is running.

To make an audio file in the library available through ActionScript, you need to provide a linkage ID.

3   Notice that the Library panel has two columns: Name and Linkage. Find the mechanical.mp3 asset in the project library and double-click the Linkage column directly next to it.

4   You can now input a linkage ID (**Figure 7.32**) specific to this object. Type **Mech**. Remember this identifier for later when you are writing your ActionScript code!

NOTE

What you input as a linkage ID basically becomes a class reference in ActionScript. You'll see how this works later in this chapter.

Using audio on the timeline

Keep in mind that when you place audio on the timeline, you're placing it inside a keyframe. It is a good idea to have a separate layer just for audio, because the keyframe will show the waveform of the audio, which can be helpful for synchronization tasks.

▶ *Video 7.14* *Using Timeline Audio*

Now you'll add some audio in your SwingingPendulum movie clip symbol.

1. First, enter the symbol edit mode by double-clicking either the symbol in the Library panel or an instance on the Stage.

2. Rename the existing layer **Swinging** and create a new layer, which you will name **Audio**. Lock the Swinging layer (**Figure 7.33**).

Figure 7.33 The SwingingPendulum layer structure

To attach the audio to a keyframe in the timeline, select the keyframe, and from the Properties panel, choose the audio file from the Name menu in the Sound subpanel. This attaches the sound to the keyframe; it will begin playing as soon as the playhead reaches that keyframe.

3. With frame 1 of the Audio layer selected, choose the tick.mp3 sound from the Name menu in the Sound section of the Properties panel and choose Stream from the Sync menu.

4. On frame 12 of the same layer, insert a blank keyframe and select the newly created keyframe.

5. In the Properties panel, choose the tock.mp3 sound, and set the sync type once again to Stream (**Figure 7.34**).

Figure 7.34 Choosing audio files

STREAM VS. START OR EVENT SOUND

While you're in the Properties panel, you'll notice a menu called Sync. It has three important options: Start, Event, and Stream.

- The Start and Event settings trigger the sound as soon as the playhead hits the keyframe and play that sound completely.

- The Stream setting also triggers the sound as soon as the playback head hits the keyframe, but it synchronizes the sound to the timeline. If the timeline stops, the sound stops. This option is best used for narration but is pretty good for clocks as well!

Using the Stream setting, you can place animated events on the timeline at the same time the sound occurs. Animate CC will keep these in sync no matter what happens. If you choose the Start or Event setting for an application like this, there will be no synchronization between the timeline animation and audio track.

SOUND EFFECTS

TIP
You should perform any heavy audio editing your tracks require before importing them into Animate CC, using a more full-featured audio-editing software package such as Adobe Audition CC.

Animate CC also has options you can set in the Properties panel to determine how the audio plays. You can access these settings using the Effect menu in the Sound subpanel. In this menu you'll find prebuilt options for fading in and across channels.

Also, next to the Effect menu you'll see a small pencil icon, which is the Edit button. Clicking this button brings up a much more capable editing dialog box that lets you trim the audio as well as control volume and panning by placing anchor points along a control line for each channel.

A Primer on ActionScript

ActionScript and Animate CC have a deep history together, and using the language to get the most out of your ActionScript-based project requires background knowledge. Let's go over some fundamentals of writing ActionScript in Animate CC projects.

Symbols and interactivity

Combining symbols with ActionScript is where things start to get interesting in Animate CC development projects. You can access both button symbol and movie clip symbol instances, and even dynamic text blocks via an instance name that you assign using the Properties panel. In this project, you've provided instance names to a number of objects on the Stage.

You can use ActionScript to directly manipulate the properties of these instances, such as text, rotation, width, height, and position. Another common interaction is using ActionScript to assign a specific event listener to a symbol instance. This allows your project to react to events that occur involving those instances. Mouse clicks, playhead movement, and asset and data loading are examples of events that can be used as triggers for other operations.

Movie clip symbols provide self-contained, reusable elements that are essential to interactive media development. Newcomers often find it difficult to decide which type of symbol to use and how to implement that symbol. But with practice you can master the art of nesting symbols and combining different types to get exactly what you want. In this project, the clock face is a complex, nested symbol.

TIMELINE FRAME LABELS

Individual keyframes can be identified by their frame number, but a better way of referencing them is to label these keyframes using the Name option in the Properties panel. The label will show up as a flag on the timeline. You've already seen the use of frame labels in HTML5 Canvas documents, and they work the same way here. You can use frame labels as a visual reference to help you better understand the organization of your project.

The label (**Figure 7.35**) can also be used as a reference for navigating a timeline when using ActionScript or JavaScript, depending on your target platform. It's usually better to navigate a timeline using frame labels instead of frame numbers, because edits to the project may cause the frame numbers to change as content is added or removed from the timeline.

TIP

Another reason to target frames with labels instead of numbers is that the numbering of frames differs across platforms. For instance, the first frame in ActionScript is frame 1, whereas in JavaScript the first frame is frame 0. Using labels avoids the need to concern yourself with this issue across different target platforms.

Figure 7.35 Frame labels

ActionScript essentials

Whether writing ActionScript in Animate CC or using a code-only editor like Adobe Flash Builder, you'll need to grasp some essential concepts if you want to start writing effective code.

VARIABLES

Variables in ActionScript are objects that hold a particular type of value that can be changed across the lifetime of the application. Variables can be just about any class type, but the most common variables in basic Animate CC projects are numbers and strings.

A number is a variable that holds a numeric value. The syntax for creating a numeric variable looks like this:

```
var myNum:Number = 7;
```

First, you define a variable with the `var` keyword, and then you give the variable the identifier `myNum`. The type of `Number` tells Animate CC what type of variable you are defining, and = `7` sets the initial value of that variable. The semicolon simply declares the end of an instruction.

Another common variable is a string. Variables typed as strings are basically blocks of text, and they can include punctuation and numerical characters. This is generally noted by using quotes around the text value, though a string can be combined, or concatenated, with other variables to form a complex string. You can define a string like this:

```
var myText:String = "Hey, Animate!";
```

Again, the `var` keyword tells Animate CC you are defining a variable, and `myText` is the identifier for that variable. The type of `String` tells Animate CC that this variable will include text data, and = `"Hey, Animate!"` sets the initial value of the variable.

Interestingly enough, you do not need to set an initial value for a variable. Also, after a variable is set, you can reassign it without the `var` keyword or specific class type, as shown here:

```
var myText:String;
myText = "Hello!";
myText = "Goodbye";
```

FUNCTIONS

When programming in ActionScript, you'll sometimes find yourself typing the same series of lines over and over. This is where functions will be of use. A function assigns a single command to a block of code. Once it's defined, you need only call the function name to run everything in that block of code and can reuse the function many times in order to simplify the code. Take a look at the following lines of code:

```
myText = "Hey, Flash!";
myNum = 7;
```

You could write a function to combine these two lines into one command:

```
function setBoth():void {
 myText = "Hey, Flash!";
 myNum = 7;
}
```

It's a little more work, but from now on, every time you want to set both of those variables, you only need to type

```
setBoth();
```

In completing this chapter's project, you will use a function to change the values associated with telling time and adjusting visual assets to reflect the current time in both digital and analog form.

EVENTS

Interactive media applications by nature are **event**-driven. When an event occurs, the code reacts to that event as if some object in the application was listening for that event. Numerous event types are built into ActionScript that allow code to be triggered on a variety of activities like mouse clicks, data loading, frame-entering, and touch gestures on mobile devices. In our clock application you'll use both timer events and mouse events to enable different types of functionality.

Writing ActionScript to Control the Clock

In Animate CC, you can attach code to any frame on any layer of a project. However, there is an active and long-held practice that all frame script code belongs in its own layer in a project's timeline. This helps a great deal in organizing layers and in keeping all of the code where it can be easily located.

1 Create a new layer named **Actions** and lock it, since you don't want any visual assets in it.

2 To begin writing ActionScript, or any code in Animate CC, you must open the Actions panel. Generally, this panel won't be opened by default, so choose Window > Actions to do so.

With the Actions panel open and frame 1 of the Actions layer selected, you're ready to continue with the project.

Importing classes

▶ *Video 7.15*
Importing Classes

To use many of the classes available in ActionScript, you'll need to import them in the project's code. You do this through use of the `import` statement, followed by the package and class name. Packages are a coding construct that keeps classes of the same name from causing collisions, and they also help with organization.

TIP

Importing classes in ActionScript will also allow Animate CC to suggest properties and values through code completion in the editor. This is very, very different from our experience working in JavaScript.

You'll import a number of classes for your project.

Type the following lines of code to import the `Timer`, `Movie Clip`, `MouseEvent`, and `TextField` classes:

```
import flash.utils.Timer;
import flash.display.MovieClip;
import flash.text.TextField;
import flash.events.MouseEvent;
import flash.events.TimerEvent;
```

`Timer` is a utility class that allows you to run a function on a schedule.

`MovieClip` and `TextField` are used in reference to visual objects you have created on the Stage.

`MouseEvent` and `TimerEvent` will allow you to listen for and respond to events of those types.

Declaring Stage variables

▶ *Video 7.16*
Declaring Stage Variables

With these classes imported, they are available for use in our application. Now you need to declare a number of variables based on those imported classes that correspond to objects already created on the Stage. Notice that you use the exact instance names given to both the `clockFace` symbol instance and `timeDisplay` text block:

```
var clockFace:MovieClip;
var timeDisplay:TextField;
```

Telling time with a timer

The first thing you need is a way to access the system clock. You do this by using the `Date` class in ActionScript. `Date` is one of a handful of classes that you don't import. These classes don't belong to any package and are called *top-level classes*. Create the `currentTime` variable directly beneath the previous ones:

```
var currentTime:Date;
```

Now you'll declare a variable called `ticker` as an instance of the `Timer` class. You set it equal to a new `Timer` instance and set the amount of time, in milliseconds, on which to have the `Timer` cycle run. In this case, the `Timer` will run every 250 milliseconds, or four times every second.

```
var ticker:Timer = new Timer(250);
```

Additionally, you'll add an event listener to the `Timer` to execute a function every time the `Timer` cycle fires. You do this by listening for the `TimerEvent.TIMER` event and execute a function called `onTick` (which you haven't created yet).

```
ticker.addEventListener(TimerEvent.TIMER, onTick);
```

To start the `Timer`, you invoke its built-in `start()` method:

```
ticker.start();
```

Let's create that `onTick` function now. Here's the completed function, followed by an explanation of what it all means:

```
function onTick(e:TimerEvent):void {
    currentTime = new Date();
    var seconds:uint = currentTime.getSeconds();
    var minutes:uint = currentTime.getMinutes();
    var hours:uint = currentTime.getHours();
    clockFace.secondHand.rotation = 360 + (seconds * 6);
```

▶ *Video 7.17*
Programming the Clock Face

▶ *Video 7.18*
Rotation and Dynamic Text

```
    clockFace.minuteHand.rotation = 360 + (minutes * 6);
    clockFace.hourHand.rotation = 360 + (hours * 30) +
    → (minutes * 0.5);
    var displayMinutes:String = minutes < 10 ? "0" +
    → minutes : "" + minutes;
    var digitalTime:String = hours + ":" + displayMinutes;
    timeDisplay.text = digitalTime;
}
```

To create any function in ActionScript, you begin with the keyword `function` followed by the function name. In this case, the function name is `onTick`, and it received an argument identified as `e`, indicated in parentheses, of type `TimerEvent` because that is the type of event that has invoked the function. You can get all sorts of data from this argument. A function will also need a return data type declared. In this function, you are doing lots in the function body but are not actually returning any data to the caller, so you declare the return data type as `void`.

The body of the function consists of the lines of code that are wrapped between the two curly braces. In the body of the function, you first refresh your `currentTime` variable with a new `Date`. The `Date` object includes methods for grabbing hours, minutes, seconds, and more, so you use specific methods built into that class to set new variables that represent those specific pieces of data.

The next part of the function will visually adjust the `rotation` property of your three clock hands by interpreting the time data gathered and performing some calculations on it to figure out the proper rotation. The math is a bit beyond the scope of this book, but you're basically converting numeric data into a rotation (measured in degrees, from 0 to 360, clockwise) value to adjust the rotation of each clock hand individually. Notice how you can refer to a nested symbol instance through dot notation like `clockFace.secondHand`? This is incredibly powerful!

Additionally, you use shorthand logic to prepend a 0 to the minutes gathered for display in the digital readout, but only if the minutes returned are single numerals. This is so the text in our `timeDisplay` text block does not shift around as the time changes.

Creating mouse interaction

▶ Video 7.19
*Creating Mouse
Interaction*

Similar to how you added an event listener to your `Timer`, you'll also add two event listeners to your `clockFace` instance. One will detect whether the mouse cursor has entered over the visual object, and the other will detect when it leaves.

1   Set the `visible` property of your text block to `false`. You don't want the digital readout to display until a `MouseOver` event occurs.

```
timeDisplay.visible = false;
```

2   Add the proper `MouseEvent` event listeners to your `clockFace` instance:

```
clockFace.addEventListener(MouseEvent.MOUSE_OVER,
 → showDigital);
clockFace.addEventListener(MouseEvent.MOUSE_OUT,
 → hideDigital);
```

3   Follow this with a new function called `showDigital` that sets the text block `visible` property back to `true`:

```
function showDigital(e:MouseEvent):void {
   timeDisplay.visible = true;
}
```

4   Apply the inverse function, setting it once again to `true`:

```
function hideDigital(e:MouseEvent):void {
   timeDisplay.visible = false;
}
```

Audio playback with ActionScript

Audio files in the library don't have to be associated with a keyframe to be played. They can also be triggered using simple ActionScript. Since you gave your mechanical.mp3 sound a linkage ID of Mech in the Library panel, you can now refer to that sound as a class called `Mech` and create instances of it through ActionScript:

```
var mechSound:Mech = new Mech();
```

Additionally, you can use all of the inherent `Sound` class methods and properties such as the `play()` method. Here you are telling the sound to play, starting at position 0 (the beginning) and to loop forever using `int.MAX_VALUE`. This will create a constantly looping, mechanical background sound:

```
mechSound.play(0, int.MAX_VALUE);
```

▶ *Video 7.20* Audio Playback with ActionScript

TIP

The ActionScript command `SoundMixer.stopAllSounds();` *is a useful instruction to stop all audio regardless of the source. It can be helpful when you are implementing a mute button or preparing to load fresh audio content.*

Completed code

The full, completed ActionScript code for this project is shown next. If you are having trouble, compare the code you have written with what's shown here. If you're not having any trouble, try modifying the code in your project to achieve different results.

```
import flash.utils.Timer;
import flash.display.MovieClip;
import flash.text.TextField;
import flash.events.MouseEvent;
import flash.events.TimerEvent;
var clockFace:MovieClip;
clockFace.addEventListener(MouseEvent.MOUSE_OVER, showDigital);
clockFace.addEventListener(MouseEvent.MOUSE_OUT, hideDigital);
var currentTime:Date;
var timeDisplay:TextField;
timeDisplay.visible = false;
var ticker: Timer = new Timer(250);
ticker.addEventListener(TimerEvent.TIMER, onTick);
ticker.start();
var mechSound:Mech = new Mech();
mechSound.play(0, int.MAX_VALUE);
function onTick(e:TimerEvent):void {
    currentTime = new Date();
    var seconds:uint = currentTime.getSeconds();
    var minutes:uint = currentTime.getMinutes();
    var hours:uint = currentTime.getHours();
    clockFace.secondHand.rotation = 360 + (seconds * 6);
    clockFace.minuteHand.rotation = 360 + (minutes * 6);
    clockFace.hourHand.rotation = 360 + (hours * 30) +
    ↪ (minutes * 0.5);
    var displayMinutes:String = minutes < 10 ? "0" +
    ↪ minutes : "" + minutes;
    var digitalTime:String = hours + ":" + displayMinutes;
    timeDisplay.text = digitalTime;
}
function showDigital(e:MouseEvent):void {
```

```
      timeDisplay.visible = true;
  }
  function hideDigital(e:MouseEvent):void {
      timeDisplay.visible = false;
  }
```

Testing an ActionScript Project

One of the worst things that can happen when you're writing interactive media applications is to release your work for distribution only to have a user discover that a problem exists with your code. Here's some advice on how to avoid that situation and produce a solid application for your client.

★ ACA Objective 5.1

ActionScript errors

You can encounter two distinct types of errors when writing ActionScript code. One is the compilation error (**Figure 7.36**). This occurs when you compile your code to run in Flash Player or Adobe AIR. This is probably the easiest type of error to catch, because when you try to test your application, it will not compile, and you'll receive detailed information regarding the specific error from Animate CC.

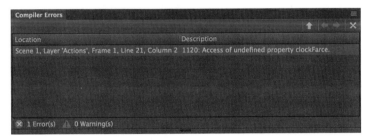

Figure 7.36 Compilation error

The second type of error is a bit more difficult to troubleshoot, because you have to compile and run the application, taking certain steps, to produce the error. These are known as runtime errors and normally require the use of a code debugger to troubleshoot. Luckily, Animate CC comes with an ActionScript debugger built in. Access this feature by choosing Debug > Debug Movie.

ActionScript comments

ActionScript programming can create some exciting interactive effects, but it can also be difficult depending on what you are programming. Help yourself out by commenting your code. Commenting involves putting notes in your code to help you find your way around at a later date.

There are two main ways of commenting: single-line and block **comments**.

You create single-line comments by starting a line with double slashes:

```
// this is just a short, single-line comment!
```

Block comments start with /* and end with */. This will let you block off larger blocks of text like this:

```
/*
This is a multi-line
comment. Use it to comment
out big chunks of code
or to make lengthy notes
to reference later
*/
```

Trace statements

The last technique we'll explore is how to trace data to the Output panel in Animate CC. The `trace()` command is a versatile way to expose the values of certain variables, or even just to fire off an alert when you hit a specific piece of code. This works very similar to using `console.log()` in JavaScript.

In your clock project, you could use this command to trace the value of rotation on your minute hand; for instance:

```
trace(clockFace.minuteHand.rotation);
```

The values are then output to the Output panel for us to monitor.

Publishing the Clock for Desktop Installation

★ *ACA Objective 5.2*

The Adobe AIR platform is an exciting addition to the output options in the Animate CC interactive media development environment. It allows the same file to be delivered across a wide variety of platforms, including mobile and desktop devices. Under the Target options in the Publish Settings dialog box, you can choose the appropriate format for the AIR output. You're targeting AIR for Desktop with this particular project, but all AIR targets share a similar development methodology since they are all written in ActionScript 3.0, no matter the specific target.

Exploring the AIR Settings dialog box

The AIR Settings dialog box provides additional options related to the publishing and delivery of an AIR file. You can access these options by clicking the wrench icon next to the Target menu in the Publish Settings dialog box. The AIR Settings dialog box contains several tabs that allow you to set up the options for the AIR application (**Figure 7.37**).

COMPLETING APPLICATION DETAILS

To complete the final details for publishing the application, choose File > AIR For Desktop Settings (if you haven't already opened the dialog box from the Properties panel). The AIR Settings dialog box opens, containing the following tabs:

Figure 7.37 AIR Settings dialog box

General: This tab contains core information about how you want to package your desktop application. You can choose to generate an AIR file or an operating system–specific installer or use the embedded runtime option. This is also the place to name your application and make decisions about window style and render mode.

Signature: All Adobe AIR applications must be signed in order to be properly installed on a user's system. This tab allows you to select a code-signing certificate from a signing authority, if you have purchased one. You can also use this tab to create a free, self-signed certificate to publish your applications.

Icons: This section allows you to specify a group of custom icons that the user will see on the desktop, on the dock or taskbar, and when the application is running just like any desktop application. You can create icons of various sizes in an application like Adobe Photoshop.

Video 7.21 *General AIR for Desktop Properties*

Video 7.22 *Using a Signed Certificate*

Video 7.23 *Creating Application Icons*

Advanced: Here is where you can specify associated file types, initial window settings, and the application installation folder. Many applications will not need to have much of anything specified here.

Language: This section is used only for mobile applications and will be disabled when using AIR for Desktop.

Publish and install

▶ *Video 7.24*
*Publishing and
Installing an AIR
Application*

To publish the AIR for Desktop application once you've finalized the Publish Settings, choose File > Publish. To use an AIR document, end users must have the Adobe AIR runtime installed on their systems. Once the AIR runtime is installed, they are able to install any AIR application. If the application was published with the embedded runtime option, the user will not even need to install the AIR runtime separately, because it is bundled into the installation package.

Once installed (**Figure 7.38**), an AIR application can be run, managed, and uninstalled just like any other application on your system. Periodically, Adobe will issue a new version of the AIR runtime. If you're using the runtime separately, you will be prompted to update. However, with an embedded runtime in use, the application will continue to use that version until the author decides to push out an update of her own.

Figure 7.38 The AIR Application Installer

Challenge!

In this project, you're using sounds that are bound to the timeline as well as those initiated through ActionScript. Right now, if you want to mute the clock sounds, you have to turn down your computer speakers. The challenge is to create a sound toggle button as part of the interface that will mute all sounds when enabled.

Conclusion

In this chapter, you've moved beyond the web browser to target the Windows and macOS desktop operating systems using ActionScript and Adobe AIR. When working with AIR for Desktop, you're taking everything available to you when targeting Flash Player and injecting it with another layer of functionality and power to create true, installable apps.

We've covered a lot of somewhat advanced concepts in this chapter. You've gone through the process of building a customizable, functional, cross-platform clock application. You've also been given a solid introduction to the fundamentals of ActionScript and how to work with ActionScript code in Animate CC to adjust visual elements on the Stage. Lastly, you've seen how simple it is to integrate sound into an application and how to publish all of this to a Windows or macOS desktop.

CHAPTER OBJECTIVES

Chapter Learning Objectives

- Work with Adobe AIR for Mobile.
- Use buttons in Animate CC.
- Master object-oriented ActionScript concepts.
- Write ActionScript classes.
- Ingest and display external data.
- Respond to user interaction.
- Compile for Apple iOS and Google Android.

Chapter ACA Objectives

For full descriptions of the objectives, see the table on pages 286–291.

DOMAIN 2.0
PROJECT SETUP AND INTERFACE
2.1, 2.4

DOMAIN 4.0
CREATE AND MODIFY VISUAL ELEMENTS
4.2, 4.7

DOMAIN 5.0
PUBLISHING DIGITAL MEDIA
5.2

CHAPTER 8

Develop a Mobile Quiz App

One of the coolest things you can do with Adobe Animate CC is to create a mobile app that can be compiled to either Apple iOS or Google Android using Adobe AIR. In this chapter, you'll take a deep look at ActionScript and build a simple mobile application.

For this project, you'll build a mobile app that can be compiled and distributed in app stores for installation on Apple iOS and Google Android. You'll create a straightforward quiz app that loads in data from a JavaScript Object Notation (JSON) file. The loaded data can then be randomized and displayed to the user, prompting a simple decision from the user via the touch of a button (Figure 8.1).

▶ *Video 8.1* *Project Overview*

Figure 8.1 The completed project

Creating an Adobe AIR
for Mobile Document

★ ACA Objective 2.1 Not only can you develop applications for desktop operating systems using Adobe AIR, you can also create apps for the two most popular mobile operating systems in the world today: Google Android and Apple iOS. Depending on which mobile operating system you want to target, you'll choose either AIR for Android or AIR for iOS in the New Document dialog box (which you access by choosing File > New).

Adobe AIR for Android

When you tell Animate CC to compile an AIR app for mobile Android, it generates an APK file. This is a standard Android app ready for distribution through Google Play, Amazon, or other app stores. Similar to the two different distribution mechanisms for desktop, with Android development you can choose whether to require the user to install the AIR runtime alongside the app or bundle the AIR runtime along with the app in a process called Captive Runtime. Just as with desktop solutions, Captive Runtime is preferable since it is much more seamless a process for the user.

GOOGLE PLAY

When distributing your mobile app through the Google Play store, you must sign your app with a self-signed certificate before uploading it to the app store. Additionally, you'll need a Google Developer account, which has a one-time cost of $25: see https://play.google.com/apps/publish/.

Adobe AIR for iOS

When building AIR apps for iOS, you don't have many choices for how to compile or distribute the app you're creating. The compiler builds a native iOS app directly from your Animate CC project since Apple does not allow separate runtimes on iOS. After compilation, you'll have a file in the IPA format (iOS App Store package) ready for testing, distribution, or whatever purpose you choose.

Setting up the AIR for Mobile project document

To create an Animate CC document that targets Adobe AIR for mobile devices, you'll make choices that will be similar to how you've begun other projects in this book.

▶ **Video 8.2** *Setting Up the AIR for Mobile Project Document*

1   On the Welcome Screen, choose Create New > AIR For Android (or AIR For iOS). Alternatively, choose File > New > AIR For Android (or iOS) to launch the New Document dialog box (**Figure 8.2**).

Your document should now be open and ready for you to modify the Stage properties.

Figure 8.2 Creating a new AIR project using the New Document dialog box

Figure 8.3 Project properties

2 Choose a width of 390 pixels and a height of 650 pixels to form a simulated mobile device view. This is scaled down from the default resolution to better fit within the Animate CC application window for the purposes of this instruction.

On iOS and Android, the application basically takes over the entire screen, so envision the entire Stage as the device screen for this project.

3 Set the background to whatever color you want. I'm using #9999CC in my example project.

4 You could leave the fps at 24 (the default), but you'll be using only a single frame for this project, so I recommend setting the FPS value to 12 (**Figure 8.3**).

Keeping the fps down a bit will save some device resources for the end user.

5 Additionally, if it's available, choose AIR 28 For Android as the publish target. If you use something a bit older, or even a newer version of the AIR SDK, that should be fine as well.

> **NOTE**
>
> *You won't use any of the new features of recent AIR versions in this project, so just about any of the publish target choices available should be fine.*

Design the App Interface Elements

One of the strengths of Animate CC is that it enables you to use the same tooling and workflows regardless of the target platform. Even though you're building a mobile application for this project, you can still design your entire user interface using the same tools available for asset creation or animation. Animate CC offers a truly unified, creative workspace.

★ *ACA Objective 4.2*

 Video 8.3 Create the App Header

Create the app header

The first thing you'll do is create an app header using the Text tool (T).

1 Double-click the existing Layer 1 layer and rename it **AppTitle**.

2 Select the Text tool from the Tools panel and use the Properties panel to adjust how your header text will appear.

3   The header text will not be changing during application runtime, so choose Static Text from the Text Type menu.

4   For the font family, choose Marker Felt if it's available and Wide as the style.

    If you need to use a different font, choose a nice big one. Choosing a 75pt font size and a nice, dark color such as #636384 will do fine (**Figure 8.4**).

5   Click anywhere on the Stage and type the header text **Quiz Me!**.

6   Once the text block is created, align it to the center along the x-axis and set the Y position value to 20px.

    You should now have a nice, bold app header at the top of the Stage.

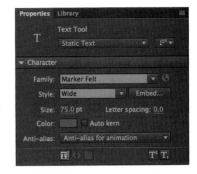

Figure 8.4 Header text properties

Create a question text element

The next two text blocks you create will be dynamic text because you'll need to change the text values at runtime. You can make them dynamic by providing each text block with an instance name, just like you've done with movie clip symbol instances in previous examples.

▶ *Video 8.4 Create a Question Text Element*

1   To begin, lock the AppTitle layer and create a new layer called **QuestionText**.

2   In the Properties panel, set the text type to Dynamic Text and for the font family choose Chalkduster.

    The font size will be 28pts and the color a neutral gray at #333333.

3   Click and drag out a nice big text block and type **Question Text Here...** for the placeholder text value.

    Again, this will be replaced by question text from your quiz bank when the app is running. With the text block created and selected, you'll now modify the instance properties in the Properties panel to finish.

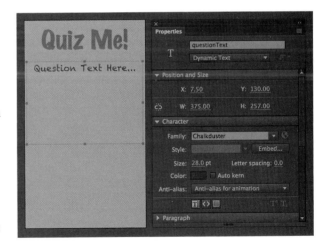

Figure 8.5 Question text properties

4   Give the text block the instance name `questionText` for ActionScript interactions later on. Make sure the text block measures 375px wide and 257px high.

5   Position the text block at 130px from the Stage top and center it along the x-axis (**Figure 8.5**).

Create a status text element

▶ **Video 8.5** *Create a Status Text Element*

The purpose of the final text element is to provide feedback to users as they make decisions about the questions presented by the app. This will once again be a dynamic text object with an instance name for later manipulation through code.

Figure 8.6 Status text properties

1 Lock all current layers and create a new layer named **StatusMsg**.

2 Choose Chalkduster as your dynamic text font once again and set the size to 52pts. Choose a nice off-red color (#993300) for the status message text so that it stands out to the user (**Figure 8.6**).

3 Click the Stage and drag out a text block measuring 320px in width.

4 Type an ellipsis (...) for a placeholder text value.

5 In the Properties panel, set the instance name to **statusMsg**. Set the Y position to 300px from the Stage top and then center the text across the x-axis.

6 Select the Free Transform tool and use it to rotate the text slightly on the Stage (**Figure 8.7**).

Figure 8.7 Rotating the status text within the project

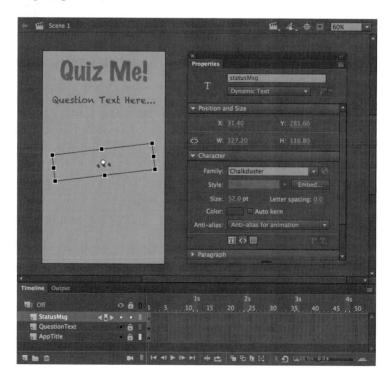

Designing the buttons

★ ACA Objective 2.4

You'll need to provide the user with a means of input. To do so, you'll create a set of buttons: one to indicate a choice of "true" and another for "false." First, you'll create the true Button symbol, and then you'll duplicate and edit the new symbol to create a false Button symbol.

▶ Video 8.6
Designing a Button

Button symbols are unique symbol types in Animate CC. They contain four specific frames: Up, Over, Down, and Hit (**Figure 8.8**). The first three indicate specific states of interaction common to buttons in general, and the Hit state indicates the active area that activates those states.

Figure 8.8 Button states

1   Create a new layer in the timeline and name it **Buttons**. Lock all other layers.

Next, you'll draw a simple visual asset to use in your Button symbols.

2   Select the Oval tool ( ) and use the Properties panel to tweak your tool settings.

3   For Stroke, choose a color of #333333 and a size of 8. Set the fill color using the green radial gradient swatch from the default swatches (**Figure 8.9**).

Figure 8.9 Oval tool properties

4   With these settings in place, hold down the Shift key and drag out a circle of 150px in diameter.

5   With this new shape selected, choose Modify > Convert To Symbol.

6   In the dialog box that appears, be sure that the symbol type is set to Button and name it **TrueButton**. Once created, give this object an instance name of **trueBtn** in the Properties panel. Switching to the project library, you will see the new Button symbol created and ready to be used (**Figure 8.10**).

You'll now add a text label to your Button symbol.

7   Double-click the Symbol entry in the project's Library panel to enter and edit the symbol itself. Notice that all four Button symbol frames are available in the internal Button symbol timeline.

Figure 8.10 Button symbol in the project library

8 Rename the existing Layer_1 layer to **Skin**.

9 Create a new layer and name it **Label**.

10 Select the Text tool and create a text block with the value of **True** in the Label layer.

11 With this text block selected, use the Properties panel to adjust the font size to 32pt with a color value of #333333 to match the stroke of your shape. Use whatever font you wish.

12 Align this text to appear below the shape, centered along the x-axis (**Figure 8.11**).

Figure 8.11 Button label created

NOTE

If desired, you can create new keyframes for each of these states and tweak the shape that's created for each specific frame. However, you're targeting a touch screen on mobile devices, so this isn't too great a concern; touch rarely exposes hover events as part of the interaction chain. Often, simply having a default Button symbol state is enough when targeting mobile.

Figure 8.12 Adjusting the gradient

Before moving on, we will add enough frames in the Skin layer to cover all four button states and extend frames in the Label layer up to the third button state.

1 Right-click the Down state in the Label layer and choose Insert Frame from the menu.

2 Right-click the Hit state in the Skin layer and, once again, choose Insert Frame.

You can also make the button look a lot nicer by simply using the Gradient Transform tool to modify its fill (**Figure 8.12**).

Now that you've completed designing the true Button symbol, you can duplicate it and then tweak a number of properties to create a false Button symbol. Duplicating a symbol in this way, no matter what the symbol type, allows you to easily create a uniform look across interactive elements in your application.

1. With the initial symbol completed, look at the Library panel once again and right-click the TrueButton Button symbol entry.

2. From the menu that appears, choose Duplicate and name the new symbol **FalseButton**.

    You'll see the new symbol immediately appear in the Library panel.

3. Double-click that symbol entry and change the text to read **False** instead of True. Additionally, select the shape that already exists. In the Properties panel, choose the red radial gradient swatch from the fill selection area.

    Both Button symbols are now completely unique in color and label. With both symbols created, you already have an instance of the TrueButton symbol on the Stage.

4. Click the FalseButton symbol entry in the Library panel and drag an instance out onto the Stage. Name this new instance `falseBtn` and align both instances close to the bottom of the Stage.

    These instances should be spaced in equal distance from one another and from each side of the screen (**Figure 8.13**).

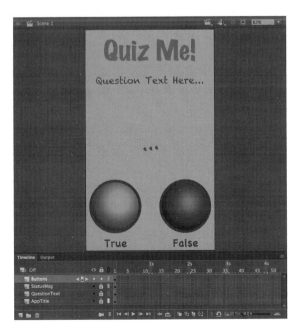

Figure 8.13 The completed mobile app interface

▶ **Video 8.7**
Duplicating the Button

▶ **Video 8.8**
Embedding Fonts

WARNING

Now that all text is in place, and since we are using dynamic text in a number of areas for this project, we must be sure to embed the font characters to be used. Click the Embed button next to the Style menu in the Character section of the Properties panel to create an embedded font and then use that newly created font for any dynamic text.

Writing the Application Classes

★ ACA Objective 4.7

In the previous chapter, you saw how to build a basic application targeting the desktop with ActionScript in the project timeline. For this project, you'll take a different approach by using the object-oriented class structures that ActionScript provides. Both methods would work for either of the projects in question. We'll use this opportunity to introduce new concepts and approaches.

Writing the QuizGame class

Classes in ActionScript are object-oriented constructs that define a set of **methods** and **properties**, which in turn define a particular object (a **method** is a function that is part of a class). For instance, `MovieClip` is a class from which all movie clip symbols are derived. `MovieClip` includes properties such as `x` and `y` and methods like `play()` and `stop()`.

An **object** is a specific **instance** of a class, whereas the class itself is more like a template. Think of the relationship between symbols in the library and instances on the Stage; it's a similar concept.

You must assign classes, methods, and properties access control namespace attributes. These declarations determine which portions of a program can access the various properties and methods of other classes. Five such attributes are built into ActionScript:

- **internal**: Visible to references inside the same package
- **private**: Visible to references in the same class
- **protected**: Visible to references in the same class and derived classes
- **public**: Visible to references everywhere
- **static**: Specifies that a property belongs to the class, as opposed to instances of the class

You declare these attributes along with variables and functions such as the following:

```
private var myVar:String = "This is private.";
```

Packages are a way to organize classes and preserve them from collisions with other classes that may be named identically. Say, for instance, you've defined a class

TIP

It's common practice to use a reverse-domain naming scheme when defining packages in ActionScript and many other programming languages. For instance, I own the domain josephlabrecque.com, so for a package name I'd use com.josephlabrecque.

called `FileEncoder` and you're also using a class named `FileEncoder` from an external library of classes. If you and the library author don't organize or identify the individual `FileEncoder` classes by package, the compiler will have no idea which class you might be referring to at any time.

CREATING A NEW CLASS

Now you'll begin to create your main class for this project.

▶ *Video 8.9* *Creating the QuizGame Class*

1   In the Properties panel, check Document Properties to ensure that no objects are selected on the Stage.

2   Note the Class field in the Publish section. On the right is a small pencil icon, signifying the Edit Class Definition function. Click this icon to reveal the Create ActionScript 3.0 Class dialog box (**Figure 8.14**).

Figure 8.14 Create ActionScript 3.0 Class dialog box

3   In the Class Name field, type **com.josephlabrecque.QuizGame** (go ahead and use your own domain if you have one).

The following class is created and opened in Animate CC:

```
package com.josephlabrecque {
  import flash.display.MovieClip;
  public class QuizGame extends MovieClip {
    public function QuizGame() {
      // constructor code
    }
  }
}
```

It's important to understand what you've created here. The first line, `package com.josephlabrecque {`, is the package definition for your class. The line `import flash.display.MovieClip;` will make the `MovieClip` class available for your use. Notice how the `MovieClip` class even has its own `flash.display` package? This is a core package definition in Flash Player and AIR.

DEFINING THE CLASS

Next, you'll define your class with `public class QuizGame extends MovieClip`. You can tell there's a lot going on here! First, you declare the class as `public`, meaning that it will be visible to other objects in the program. Then you declare your intention to define a class with the `class` keyword, followed by the name of the class. Any class that is the main class of an Animate CC application like this must extend either the `MovieClip` or `Sprite` core class, so in this case, you're extending the `MovieClip` class previously imported. That way, you can make use of everything that `MovieClip` has to offer in terms of properties and methods, while adding your own custom members as well. This is known as *inheritance*, and it's a core object-oriented programming concept.

The last part, `public function QuizGame()`, defines your constructor function. This is a method with the same name as the class that will run by default, meaning you never have to invoke this class. It runs once the class is instantiated. Notice that there's never any return data type declared in a constructor function.

SAVING THE CLASS

Before moving on, you need to save this class as a file:

1 Choose File > Save and navigate to the location of your existing FLA document. From here, you must replicate a folder directory from your package name.

2 Create a new directory named **com** and enter it. Then create a new directory within that called **josephlabrecque** and enter it as well.

3 Finally, save the file to that directory and name it **QuizGame.as** (**Figure 8.15**). Once the file is saved, click the tab in Animate CC that represents your FLA document and save that as well.

Figure 8.15 Package structure

Notice in Figure 8.15 how the package definition and the file structure are identical. Additionally, the name of the class file and the name of the class definition are identical. This is important; your classes won't work unless these items match exactly with one another.

Writing the QuestionBank class

The `QuizGame` class you just created will contain the majority of program logic for your application, but it's useful to delegate specific duties to additional classes whenever possible. Next, you'll define an additional class to assist you in handling the loading and management of your question data.

▶ *Video 8.10* *Writing the QuestionBank Class*

1   To create this new class, choose File > New.

The New Document dialog box appears.

2   For the document type, select ActionScript 3.0 Class from the menu on the left (**Figure 8.16**).

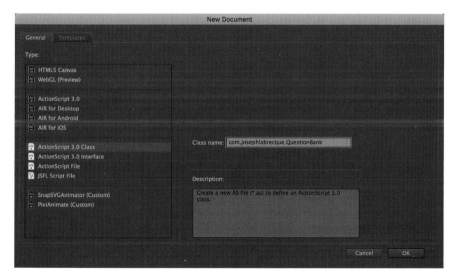

Figure 8.16 Choosing ActionScript 3.0 Class for the new document

3   Note how similar the options presented to you are compared to what you saw when constructing your initial class. In the Class Name field, type `com.josephlabrecque.QuestionBank`. (Again, use your own domain if you have one.) Then click OK.

The following class is created and opened in Animate CC:

```
package com.josephlabrecque {
  public class QuestionBank {
    public function QuestionBank() {
      // constructor code
    }
  }
}
```

Note a number of differences between this class and the previous one. You're not extending any other classes here; this is not a main class and thus isn't bound to any timeline. Similarly, you don't import any classes to extend. You need to save this file as well.

4 Choose File > Save and navigate to the location of your existing ActionScript class file in the package directory structure you created earlier.

5 Name this file **QuestionBank.as** and save it alongside the QuizGame.as class file.

DEFINING STAGE OBJECT REFERENCES

▶ *Video 8.11*
*Defining Stage
Object References*

This step isn't exactly necessary, but it provides a lot of benefits to your coding experience, including auto-completion and code hinting. These features won't be available to you unless you import the classes you need and then declare variables with the same instance name as the instances on your Stage.

You'll add these to the main QuizGame class.

```
import flash.text.TextField;
import flash.display.SimpleButton;
```

In this example, you have two Button symbol instances on the Stage and two TextFields. All four have instance names. Notice that you declare only the variables; you're not creating new instances of anything, since the instances already exist on your Stage. This is done only to improve the coding experience and allows Animate CC to suggest methods and properties of these instances from among those that are available in the imported class type.

```
public var trueBtn:SimpleButton;
public var falseBtn:SimpleButton;
```

```
public var questionText:TextField;
public var statusMsg:TextField;
```

At this point, you can also modify any of your Stage objects. For instance, I'll set the `statusMsg` text to an empty string when initializing the game. You can place this instruction in the `QuizGame` constructor function, and it will run immediately when the app is fired up:

```
public function QuizGame() {
    statusMsg.text = "";
}
```

Creating a Bank of Questions

You could build the data for this application in the ActionScript code, but doing so would mean that every time you wanted to tweak the wording or add new questions, you'd have to edit the code and recompile the app. That's not very convenient, and data doesn't belong with application structures and logic anyway.

It's much better to create a service to call over the Internet, or even a local data file (as you'll do next). This approach not only separates the data from the app code but also allows much simpler modification.

Building the JSON file

JSON is a data interchange format created with the intention of being human-readable and at the same time easy for programs to ingest and parse. JSON is a popular data format for the web and has been natively supported in Adobe AIR since AIR 3 and is also available in Adobe Flash Player. For your application, you'll use this format to build a bank of questions and accompanying answers to populate your mobile app.

> ▶ *Video 8.12*
> *Building the*
> *JSON File*

> **NOTE**
> *For complete information about the JSON format, visit www.json.org.*

To create the JSON file, use a simple text editor such as Notepad, TextEdit, Brackets (http://brackets.io), or Visual Studio Code (https://code.visualstudio.com).

Begin with a blank text document and enter the following structure:

```
{
    "questions":[
    {"q":"", "tf":""},
    {"q":"", "tf":""},
    {"q":"", "tf":""}
    ]
}
```

This establishes your JSON structure using standard syntax. The initial curly braces ({}) establish the root object, followed by a `"questions"` array defined with array-syntax braces ([]) that contains a comma-delimited set of additional objects all defined by curly braces. Each object here represents a question-and-answer set. The `question` property of the object is a string that contains the question statement text. The `tf` property is an indicator specifying whether the statement is true or false (**Figure 8.17**).

When your JSON file is completed, create the **data** directory in the same location as your FLA document, and in that directory, save the file as **questions.json**.

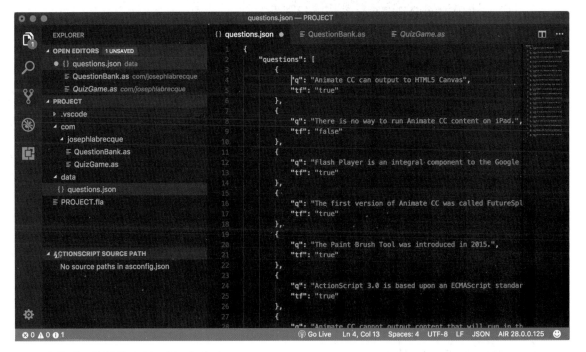

Figure 8.17 The JSON file in Visual Studio Code

THE COMPLETED JSON FILE

I've completed the JSON file with a set of 20 statements on Animate CC, Flash Player, ActionScript, and AIR. You can make your version of the quiz on any subject you like. Here is the fully completed JSON structure you'll use in our examples:

```
{
    "questions":[
        {"q":"Animate CC can output to HTML5 Canvas",
        → "tf":"true"},
        {"q":"There is no way to run Animate CC content
        → on iPad.", "tf":"false"},
        {"q":"Flash Player is an integral component to the
        → Google Chromebook experience.", "tf":"true"},
        {"q":"The first version of Animate CC was
        → called FutureSplash Animator.", "tf":"true"},
        {"q":"The Paint Brush Tool was introduced in 2015.",
        → "tf":"true"},
        {"q":"ActionScript 3.0 is based upon an ECMAScript
        → standard.", "tf":"true"},
        {"q":"Animate CC cannot output content that will
        → run in the iPhone web browser.", "tf":"false"},
        {"q":"When targeting HTML5 Canvas, Animate CC
        → leverages the CreateJS libraries.", "tf":"true"},
        {"q":"Flash Player is built into Google Chrome,
        → Internet Explorer, and Microsoft Edge.",
        → "tf":"true"},
        {"q":"Using Animate CC, you can build apps which run
        → on iOS.", "tf":"true"},
        {"q":"Animate CC is an industry standard animation
        → and interactivity tool.", "tf":"true"},
        {"q":"As of September 2015, there have been over
        → 4 BILLION Adobe AIR application installs.",
        → "tf":"true"},
        {"q":"Animate CC content cannot be packaged as
        → OAM files.", "tf":"false"},
        {"q":"The current version of ActionScript (as of 2018)
        → is AS4.", "tf":"false"},
        {"q":"JavaScript can be edited directly in the Actions
        → Panel.", "tf":"true"},
        {"q":"Animate CC can be used to produce
        → ActionScript 2.0 content.", "tf":"false"},
```

```
{"q":"Flash Player cannot access a system webcam or
→ microphone.", "tf":"false"},

{"q":"The final version of Animate CC from
→ Macromedia was Flash Professional 8.", "tf":"true"},

{"q":"As of September 2015, Flash Player is downloaded
→ 1.2 BILLION times per month from Adobe.com.",
"tf":"true"},

{"q":"Adobe continues to develop Flash Player for
→ Android.", "tf":"false"}

  ]

}
```

Loading the JSON data

To load the JSON data into your application, you'll leverage the `QuestionBank` ActionScript class. You'll import three additional classes into `QuestionBank` to deal with loading the JSON file. Add the following lines right beneath the package definition:

```
import flash.net.URLRequest;
import flash.net.URLLoader;
import flash.events.Event;
```

Now, immediately after the class definition, you'll enter some variables. Here's a quick overview of what these variables are named and their role in the application:

- **JSON_URL**: A constant that defines the location of your JSON file
- **jsonRequest**: A URLRequest object that defines the URL you want to load
- **jsonLoader**: A URLLoader object that uses the URLRequest object to load in your JSON
- **questionArray**: The Array object you'll use to store all the parsed objects from your external JSON

The code will look like this:

```
private const JSON_URL:String = "data/questions.json";
private var jsonRequest:URLRequest;
private var jsonLoader:URLLoader;
private var questionArray:Array;
```

In your `QuestionBank` constructor function, you'll initialize the `Array` object by stating `questionArray = new Array();` and then invoke a method to load in your JSON via `loadJSON();` using the `URLRequest` and `URLLoader` objects. The completed constructor function looks like this:

```
public function QuestionBank() {
  questionArray = new Array();
  loadJSON();
}
```

To load the JSON, you must use the `loadJSON` method that first defines your `URLRequest`, with the `String` constant declaring your file path to the JSON file. A `URLLoader` is then created that's instructed to invoke a method called `jsonLoaded` when the file load completes. Finally, you tell the `URLLoader` to load your `URLRequest`:

```
private function loadJSON():void {
  jsonRequest = new URLRequest(JSON_URL);
  jsonLoader = new URLLoader();
  jsonLoader.addEventListener(Event.COMPLETE, jsonLoaded);
  jsonLoader.load(jsonRequest);
}
```

Once the file has completely loaded into your application, the `jsonLoaded` method is triggered, which uses the native JSON parser in ActionScript to parse the event target data and save it to a new object named `jsonData`. This object is then processed in a for each loop in order to add each question object to the array you created previously:

```
private function jsonLoaded(e:Event):void {
  var jsonData:Object = JSON.parse(e.target.data);
  for each (var question:Object in jsonData.questions){
    questionArray.push(question);
  }
}
```

Integrating the QuestionBank class

▶ **Video 8.14**
*Integrating the
QuestionBank
Class*

Now you've created two completely independent classes. Your `QuizGame` class is tied to the FLA document, but the `QuestionBank` class isn't connected to anything. To have a working application, you'll need to integrate the `QuestionBank` class into your main `QuizGame` class so that it can be used from there.

PREPARING THE QUIZGAME CLASS

NOTE

*Simply declaring the
variables like this does
not instantiate them or
make them available
for use in the applica-
tion. It merely provides
the intention to use
named variables as
specific data types.*

The way you use one class from within another is something you've already done, though you may not fully realize it yet. Basically, any time you've imported classes and then instantiated variables from those classes, you've taken the same steps needed to integrate your `QuestionBank` class into `QuizGame`.

1 In the QuizGame.as file, import the core `Event` class from the `flash.events` package. You'll use this to listen for events broadcast from your `QuestionBank` class.

    ```
    import flash.events.Event;
    ```

2 Import the `QuestionBank` class from the `com.josephlabrecque` package:

    ```
    import com.josephlabrecque.QuestionBank;
    ```

3 Declare two objects: one as a `QuestionBank` instance and one as an `Array`. Place these lines of code alongside the previous declarations:

    ```
    private var questionBank:QuestionBank;
    private var questionArray:Array;
    ```

    Now in the `QuizGame` constructor function, you'll perform some setup opera-tions. You already have a line of code that clears out your status message text.

4 Right below that line of code, set `questionArray` to a new `Array` object. This action makes the `Array` object available for use.

5 Below that, set `questionBank` as a new `QuestionBank` object. The `questionBank` variable has now been instantiated, and you're able to read properties from it or invoke the methods that belong to it. Listen for an event to be broadcast from the `questionBank` instance so that you know exactly when the question data has been retrieved and made available for use.

6   Add an event listener of type `Event.COMPLETE` to your instance.

When this event is detected, an additional method called `dataReady` will execute:

```
public function QuizGame() {
statusMsg.text = "";
questionArray = new Array();
questionBank = new QuestionBank();
questionBank.addEventListener(Event.COMPLETE, dataReady);
}
```

7   To create the method, create a new private function, name it `dataReady`, and pass through the `Event` from your listener as an argument.

If any method is invoked with argument data passed through, the receiving function must be configured to accept that data or the compilation will fail. The return data type is set to `void` since this method doesn't return any data.

8   In the body of your function, set `questionArray` equal to `questionBank.buildBank()`.

This will invoke the `buildBank` method, which you have yet to create, from the `questionBank` instance and will return that `Array` data to `questionArray` for your use in the main `QuizGame` class.

9   Grab a question from the bank by invoking a method named `grabQuestion` that doesn't yet exist.

```
private function dataReady(e:Event):void {
   questionArray = questionBank.buildBank();
   grabQuestion();
}
```

FINISHING THE QUESTIONBANK CLASS

By now you've prepared your main `QuizGame` class to listen for events emerging from the `QuestionBank` class and to respond to such events appropriately. However, the `QuestionBank` class needs to be modified in order to be able to broadcast such events. In the `QuestionBank` class, the first thing you must do is import the `EventDispatcher` class from the `flash.events` package:

▶ *Video 8.15*
Finishing the
QuestionBank Class

```
import flash.events.EventDispatcher;
```

Similar to how you extended the `QuizGame` class from `flash.display.MovieClip`, you'll extend the `QuestionBank` class from `flash.events.EventDispatcher`. That way, your `QuestionBank` class can dispatch events to other parts of the application. On the existing class definition, simply add `extends EventDispatcher` right after `public class QuestionBank` to enable this:

```
public class QuestionBank extends EventDispatcher
```

Now you'll broadcast, or dispatch, your event. In the final line of your `jsonLoaded` method, right after the `for` loop, use the `dispatchEvent` method to broadcast a completion event to the rest of your application. You'll be able to catch this event in your main `QuizGame` class since you've already added an event listener to do so. To your `for` loop, add the following line of code immediately after the closing curly brace:

```
dispatchEvent(new Event(Event.COMPLETE));
```

Additionally, you must create a way of getting all the question data now contained in the `QuestionBank` class over to your main `QuizGame` class for use in the app. To populate your `Array` in `QuizGame`, you're invoking a nonexisting method of `QuestionBank` named `buildBank`. You'll create this method now:

1 Create a new public function named `buildBank` with a return data type of `Array`.

2 In the function body, create a temporary `Array` named `b`.

   This is what will eventually be returned to the `QuizGame` class. Additionally, you'll create another variable, `max`, which is an int.

3 Set the value of this variable to the length of `questionArray`.

   This lets you know how many questions you have to deal with.

The next thing you need to do is establish a `for` loop that counts from 0 to the value of `max`. For each iteration of this loop, you use the `Array.push()` method to add specific values from your main `Array` into the temporary `Array`. Once all the questions have been added, the `for` loop ends, and you use the `return` command to send the temporary `Array` and all of its data back to the class that invoked this method:

```
public function buildBank():Array {
  var b:Array = new Array();
  var max:int = questionArray.length;
```

```
      for(var i:int=0; i<max; i++){
        b.push({q:questionArray[i].q, tf:questionArray[i].tf});
      }
      return b;
  }
```

THE COMPLETED QUESTIONBANK CLASS

You've now constructed the entire `QuestionBank` class. Yours should appear identical to the class shown here:

```
package com.josephlabrecque {
    import flash.net.URLRequest;
    import flash.net.URLLoader;
    import flash.events.Event;
    import flash.events.EventDispatcher;
    public class QuestionBank extends EventDispatcher {
        private const JSON_URL:String = "data/questions.json";
        private var jsonRequest:URLRequest;
        private var jsonLoader:URLLoader;
        private var questionArray:Array;
        public function QuestionBank() {
            questionArray = new Array();
            loadJSON();
        }
        private function loadJSON():void {
            jsonRequest = new URLRequest(JSON_URL);
            jsonLoader = new URLLoader();
            jsonLoader.addEventListener(Event.COMPLETE, jsonLoaded);
            jsonLoader.load(jsonRequest);
        }
        private function jsonLoaded(e:Event):void {
            var jsonData:Object = JSON.parse(e.target.data);
            for each (var question:Object in jsonData.questions){
                questionArray.push(question);
            }
        }
```

```
            dispatchEvent(new Event(Event.COMPLETE));
        }
        public function buildBank():Array {
            var b:Array = new Array();
            var max:int = questionArray.length;
            for(var i:int=0; i<max; i++){
                b.push({q:questionArray[i].q,
                → tf:questionArray[i].tf});
            }
            return b;
        }
    }
}
```

App Logic and Flow

★ ACA Objective 4.7

You have the interface designed, the basic classes written, and the data loading in. Your mobile app is nearly finished! You do have an essential task to complete, though: the interactive part. You must have the app respond to user input, check the choices the user provides, and give feedback once all this has occurred. You'll establish all this functionality through modifications to your main `QuizGame` class.

Showing questions to the user

▶ Video 8.16
Showing Questions
to the User

To manage your set of questions, you'll define a number of variables in the application. Directly below the other variable declarations that exist in the `QuizGame` class, you'll define an additional set of variables for this purpose. `questionMax` is an int and a constant, meaning that once a value has been set, it should never change. This defines how many questions, from the full pool of questions, you want to show your user. The `questionCount` variable keeps track of how many questions have been asked so far, and the `currentAnswer` variable holds the answer data, gathered from your internal `Array` of questions.

```
private const questionMax:int = 5;
private var questionCount:int = 0;
private var currentAnswer:String;
```

In your `dataReady` function, you're invoking a method called `grabQuestion` to pull a question object from the pool and show it to the user. This isn't something you've written yet, so you'll define a new private function with the name of `grabQuestion`, which returns nothing, typed as `void`. In this function, you'll look to see if your current question count is less than the maximum amount of questions you want to ask in the app. If it is, then you'll pull a random question from the `Array` by using the `Math.random()` function.

You're pulling the question object from the `Array` by using the `Array.splice()` command, which will remove the object completely from the `Array`, making the length of the `Array` one index shorter each time `grabQuestion` is run. This ensures that you never present the user with the same question twice. The question data is placed in a temporary `Array` named `ta`, and the question statement is immediately pulled from this `Array` and placed in the `questionText` text block on the Stage, effectively making the statement visible to the user in the app. You do this by setting the value of `questionText.text` equal to `ta[0].q`. When you see something like `[0]` in ActionScript, this is `Array` syntax, simply requesting the data at position 0 of your `Array`.

Your `currentAnswer` variable will always contain the exact answer data pulled from this `Array` so you can easily check the user response against the correct answer. Similar to how you retrieve the question statement text from your temporary `Array`, you'll once again use this syntax to retrieve the correct answer to the statement. You do this by setting the value of `currentAnswer` equal to `ta[0].tf`. This will set the value of `currentAnswer` to a `String` of either `"true"` or `"false"` for each specific question statement.

Lastly, you increment your `questionCount` variable by 1, keeping a tally of how many questions you've presented to the user. This allows you to determine when to invoke your `gameOver()` method.

```
private function grabQuestion():void {
    if(questionCount < questionMax){
        var max:int = questionArray.length-1;
        var rq:int = Math.floor(Math.random() * (max - 0 + 1));
        var ta:Array = questionArray.splice(rq, 1);
        questionText.text = ta[0].q;
        currentAnswer = ta[0].tf;
        questionCount++;
```

```
    } else{
        gameOver();
    }
}
```

The gameOver() method is fairly simple. You define a new private function with
the name of gameOver, which accepts no arguments and returns nothing as well.
In the body of this function, you display the number of calculated points from the
currentScore variable and change the questionText text value to read "Game
Over!".

```
private function gameOver():void {
    statusMsg.text = currentScore + "/100 points ";
    questionText.text = "Game Over!";
}
```

As for keeping track of the score, this is something done with each button press
from the user, and it's the last bit of code you need to write.

Building button interactivity

▶ Video 8.17
Building Button
Interactivity

You've now arrived at the final part of this project: allowing the user to interact
with the mobile app and then reacting to choices the user has made in the application flow.

The first thing you need to do is import a couple more classes. The MouseEvent
class will allow you to set up event listeners in response to mouse and touch events;
setTimeout will enable you to perform a delayed function call following the user
interaction.

```
import flash.events.MouseEvent;
import flash.utils.setTimeout;
```

To keep score based on user choices, you'll establish a new variable called
currentScore. This will start with a value of 0 and be updated every time the user
correctly responds to each statement.

```
private var currentScore:int = 0;
```

Back in the QuizGame constructor function, you'll add an event listener to both of
the SimpleButton instances on the Stage. Each will invoke a method to respond

to the user's choice, based on the `currentAnswer` variable, determining whether to add to the user's score, and proceeding with the next question.

```
trueBtn.addEventListener(MouseEvent.CLICK, truePressed);
falseBtn.addEventListener(MouseEvent.CLICK, falsePressed);
```

Scroll down in the class and add a method to control responses to your user interaction. First, you create a new private function named `truePressed`. This method fires off whenever the user selects the `trueBtn` instance on the Stage. In the body of this function, you first check to see whether a status message is present. If a status message exists, it means that you should not allow the user interaction to count, because you're between questions.

Then you check whether the user's choice matches the `currentAnswer`. If it matches, then you increment the score based on how many total questions you'll be displaying and set the status message text to `"CORRECT!"`. If it's incorrect, you set it to `"WRONG!"`. No matter which answer is chosen, you then use the `setTimeout` method to be sure the status message stays on the screen for a full second before invoking the `newQuestion` method to retrieve the next statement.

```
private function truePressed(e:MouseEvent):void {
    if(statusMsg.text == ""){
        if(currentAnswer == "true"){
            currentScore += 100/questionMax;
            statusMsg.text = "CORRECT!";
        }else{
            statusMsg.text = "WRONG";
        }
        setTimeout(newQuestion, 1000);
    }
}
```

Basically, you do the same thing for the `falsePressed` function. The only real difference is that you're checking whether `correctAnswer` is false. Everything else is practically identical.

```
private function falsePressed(e:MouseEvent):void {
    if(statusMsg.text == ""){
        if(currentAnswer == "false"){
```

```
        currentScore += 100/questionMax;
        statusMsg.text = "CORRECT!";
      }else{
        statusMsg.text = "WRONG";
      }
      setTimeout(newQuestion, 1000);
    }
  }
```

The last method you need to build is the newQuestion function, which gets called from each button press method. All this does is clear out the status message text and then invoke the grabQuestion method. Again, this newQuestion method call is delayed by one full second to ensure that users will see the status message feedback to their selection before it's cleared and the new question appears.

```
  private function newQuestion():void {
    statusMsg.text = "";
    grabQuestion();
  }
```

THE COMPLETED QUIZGAME CLASS

That completes all of your ActionScript code for this project! The completed code for QuizGame.as is included here for your reference.

```
package com.josephlabrecque {
    import flash.display.MovieClip;
    import flash.text.TextField;
    import flash.display.SimpleButton;
    import flash.events.Event;
    import com.josephlabrecque.QuestionBank;
    import flash.events.MouseEvent;
    import flash.utils.setTimeout;
    public class QuizGame extends MovieClip {
      public var trueBtn:SimpleButton;
      public var falseBtn:SimpleButton;
      public var questionText:TextField;
      public var statusMsg:TextField;
```

```
private var questionBank:QuestionBank;
private var questionArray:Array;
private const questionMax:int = 5;
private var questionCount:int = 0;
private var currentAnswer:String;
private var currentScore:int = 0;
public function QuizGame() {
   statusMsg.text = "";
   questionArray = new Array();
   questionBank = new QuestionBank();
   questionBank.addEventListener(Event.COMPLETE,
   → dataReady);
   trueBtn.addEventListener(MouseEvent.CLICK, truePressed);
   falseBtn.addEventListener(MouseEvent.CLICK,
   → falsePressed);
}
private function truePressed(e:MouseEvent):void {
   if(statusMsg.text == ""){
      if(currentAnswer == "true"){
         currentScore += 100/questionMax;
         statusMsg.text = "CORRECT!";
      }else{
         statusMsg.text = "WRONG";
      }
      setTimeout(newQuestion, 1000);
   }
}
private function falsePressed(e:MouseEvent):void {
   if(statusMsg.text == ""){
      if(currentAnswer == "false"){
         currentScore += 100/questionMax;
         statusMsg.text = "CORRECT!";
      }else{
         statusMsg.text = "WRONG";
      }
```

```
                    setTimeout(newQuestion, 1000);
                }
            }
            private function dataReady(e:Event):void {
                questionArray = questionBank.buildBank();
                grabQuestion();
            }
            private function newQuestion():void {
                statusMsg.text = "";
                trace(currentScore);
                grabQuestion();
            }
            private function grabQuestion():void {
                if(questionCount < questionMax){
                    var max:int = questionArray.length-1;
                    var rq:int = Math.floor(Math.random() *
                    → (max - 0 + 1));
                    var ta:Array = questionArray.splice(rq, 1);
                    questionText.text = ta[0].q;
                    currentAnswer = ta[0].tf;
                    questionCount++;
                }else{
                    gameOver();
                }
            }
            private function gameOver():void {
                statusMsg.text = currentScore+"/100 points";
                questionText.text = "Game Over!";
            }
        }
    }
```

Publishing the App for Distribution

Now that you've completed the application and made it ready for distribution, consider some additional options. The AIR Settings dialog box provides settings related
to the publishing and delivery of an Android or iOS app. You can access these
options by clicking the wrench icon next to the Target menu in the Publish Settings
dialog box. The AIR Settings dialog box contains several tabs that allow you to set
up the options for the AIR mobile app.

★ *ACA Objective 5.2*

Completing application details

To complete the final details for publishing the application, if these settings are not
already opened from the Properties panel, choose File > AIR For Android Settings.
The AIR Settings dialog box (**Figure 8.18**) opens, containing the following tabs:

▶ *Video 8.18*
Publishing the App
for Distribution

- **General:** This screen contains core information about how you package your mobile
  application. You can choose to generate an
  AIR file, use an OS-specific installer, or use
  the embedded runtime option. This is also
  the place to name your application and make
  decisions about aspect ratio, orientation, and
  render mode.

- **Deployment:** All Adobe AIR applications must
  be signed in order to be properly installed on a
  user's device. This screen allows you to create
  a free, self-signed certificate to publish your
  applications to Android. If you're targeting
  iOS, you can input all the information about
  your provisioning profile and certificate from
  Apple.

- **Icons:** This section allows you to specify a
  group of custom icons that represent the
  mobile application. You can create icons of
  differing sizes in an application like Adobe
  Photoshop CC.

Figure 8.18 AIR Settings dialog box

- **Permissions:** This is a list of permissions you can check off, indicating which specific permissions are needed for Android. This screen does not appear if you're targeting iOS, since it handles permissions differently.
- **Language:** In this section, you indicate the languages used in your mobile application.

Challenge!

There are a *lot* of different resolutions and aspect ratios to deal with when targeting mobile devices. The way you've built this project doesn't take this fact into account, but using ActionScript, you can make the user interface elements completely responsive in regard to different screen sizes. It requires many of the concepts you've learned so far: instance names and the ability to adjust X and Y positions and other attributes through code.

Conclusion

In this chapter, you've worked in Animate CC to create a mobile app that can be compiled to either Apple iOS or Google Android using Adobe AIR technology. You spent a lot of time with ActionScript and had a deeper look at the object-oriented syntax and rich capabilities of the language structures needed to build a real, cross-platform mobile app.

You've dug deeper into ActionScript to properly organize your code into packages and classes, all while learning more of the functionality available to you when ingesting external data and forming complex data structures. You've also learned how to listen for and respond to user interaction through something as straight-forward as button presses.

CHAPTER OBJECTIVES

Chapter Learning Objectives

- Edit and evaluate your interactive media content.

- Test usability and accessibility.

- Work with focus groups and beta testers.

- Identify useful web resources for Animate CC users.

Chapter ACA Objectives

For full descriptions of the objectives, see the table on pages 286–291.

DOMAIN 5.0
PUBLISHING DIGITAL MEDIA
5.1

CHAPTER 9

Wrapping It Up!

Congratulations! You've made it to the end of this book, and by now you should be pretty good at using Adobe Animate CC to create interactive media projects targeting a variety of publishing targets and formats. As you've seen through the projects we've worked on, Animate CC is capable of a diverse array of project types.

Before we close, let's tie things up with a few words about content evaluation and testing, along with some resources for exploring more of what Animate CC has to offer.

Evaluating Interactive Media Content

Interactive content created in Animate CC can be complex depending on the type of project you're working on. Being able to properly evaluate and test a project is a task that you should always undertake before you consider a project complete. Be prepared for several rounds of editing in your project plan. Define your procedures and processes to make editing as painless as possible.

★ *ACA Objective 5.1*

Many people are drawn to interactive media development because it is dynamic and flashy. Evaluating, proofing, and editing interactive media files isn't as glamorous as creating cool interface elements or manipulating video, but it's essential to getting your work out the door. You may be tempted to try passing this tedious task off to others. That isn't a good idea. Remember that no one else knows the files like the designer or developer who put it all together.

Types of evaluation

You can evaluate interactive media content from multiple vantage points, but in any case, it's best to keep your objectives specific. Your evaluation process can involve testing technical aspects of an interactive media document to search for bugs, broken links, and other glitches. You can perform a separate round of evaluation on the contextual information to make sure it accurately reflects the intent of the storyboards. Usability should always be the final evaluation in each cycle, to test to see how end users receive the interactive media document. A good starting point is to evaluate the technical, content, and usability aspects of your interactive media piece.

TECHNICAL EVALUATION

To conduct a technical evaluation of interactive media content, you'll examine the work for any coding errors, playback issues, and deployment problems. This evaluation doesn't include addressing usability or proofreading the content against the working documents. Breaking down the tasks for this technical evaluation will help you focus on specific problems and not get overwhelmed. You also may find that solving one issue will fix other issues. Conversely, you might create or find new problems as you attempt to resolve issues.

There is always some overlap in the evaluation processes, but when evaluating an interactive media application for technical issues, you should be focusing on the functionality of the content delivery system, not the content itself. Errors and warnings in the ActionScript or JavaScript, bugs, broken links, excessive load times, and navigation errors are some of the issues that fall into this category.

INITIAL EVALUATION

TIP

Do your preliminary technical testing before you perform any usability testing, because a technical bug may skew the usability results.

You can perform your initial technical evaluation on the development platform, but as you enter the final cycles of editing, make sure that the content is running on the actual target platform. This is especially important if the interactive media content is to be delivered via mobile devices.

Bugs are the major target of a preliminary technical evaluation. Test the interface and functionality thoroughly to determine whether any errors were made in scripting or naming of instances. It's never acceptable to ship a final version of a product with a **bug** or error in the ActionScript or JavaScript. To prevent this from happening, you'll need to schedule enough time with testers to test every element in every way that it might be used (or misused).

This is a good time to call others in to help. Because you're familiar with the code and functionality, you may never even imagine how the interactive media content could be misused. Another set of hands on the keyboard and mouse can reveal issues that you may not have considered when you were building the project.

DEPLOYMENT TESTING

Most interactive media content designers and developers have powerful machines that let them quickly create and manipulate video, animations, and sound files. However, when it comes to evaluating how your interactive media application will run in the real world, all this horsepower can actually be a bad thing.

Depending on your target user, you may want to test on a machine with minimum specifications. Even running the Flash Player–based SWF file from an integrated version of Flash Player instead of running it from the browser (and even multiple browsers) can reveal unexpected results.

CONTENT EVALUATION

Content is king, and even the slickest interface can't save you if your content is inaccurate or poorly implemented. At some point in the evaluation process, a meticulous editor must proof the content. The editor should look for inconsistencies and typos by comparing the working documents to the onscreen content. Subject matter experts (SMEs) can also be called in at this point to make sure the intended concepts reflect accurately in the interactive media format.

What to look for

During the content evaluation, look for errors in the text, proper use of imagery, correct navigation points, and so on. It all begins with basic proofreading. There are other considerations, too. Recall our discussion of using type specifications, graphic treatment, placement, and color to reinforce the purpose of elements in an interactive media application. During the content evaluation, make sure that the style guide outlining those treatments is followed consistently. Look not only at the text and images but also at how those images appear and whether their appearance conforms to the style guidelines.

SPELLING CHECK

Checking spelling is the single easiest form of evaluation and can reveal problems that may have occurred while the text was imported or pasted from the working documents. Animate CC does not include an integrated spell check, so you must do this manually.

USABILITY EVALUATION

Many aspects of technical evaluation and content evaluation may be executed concurrently, but the usability evaluation should always be the last evaluation in the cycle (or cycles).

Poorly proofed and executed interfaces will affect how your audience perceives the experience, and they can increase the end user's sensitivity to how the interactive media is presented. Suddenly that very cool interface element may appear too complex or busy. Or maybe the background graphic that was just perfect for the content now seems distracting.

It is best for your project to be clean, error-free, and functioning seamlessly by the time you test it for usability so that the testers focus on just usability and don't get distracted by anything else.

What to look for

Usability includes not only testing the interface to see how end users operate the interactive media application but also evaluating how users react and work with the content. You could have a fantastic interface that is crippled by content that isn't properly organized. Even the delivery device could cause some unintended problems, like buttons that are being tapped accidentally because of proximity or something being obstructed because you need to hold the device in a certain way. You may not spot this type of issue unless you throw it out there and let the testers start beating on it.

There isn't a set checklist for usability, because the content and audiences vary. However, you could make some general guidelines to follow in your evaluation as you assess the interface, the content, and the experience.

ACCESSIBILITY EVALUATION

Accessibility is important. Although it's challenging to work with certain Animate CC projects in an accessible way, it's not impossible to do so. When targeting Flash Player, you have access to the accessibility portion of the Properties panel (**Figure 9.1**) when working with the document or movie clip properties. The choices allow you to make the entire project and specific child objects accessible.

You can input metadata regarding object name and description and, in the case of movie clip symbol instances, choose keyboard shortcuts and tab order. It's important to note, however, that there are many commonsense ways of making any piece of interactive media more accessible. These include consistent navigation, color choices, and the typefaces used.

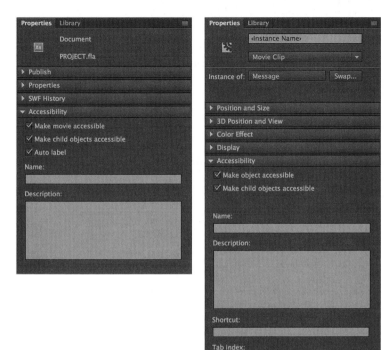

INFORMAL TESTING

How you execute the usability testing depends on the scope of the project and its intended audience. For smaller projects, a simple random group from around the office may suffice. Have your colleagues run the application and take notes as they go. Be sure that the people selected are representative of the target end users. For instance, if special subject knowledge is required to understand the content, make sure the informal group has that knowledge.

FOCUS GROUPS

A focus group can be a big help in understanding how end users will react to an interactive media experience. When an organization conducts a focus group, they invite individuals from the target audience to sit in and evaluate a product. They use the product and are encouraged by a facilitator to make comments on their experience. You may need to pay each evaluator or offer them a free gift to entice them to participate.

NOTE

Many people think it's their job to criticize. In this case, they would be correct. Don't let it get to you, and don't lose sleep if only one member of the group has a problem with something. You're looking for patterns in the opinions.

Observe your evaluators via video or through a one-way window. The point is not to spy on them as much as it is to get an honest reaction. Many people will not tell you what you need to hear when you're standing right in front of them. The anonymity of a focus group allows people to loosen up and express what they really think. A focus group also shows you how users react to the interface. You understand it because you created it, but someone viewing it for the first time may have a different reaction.

BETA TESTING

Beta testing is another valuable tool in determining usability. This involves getting potential users to agree to use preliminary releases of a product and report back with their recommendations. The big benefit of beta testing is that it involves real end users using the product in a real environment. Feedback from beta testing can be gathered via phone calls, interviews, questionnaires, or other means.

Revisions

No matter how carefully you plan or proof an interactive media application, you'll always have room for improvement. The evaluation process doesn't stop after you deliver the product. Many interactive media applications are delivered without any physical medium; this means that making improvements and revisions can be an ongoing process.

But just because you can revise it later doesn't excuse you from thoroughly evaluating an application before it goes out the door. You have only one chance at making a good first impression.

If you do a great job creating interactive media content, the development path is circular, not linear.

Where to Go Next

You may be wondering what is next for Adobe Animate CC and how you can stay up to date on all things "Flash." Like many of the Adobe Creative Cloud desktop applications, Animate CC receives a number of major updates every year.

Animate CC resources

Adobe has a number of web-based resources that are designed to serve the Animate CC user and developer community, including the following:

Animate CC at the Adobe Blog (*https://theblog.adobe.com/creative-cloud/animate/*): Here you'll find the latest news, tips, and insights directly from the Adobe Animate CC team and articles tagged to Animate CC.

Adobe AIR and Adobe Flash Player Team Blog (*https://blogs.adobe.com/flashplayer/*): This blog offers news, commentary, and insights from the Flash Player and Adobe AIR product and engineering teams.

Animate CC | Product Page (*www.adobe.com/products/animate.html*): "Create animations for any device or platform."

Animate CC | New Features (*www.adobe.com/products/animate/features.html*): "With Animate CC, you always have access to new features as soon as they're released."

Animate CC | Learn & Support (*https://helpx.adobe.com/support/animate.html*): "Get started or go deeper with our library of tutorials, projects and articles."

Animate CC |ActionScript Reference (*https://help.adobe.com/en_US/FlashPlatform/reference/actionscript/3/*): "The ActionScript 3.0 Reference for the Adobe Flash Platform contains the ActionScript language elements, core libraries, and component packages and classes for the tools, runtimes, services, and servers in the Flash Platform."

CreateJS | Website (*www.createjs.com*): "A suite of modular libraries and tools which work together or independently to enable rich interactive content on open web technologies via HTML5." This is the set of JavaScript libraries behind HTML5 Canvas projects in Animate CC. You can find a full code reference along with robust documentation.

Goodbye!

I hope you've had fun learning about interactive media with Animate CC and that you now have a deeper understanding of what can be accomplished with this powerful, modern application. You can design and produce an enormous variety of projects using Animate CC—so have at it!

ACA Objectives Covered

DOMAIN OBJECTIVES	CHAPTER	VIDEO
Domain 1.0 Working in the Animation Industry		
1.1 Identify the purpose, audience, and audience needs for preparing media.	**Ch 11** Who You're Talking For and Who You're Talking To, 11-4 **Ch 11** Identifying your client's ideal customer, 11–6	**11.2** Discovering Client Goals **11.3** Finding the Target Audience
1.2 Communicate with colleagues and clients about design plans.	**Ch 11** The golden rule for client projects, 11-7 **Ch 11** Think like a boss, 11-14 **Ch 11** Project Management, 11-14 **Ch 11** Setting Project Requirements, 11-19 **Ch 11** Feedback Loop, 11-22	**11.9** Project Management Intro **11.10** Project Management—Understand the Problem **11.13** Project Management—Avoiding Creep **11.14** Project Management—Make it So
1.3 Determine the type of copyright, permissions, and licensing required to use specific content.	**Ch 11** Copyright Happens, 11-9 **Ch 11** Playing Fair with Copyrighted Material, 11-10 **Ch 11** Licensing, 11-12 **Ch 11** People Permissions, 11-13	**11.5** About Copyright **11.7** Fair Use and Copyright **11.8** Licensing: Strict and Free
1.4 Demonstrate knowledge of key terminology related to animation and interactive media.	**Ch 1** Animate CC: Common Terminology, 4 **Ch 2** Creating the Project Document, 20 **Ch 3** Generating a Static Image, 77 **Ch 4** Creating a New HTML5 Canvas Document, 90 **Ch 5** Video in Animate CC, 162 **Ch 7** About Adobe AIR for Desktop, 211	
1.5 Demonstrate knowledge of basic design and animation principles and best practices employed in industry.	**Ch 10** Leveling Up with Design, 10-3 **Ch 10** The Elements of Art, 10-10 **Ch 10** The Element of Type, 10-30 **Ch 10** The Principles of Design, 10-38	

continues on next page

continued from previous page

DOMAIN OBJECTIVES	CHAPTER	VIDEO
2.5 Manage colors, swatches, and gradients.	**Ch 4** Applying Colors and Gradients, 99 **Ch 6** Designing Layout Elements, 170	**4.3** Drawing the Background **4.9** Using Gradients **6.5** Design the Background
2.6 Manage brushes, filter presets, and motion presets.	**Ch 4** Drawing the Frame with Variable-Width Strokes, 96 **Ch 5** Creating the Rotation Effect for your Headshot, 144 **Ch 5** Animating with Motion Presets, 151 **Ch 6** Changing the View with Camera Motion, 188	**4.4** Decorating with Art Brushes **4.13** Drawing the Stalk **5.7** Stylize the Headshot **5.15** Animating with Motion Presets **6.15** Easing the Camera Motion
Domain 3.0 Organization of Documents		
3.1 Use Timeline panel to manage layers.	**Ch 2** Controlling Layers and Folders, 27 **Ch 3** Dealing with the Timeline and Layers, 65 **Ch 3** Adjusting the Timeline, 81 **Ch 4** Grouping the Layers within a Folder, 97 **Ch 6** Organizing the Timeline, 168 **Ch 6** Advanced Layers Mode, 174 **Ch 6** Changing the View with Camera Motion, 186	**3.8** Hiding Content with a Mask **3.13** Prepare the Timeline for Animation **5.19** Duplicating Layers and Swapping Symbols **6.3** Creating Timeline Layers **6.13** Camera Overview **6.16** Attaching Layers to the Camera
3.2 Modify layer visibility using transparency and masks.	**Ch 2** Setting Layer Properties on the Timeline, 27 **Ch 5** Creating Dynamic Backgrounds with Animated Shape Masking, 134	**3.2** Setting Up Our Project **5.4** Create a Star Mask **5.5** Animating the Mask
Domain 4.0 Create and Modify Visual Elements		
4.1 Use core tools and features to create visual elements.	**Ch 1** Commonly Accessed Tools, 10 **Ch 2** Additional Vector Creation Tools, 32	**2.4** Drawing the Floor **2.5** Drawing the Ball **3.8** Hiding Content with a Mask

continues on next page

continued from previous page

DOMAIN OBJECTIVES	CHAPTER	VIDEO
4.4 Transform digital graphics and media within an animation.	**Ch 2** Adding Some Impact, 42 **Ch 3** Adjusting the Image Layout on the Stage, 64 **Ch 4** Animating the Flower Stalk with Inverse Kinematics, 107 **Ch 5** Animating the Mask, 136 **Ch 5** Creating the Rotation Effect for your Headshot, 145 **Ch 7** Animating the Clock Pendulum, 225	**4.15** Managing Armature Poses **4.18** Animating the Flower Head **5.5** Animating the Mask **7.12** Animating the Pendulum
4.5 Use basic reconstructing and editing techniques to manipulate digital graphics and media.	**Ch 3** Using Trace Bitmap, 67 **Ch 4** Drawing the Frame with Variable-Width Strokes, 96 **Ch 5** The 3D Rotation and 3D Translation Tools, 142 **Ch 5** Employing Variable-Width Stroke Options, 158 **Ch 6** Designing Layout Elements, 170 **Ch 7** Creating the Clock Hands, 221	**3.7** Using Trace Bitmap **4.5** Making a Frame **5.20** Variable-Width Motion Guides **6.5** Design the Background **7.9** Building Vector Art Clock Hands
4.6 Modify appearance of design elements using effects and graphic styles.	**Ch 5** Creating the Headshot Movie Clip, 139 **Ch 6** Using CSS to Style Your Components, 181 **Ch 6** Attaching Layers to the Camera, 188 **Ch 7** Building the Clock Face Movie Clip, 220	**5.9** Introduction to 3D Tools **6.12** Adding CSS to your Project **6.13** Camera Overview **6.14** Setting Camera Properties **7.8** Create a Clock Face Movie Clip Symbol
4.7 Add interactive or dynamic content to a document.	**Ch 2** Time to Animate!, 38 **Ch 4** Using JavaScript Code to Stop the Playhead, 123 **Ch 5** Applying Filters and Color Effects, 146	**2.8** Frames and Keyframes **2.9** Animating with Shape Tweens **4.23** Stopping the Playhead **5.9** Introduction to 3D Tools **5.10** Creating the Rotation Effect **5.11** Employing Blur Filter Effects **6.17** Create Dynamic Text

Glossary

3D Three-dimensional image or video that gives the viewer a perception of depth. To achieve this using the tools in Animate CC, a third position axis, "z," is added to the x and y axes.

accessibility Software designed with specific or general people with disabilities in mind.

ActionScript An object-oriented programming language based upon the ECMAScript standard and originally developed my Macromedia before being acquired by Adobe. ActionScript is the programming language used to build interactive and dynamic projects for Flash Player and Adobe AIR.

additive color Created by combining light.

AIR Adobe AIR allows the creation of standalone applications using Flash technology for installation on Microsoft Windows, Apple OS X, Apple iOS, and Google Android.

alignment Indicates how the lines are aligned on the right and left edges, such as left, centered, and right.

all caps Uses only uppercase letterforms for each letter.

analogous Colors that are side by side on the color wheel. They create gentle and relaxing color schemes.

Android A mobile operating system meant for touchscreen devices such as smartphones and tablets. Android is developed by Google.

Animate CC Adobe Animate CC is the rebranded version of the revered animation and interactivity application known as Flash Professional CC. Animate CC retains all of the functionality present in Flash Professional CC...and even more.

anti-aliasing A software rendering technique of which the primary goal is to soften or eliminate jagged lines. Often applied to text.

API Application Programming Interface: A documented set of functions and protocols that allows one piece of software to communicate with another or allows one piece of code to take advantage of another in its execution.

APK Android Application Package: An APK can be installed on an Android device as an executable program. The iOS equivalent is IPA.

armature An armature in Animate CC allows for movement through inverse kinematics. Armatures can be composed of multiple Movie Clip Symbol instances or through a simple shape.

array An array is a structured, index-based object type that allows a number of different values or references to be stored in a single object. Arrays in ActionScript begin with index 0.

asymmetrical Achieves balance with different elements with different weights on each side (or the top and bottom) of an image.

attribution Written acknowledgment provided with the name of the original copyright holder of the work. Creative Commons and other licenses feature different kinds of attribution requirements.

balance Evenly distributed, but not necessarily centered or mirrored.

beta Considered an unstable program. Generally, when a program is in beta, it must be tested in various ways before being considered stable.

bitmap Images represented by stored pixel data within a grid. Scaling a bitmap will degrade the visual representation of the image.

blackletter fonts Also known as old English, Gothic, or Textura. Feature an overly ornate style. Convey a feeling of rich and sophisticated gravitas.

blank keyframe A keyframe with no content whatsoever. Represented in Animate CC with an unfilled circle.

bug Generally an error, fault, or failure in a piece of code that needs to be addressed.

canvas An HTML5 element that allows the rendering of complex graphics and interactivity through JavaScript.

captive runtime The AIR runtime when packaged with an AIR application. This removes the requirement that the end-user install AIR separately; but it makes the application file size larger.

cast shadow The shadow cast on the ground and on any objects that are in the shadow of the form. Shadows fade as they get farther from the form casting the shadow.

chaotic lines Look like scribbles and feel unpredictable and frantic. Convey a sense of urgency, fear, or explosive energy.

class A class is a template through which code instances can be created. This is very similar to the relationship between Symbols and instances in Animate CC.

color The perceived hue, lightness, and saturation of an object or light.

color harmonies Color rules that are named for their relative locations on the color wheel.

comments Commenting code will prevent that code from being executed. Comments can also be added to code for reasons of documentation.

compiler A sort of translator for computer languages, usually for converting a human-readable language into machine code.

complementary Colors that are opposite each other on the color wheel. They are high in contrast and vibrant.

contrast Creates visual interest and a focal point in a composition. It is what draws the eye to the focal point.

Creative Commons Ways that artists can release their works for limited use and still choose the way the works are used and shared: Public Domain, Attribution, ShareAlike, NoDerivs, and NonCommercial.

CSS "Cascading Style Sheets" is a coding language for style sheets that work within HTML pages. Using CSS allows web designers to separate the look and formatting of a page from its content.

curved (line) Expresses fluidity, beauty, and grace.

decorative fonts Also known as ornamental, novelty, or display fonts. They don't fall into any of the other categories of fonts. Convey a specific feeling.

debug Find errors in computer code ("bugs") and fix them.

deliverables A predetermined list of items that will be delivered to the customer.

demo reel A video or audio presentation meant to showcase your work. Almost like a portfolio of work but specific to video and audio formats.

deprecation A status applied to a piece of code or other functionality that is meant to steer people away from using a particular feature. Most often, the user will be urged to adopt a replacement.

design elements The building blocks of art defined by artists to provide a framework for creating art.

design principles The essential rules or assembly instructions for art.

diagonal (lines) Lines traveling neither on a vertical nor on a horizontal path. Express growth or decline and imply movement or change.

dingbat fonts Also known as wingdings. They are a collection of objects and shapes instead of letters.

direction A common way to describe lines, such as vertical, horizontal, diagonal.

DRM Digital Rights Management: A general term referring to protections and licensing enforcement upon a piece of media.

ECMAScript A scripting language specification standardized by ECMA International. Both ActionScript and JavaScript are implementations of the ECMAScript standard.

elements of art The building blocks of creative works. They are the "nouns" of design, such as space, line, shape, form, texture, value, color, and type.

emphasis Describes the focal point to which the eye is naturally and initially drawn in a design.

event Events can generally be listened for, and reacted against, in various programming languages. Some common events to listen for are those broadcast when a mouse is clicked or a key is pressed.

fade-in Sometimes referred to as a "dissolve" or simply a "fade." A fade-in is a basic transition technique where the opacity of one layer is changed over time to either transition to or reveal additional content.

fair use A set of rules that specify how and when copyrighted material can be used and that make sure copyright protection doesn't come at the cost of creativity and freedom.

feedback loop A system set up to continually encourage and require input and approval on a project's direction.

filters Filters in Animate CC can be added to certain object types to apply different effects like glows or drop shadows. Filters can be stacked, and one object can have multiple filters applied to it.

Flash Player Adobe Flash Player is the web browser plugin that has pushed creativity forward on the Internet—even when web standards stagnated. While much functionality can be achieved with native web technologies, Adobe Flash Player is still an integral technology for games, premium video, and even more.

Flash Professional CC For nearly 20 years now, Adobe Flash Professional CC has enabled rich creativity on the web and beyond. In early 2016, Adobe will release a rebranded version of this application named Animate CC.

flow A design element related to the energy conveyed by lines and shapes.

focal point What the design is all about. The call to action or the primary message you are trying to get across.

font A subset of a typeface, consisting of characters of a specific size and style.

form Describes three-dimensional objects, such as spheres, cubes, and pyramids.

FPS "Frames per second" is a way to describe the speed of an animation.

frame Frames are a unit of measurement in Animate CC. An animation will run at a specific speed measured in frames per second (FPS) and the number of frames that the animation contains, along with its FPS, determine its length.

function A defined group of commands and logic that can be invoked by a program to fulfill a certain task.

geometric (lines) Tend to be straight and have sharp angles. Look manmade and intentional. Communicate strength, power, and precision.

geometric shapes Predictable and consistent shapes, such as circles, squares, triangles, and stars. They are rarely found in nature and convey mechanical and manufactured impressions.

GIF Graphics Interchange Format: A lossless bitmap image format limited to 256 colors. Best used for simple images due to the limited palette. GIF images can also be animated.

glyph Each character of a font, whether it is a letter, number, symbol, or swash.

gradients A gradient in Animate CC is a type of color swatch consisting of two or more colors that visually blend into one another via a transition of properties.

H.264 MPEG-4 Part 10, Advanced Video Coding: The most common video format for web-based video. Sometimes referred to as "AVC" or "MPEG-4 AVC."

hand-drawn lines Appear as though created using traditional techniques, such as paints, charcoal, or chalk.

handwritten fonts Also known as hand fonts, they simulate handwriting.

HD Video "High-definition video" generally refers to video whose resolution is higher than 480 (North America) or 576 (Europe) vertical lines.

headshot A realistically photographed portrait used for branding, casting, and social media.

highlight The area of a form that is directly facing the light and that appears lightest.

horizontal Moving from left to right; for example, the horizontal line in an "H." Expresses calmness and balance.

horizontal scale Describes the function of stretching letters and distorting the typeface geometry.

HTML5 Version 5 of the Hyper Text Markup Language. HTML defines the page markup elements used for layout and content and can be interpreted and displayed by a web browser.

HTML5 Canvas See "canvas."

hyphenation Determines if and when words should be split with hyphens when wrapping to the next line.

ideographs (ideograms) Images that represent an idea, such as a heart representing love.

implied lines Lines that aren't depicted literally but are implied by shapes, such as dotted or dashed lines, people waiting in lines, or the margins of a block of text.

indent Settings that determine how far an entire paragraph is indented from the rest of the text on each side or in just its first line.

instance When a class is instantiated with the "new" keyword in ActionScript, a new instance of that class is created that we can then work with.

instances Instances are objects used within a project that are based upon Symbols created and stored within the project Library. Instances can have many properties adjusted individually, apart from the Symbol itself.

inverse kinematics At times this is referred to as IK. Inverse kinematics is a model of movement employed by Animate CC for use upon armatures. It is a system of bones and joints that all interact with one another, creating natural movement.

iOS A mobile operating system meant for touchscreen personal computing devices such as smartphones, tablets, and smartwatches built by Apple, who is the owner and developer.

iterations New versions of a design that successively become closer to the desired result.

iterative work Work that is shared as it is completed, allowing the customer to chime in with comments while it is still easy to make a change.

JavaScript The programming language used for the native web. Alongside HTML and CSS, JavaScript is an essential technology component for the modern web. Animate CC allows the use of JavaScript in project types that support it through the Actions panel.

JPG Joint Photographic Experts Group: A lossy bitmap image format used heavily on the web. Suitable for complex images like photographs. Also represented in the form JPEG.

JSON JavaScript Object Notation: A human-readable way to structure data that is also easily ingested and parsed by software.

justified Aligns text to a straight edge on both the right and left edges of a paragraph.

kerning The space between specific letter pairs.

keyframe In animation, a frame on the timeline whose state (whether an image or location or other parameter) defines the starting or ending point of a smooth transition.

layer Layers exist as part of the Animate CC timeline and serve the dual functions of containing image, sound, code, and other data as well as to provide a mechanism to arrange the visual stacking order of content.

leading The amount of space between the baselines of two lines of text.

licensing A way to legally use copyrighted material for a certain time and in a certain way, usually associated with paying a fee established by the copyright holder.

ligatures Special characters used to represent letter combinations, such as "fi", which represents "fi".

light source The perceived location of the lighting in relation to the form.

line A mark with a beginning and end points.

loop A programming construct that repeats a certain piece of code a certain number of times depending upon some logical operator.

mask Layers in Animate CC can use their contents to mask other layers grouped beneath them. Any content covered by the mask object will appear visible, while any content outside of that overlay will not be visible.

meme An idea, often expressed on the Internet through images and video, which spreads from person to person, often becoming culturally significant.

metadata Information that is included in a document but is hidden, such as copyright, lens information, location via GPS, camera settings, and more.

methods Methods are functions that exist as members of a class in ActionScript.

model releases The permission that is required when a person's face is identifiable in a photo and the image will be used to promote something—whether it's a product or idea.

monochromatic Different shades and tints of the same color. Communicates a relaxed and peaceful feeling.

monospaced fonts Fixed-width or non-proportional fonts that use the same amount of horizontal space for each letter.

movement Visual movement within an image, such as the natural tracking of the eye across an image as the eye moves from focal point to focal point.

MP3 MPEG-2 Audio Layer III: A lossy audio file format and the most common audio file format on the web.

negative space Blank areas in a design. Also known as white space.

nesting In programming, embedding a process within another process, or an object within another object.

NoDerivs (ND) Creative Commons licensing. Requires that you not change material when you incorporate it into your own work. It can be used freely, but you must pass it along without change.

NonCommercial (NC) Creative Commons licensing. Means you can use work in your own creative work as long as you don't charge for it.

number The most flexible and general numeric data type in ActionScript. Used to store numeric data within variables.

object A generic object type in ActionScript that can have properties and data values assigned to it.

object shadow The area of the form that is facing away from the light source and appears darkest.

organic lines Lines that are usually irregular and imperfect. Found in nature.

organic shapes Are random or generated by something natural. They are usually asymmetric and convey natural, homemade, or relaxed feelings.

package Using packages in ActionScript is a way to organize your classes and ensure that no code collisions are possible between properties or methods that may share the same name.

paragraph settings Format settings that affect an entire paragraph rather than selected words. These settings include alignment, hyphenation, and so on.

paragraph spacing The distance between a paragraph and the preceding or following paragraph.

Pattern A repetitive sequence of different colors, shapes, or values.

pictograph (pictogram) Graphic symbol that represents something in the real world. Computer icons are pictographs that suggest the function they represent, such as a trash can icon to delete a file.

pixel A single dot representing the values of lightness and color at one location in a raster image. Pixel is short for "picture element."

playhead In animation and video, an interface element that identifies the currently visible frame on the timeline.

PNG Portable Network Graphics: A lossless bitmap image format useful for complex photographic elements and simpler images as well. PNG may include a full alpha channel, allowing for nuanced transparency.

Point A unit of measure for typography and print design that is equal to 1/72 of an inch.

Ppi Stands for pixels per inch and is a setting that affects only printed images. Higher ppi affords more detail in printed images.

primary colors Red, blue, and green. These can be combined to create every other color in the visible spectrum.

project creep Unplanned changes that increase the amount of work, or scope, that a project requires. When the project loses focus and spins out of control, eating up more and more time and effort.

project deadlines Dictates when work needs to be completed.

project scope Outlines the amount and type of work to be completed.

properties Properties are variables and constants that are members of a class in ActionScript.

proportion (scale) Describes the relative size and scale of elements.

public domain A work is said to be in the public domain when its copyright has expired or has been released and no longer applies to the content or when an artist releases their work. The work can be used without worrying about infringement. In the Creative Commons licensing program, public domain is covered under CC0 ("CC Zero").

radial In design, a type of balance achieved among elements arranged around the center of the design, rather than reflected across a central plane.

Raw Whether talking about video or any other medium, the term "raw" refers to the fact that the data has not been compressed, encrypted, or processed by any means.

reflected highlight Area of a three-dimensional form that is lit by reflections from the ground or other objects in a scene.

repetition Repeating an element in a design.

representative shapes Shapes used to represent information. They are helpful in communicating with multicultural and multilingual audiences.

rhythm A quality of design that describes the relationship among elements that don't adhere to a consistent pattern or sequence, but are placed in a creative and expressive arrangement.

rule of thirds A technique for laying out the space of your page to provide a focal point. Two vertical and two horizontal lines evenly divide the space into nine equal boxes, as in a tic-tac-toe board.

Runtime A piece of software that executes specifically targeted code. The Adobe Runtimes include both Flash Player and AIR.

sans serif fonts Text without serifs. Often used for headlines and titles for their strong, stable, modern feel.

scale *See* proportion.

script font A font that mimics handwriting. It conveys a feeling of beauty, grace, or feminine dignity.

SDK Software Development Kit: A set of tools and software packages or frameworks that allows the development of applications or games based upon a specific platform.

secondary colors Created by combining primary colors.

serif fonts Associated with fonts created by typewriters. They convey tradition, intelligence, and class.

shape An area enclosed or defined by an outline, such as circles, squares, triangles, or even clouds.

ShareAlike (SA) Creative Commons licensing. Allows you to use an item (design) in any way you want as long as your creation is shared under the same license as the original work.

sketches Representative drawings of how to lay out a document or web page. These are sometimes one of the deliverables of a project.

skin A customizable set of graphic elements that define the appearance of a piece of software.

slab serif fonts Squared-off versions of a typical serif font. Also known as Egyptian, block serif, or square serif. Convey a machine-built feel.

small caps Uses only uppercase letterforms for each letter and appears in a smaller size.

space The canvas, or working area. Its dimensions are determined by the resolution of the page you are creating.

specifications Detailed written goals and limits for a project. These are sometimes one of the deliverables of a project.

spritesheets In order to require as few server calls as possible, bitmap images can be packed together into a single image that is loaded only once. The loaded image can then be parsed in accordance with an accompanying data file.

Stage The portion of an Adobe Animate CC project that will be visible to the end user.

stock photos Images for which the author retains copyright but for which a license for use is available.

string A sequence of characters assigned to a variable. Generally, a piece of text.

style (line) An effect applied to a line, such as varying width, hand-drawn, and implied.

subtractive color Created by subtracting light.

SVG Scalable Vector Graphics: An XML-based scalable vector format used for the representation of image data. Can be viewed on the web and may include animation and interactivity.

swashes Special characters with flowing and elegant endings for the ascenders and descenders.

Symbols Symbols in Animate CC primarily allow the re-use of assets as instances within a project. Symbols are stored within the project Library. Editing a Symbol will edit all instances of that Symbol.

symmetrical Occurs when you can divide an image along its middle, and the left side of the image is a mirror image of the right (or the top reflects the bottom). Conveys an intentional, formal, and mechanical feeling.

tertiary colors Created by mixing primary and secondary colors.

texture Describes the actual tactile texture in real objects or the appearance of texture in a two-dimensional image.

Timeline The sequence of events in an Adobe Animate CC project in chronological order. A project's timeline is displayed in the Timeline panel.

tracking The overall space between all the letters in a block of text. It allows you to compress or expand the space between the letters as a whole rather than just between specific pairs, as you do with kerning.

transcode Encoding a piece of media from one format to another. Animate CC works in conjunction with Adobe Media Encoder to encode and transcode video files from one format to another.

type size A font's height from the highest ascender to the lowest descender.

typeface Specific letterform set, such as Helvetica, Arial, Garamond, and so on. It is the "look" of letters.

unity Also known as harmony and sharing similar traits. Low contrast. Things that go together should look like they belong together. The opposite of variety.

usability The ease of use or learnability of a piece of software.

value Describes the lightness or darkness of an object. Together with color, value represents the visible spectrum, such as a gradient.

variety High contrast. The opposite of unity.

variable In coding, a placeholder for a value used in a program. A variable can be associated with a data type.

varying width lines Expresses flow and grace.

vector Graphics generated through mathematical expressions. Vectors can be infinitely scaled without any loss in visual fidelity.

vertical Moving from top to bottom. Vertical lines tend to express power and elevation.

vertical scale Describes the function of stretching letters and distorting the typeface geometry.

viewport In computer graphics, the visible part of a larger area. In Animate CC, the Stage acts as a viewport, defining the visible area of the overall artwork.

WebGL A graphics language that is able to render GPU-accelerated 2D and 3D content using HTML5 Canvas.

weight (line) The thickness of a line.

Welcome Screen A special user interface element that provides quick access to recent documents and the creation of new documents.

Wireframe A schematic sketch of a project, commonly used for interactive projects.

XML Extensible Markup Language: HTML and other content delivery formats are often based upon this simple, node-based structural language.

Index

NUMBERS

3D rotating headshot, 139–141
3D Rotation tool, 91, 142–145
3D Translation tool, 91, 142
3D view, simulating, 143

A

ACA (Adobe Certified Associate)
    exam, preparation, 6
ACA Objectives
    3D tools, 142
    ActionScript 3.0, 208–210
    ActionScript 3.0 document, 21
    Adobe AIR for Mobile
        document, 246–248
    Advanced Layers mode, 174
    animated shape masking,
        134–138
    animating, 38–42
    app logic and flow, 268–274
    application classes, 254
    background elements, 93–97
    background for virtual
        clock, 214
    base elements, 173–174
    Brush Library panel, 173
    buttons for mobile quiz
        app, 251–253
    camera-motion views,
        186–188
    centering published
        content, 204
    CSS style rules, 181
    document and Stage
        properties, 168
    drawing frames, 96–97
    dynamic backgrounds,
        134–138
    dynamic text, 190–191
    evaluating interactive media
        content, 279–284
    external graphics, 61–65
    graphic symbols, 100
    headshot movie clip, 139–141
    hiding content with
        masking, 69–70
    HTML5 Canvas Document,
        90–93
    importing backgrounds,
        133–134
    interface features, 12–16
    inverse kinematics, 107–111
    Lasso tool, 171
    layer properties, 27
    layout elements, 170–174
    Motion Editor, 145–147
    names in movie clips, 149–151
    personalized text message,
        117–122
    publishing app for
        distribution, 275–276
    publishing for HTML5 canvas,
        125–128
    raw video, 159
    saving documents, 24
    sizing and positioning
        instances, 177
    Stage and timeline, 25–26
    timeline layers, 168–170
    tools, 10
    Video in Animate CC,
        162–165
    video project setup, 132–134
    web fonts, 191–194
accessibility evaluation, 282–283
Actions layer and Camera
    layer, 194
Actions panel, 123, 210
Actions Wizard, using, 197–198
ActionScript 3.0
    Actions panel, 210
    attributes, 254
    body of function, 199
    classes, 254
    comments, 239–240
    document, 21
    errors, 239
    events, 233
    functions, 232–233
    instances, 254
    `interval` attribute, 254
    vs. JavaScript, 209
    methods, 254
    numbers, 232
    objects, 254
    packages, 254–256
    `private` attribute, 254
    properties, 254
    `protected` attribute, 254
    `public` attribute, 254
    Publish settings, 48–52
    reverse-domain naming, 254
    Stage object references,
        258–259
    `static` attribute, 254
    strings, 232
    symbols and interactivity,
        230–231
    trace statements, 240
    variables, 232
    versions, 208–209
    writing to control clock,
        233–239
ActionScript 4.0, 209
ActionScript projects, 13
Add Anchor Point tool, 34
Adobe AIR for Desktop, 211–213
Adobe AIR for Mobile
    Android, 246
    app interface elements,
        248–253
    app logic and flow, 268–274
    application classes, 254–259
    bank of questions, 259–268
    iOS, 246–247
    project document, 247–248
    publishing for distribution,
        275–276
Adobe Media Encoder, 160–161
Advanced Layers mode, using,
    174–175. *See also* layers
AIR for Mobile
    button interactivity, 270–274
    deployment, 275
    icons, 275
    languages, 276
    permissions, 276
    project overview, 245
    publishing for distribution,
        275–276
    questions to user, 268–270

D

Debug Console, revealing, 13
Debug workspace, 13
Delete Anchor Point tool, 34
Delete Layer icon, 105
demo reel, 131
deployment testing, 281
descriptor text
    building, 152–154
    classic motion guides,
        154–157
Designer workspace, 14
Developer workspace, 14
Dither option, 79
document file, 21
document types
    choosing, 20
    setting, 22–25
documents
    saving, 24
    tracking current location, 30
drawing
    ball, 31
    flower stalk, 105–106
    flowerpot, 97–101
    mask shape, 135–136
    shapes, 31–32
drawing objects, constraining, 29
DRM (digital rights
        management), 160
Drop Shadow settings,
        choosing, 120
dynamic backgrounds, 134–138.
        See also background images
dynamic text, creating, 74–75,
        190–191. *See also* text

E

ease presets
    using with camera, 188
    using with shape tweens,
        45–46
ease values, 44
easing animations, 42–46
ECMAScript specification, 209
Edit Stroke Style icon, 95

editing
    flower graphic symbol,
        102–106
    flower symbol, 104–105
    symbols, 153
embedding
    fonts, 75, 253
    video files, 163–164
Essentials workspace, 14
evaluating interactive media
        content, 279–284
exporting
    animated GIF image, 83–85
    as GIF (Graphics Interchange
        Format), 78–79
    as JPEG, 77–78
    as PNG (Portable Network
        Graphics), 79–80
    as SVG (Scalable Vector
        Graphics), 80
    video from Animate CC,
        159–162
external graphics
    adjusting image layout, 64
    bitmap images, 61
    importing, 63–64
    Timeline and layers, 65
eye icon, 27
Eyedropper tool, 37

F

F4V format, 163
fade-in, using with headshot, 148
file types, 21, 24
filters and color effects, applying,
        146–147
FLA file type, 21
Flash Player, 6, 21, 47–48
Flash Professional CC, vs.
        Animate CC, 5–7
Floor layer, 31
flower, emerging from bud,
        115–117
flower graphic symbol, editing,
        102–106. *See also* graphic
        symbols

flower head
    animating along stalk,
        113–115
    drawing, 112–113
flower stalk, animating with
        inverse kinematics, 105–111
flowerpot, drawing, 97–101
FLV format, 162–163
focus groups, 283–284
folders
    grouping layers in, 97
    icon, 26
    and layers, 26–27
fonts, embedding, 75, 253.
        See also web fonts
FPS (frames-per-second), 11, 46
frame labels, adding, 169–170
Frame Picker, using with text
        message, 121–122
frame span, inserting, 38–39
frame-by-frame animation, 42
frames, 5, 11
framing vector shapes,
        creating, 71–72
Free Transform tool, 42–43,
        99, 113
function, body of, 199

G

gameOver() method, 270
GIF (Graphics Interchange
        Format), exporting as, 78–79
global variables, setting in
        JavaScript, 195–196. *See also*
        variables
Google Fonts, 192
Google Play, app
        distribution, 246
Gradient Transform tool, 99, 172
gradients and colors, applying, 99
graphic symbols. *See also* flower
        graphic symbol; Messages
        graphic symbol; symbols
    converting to, 100
    and movie clip symbols, 103
    using, 101
graphics. *See* external graphics
grid, enabling, 25, 60

M

Macromedia Flash 4, 13
Magic Wand, 36
mask shape, drawing, 135–136
masks. *See also* animated shape
    masking
    animating, 136–138
    using to hide content, 69–70
meme image. *See also* image
    layout
    animated GIF, 81–85
    bitmaps, 65–70
    completed version, 58
    external graphics, 61–65
    framing vector shapes, 71
    in Library panel, 64
    project document, 58–59
    project setup, 59–61
    static image, 77–80
    text elements, 72–76
Merge Drawing, 30
Messages graphic symbol,
    creating, 121. *See also*
    graphic symbols
methods and classes
    gameOver(), 270
    MouseEvent, 270
    using, 125
    using in ActionScript, 254
mobile quiz app
    button interactivity, 270–274
    deployment, 275
    icons, 275
    languages, 276
    permissions, 276
    project overview, 245
    publishing for distribution,
        275–276
    questions to user, 268–270
Motion Editor, using, 145–147
motion presets, animating names
    with, 149–152
motion tweens. *See also* tweening
    applying to shapes, 41
    creating, 114
MouseEvent class, 270
movie clip symbols
    3D rotating headshot,
        139–141

descriptor text, 152–154
and graphic symbols, 103
swapping out, 157
using, 101
MP4 file format, 161, 163
MP4 video, adding as guide, 164

N

navigation buttons, creating,
    176–178
nesting hierarchy, 141
New Layer button, 26, 92
next and back functions, writing,
    197–198

O

Object Drawing, 30
object instances, using in project
    library, 62. *See also* instances
objects
    constraining, 29
    using in ActionScript, 254
onion skinning, 43
Options area, described, 10
outline icon, 27
Output Name option, 50
Oval Primitive tool, 216
Oval tool, 29–30, 98, 216, 251
overlapping shapes, 98

P

packages, using with
    ActionScript, 254–256
page icon, 26
Paint Brush tool, 33, 94–95
Paint Bucket tool, 37
panels
    Actions, 123, 210
    Brush Library, 173
    Code Snippets, 124
    collapsing, 13
    Color, 37–38
    Library, 64
    managing, 12–13
    Properties, 8–9
    Swatches Panel, 37
    Timeline, 11–12

Tools, 9–10
Variables, 13, 264
Paste in Place, 40
pasteboard, 15–16
Pattern brushes, using, 139
Pen tool, 34
Pencil tool, 32
Photoshop, importing graphics,
    63–64
placing content with
    keyframes, 38
platform targets, 20
playback of video, 164–165
Playback Security, 51–52
playhead
    stopping, 123–125, 194
    in timeline, 11
PNG (Portable Network Graphics),
    exporting as, 79–80
poem generator
    background and layout
        elements, 174
    building and displaying,
        201–203
    overview, 167
    project overview, 167
Polygon tool, 36, 135
PolyStar tool, 34, 135
presets, using, 13–14
Profile settings, 49
progressive download, using
    for playback, 164
project libraries, 62
project type, choosing, 59
projectors, generating, 53
promotional video. *See also*
    videos
    3D rotating headshot,
        138–148
    animated shape masking,
        134–138
    animating names, 149–152
    dynamic animation, 152–159
    dynamic backgrounds,
        134–138
    embedding files, 163–164
    exporting, 159–162
    motion presets, 149–152
    project setup, 132–134